S0-FLP-790

CFA Institute

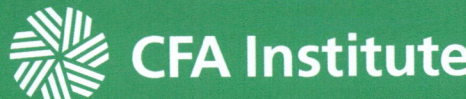

# Claritas®
## Investment Certificate

# 2013–2014
### VOLUME 2: MODULES 5–7

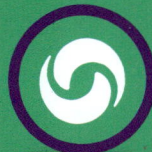

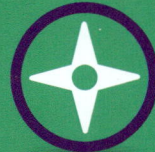

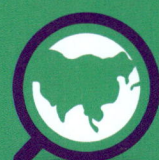

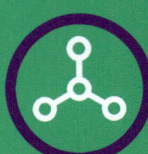

©2013 by CFA Institute

All rights reserved. No part of this publication may be reproduced or transmitted in any form or by any means, electronic or mechanical, including photocopy, recording, or any information storage and retrieval system, without permission of the copyright holder. Requests for permission to make copies of any part of the work should be mailed to: CFA Institute, Permissions Department, 560 Ray C. Hunt Dr., Charlottesville, VA 22903.

CFA®, Chartered Financial Analysts®, AIMR-PPS®, and GIPS®. are just a few of the trademarks owned by CFA Institute. To view a list of CFA Institute trademarks and the Guide for the Use of CFA Institute Marks, please visit our website at www.cfainstitute.org.

ISBN: 978-1-937537-59-3

June 2013

# Contents

## Volume 1

| | | |
|---|---|---|
| **Module 1** | **Industry Overview** | **1** |
| **Chapter 1** | **The Investment Industry: A Top-Down View** | **3** |
| | Learning Outcomes | 4 |
| | Introduction | 5 |
| | How Economies Benefit from the Existence of the Investment Industry | 7 |
| | How Individuals Benefit from the Existence of the Investment Industry | 9 |
| | Investment Industry Participants | 12 |
| | Key Forces Driving the Investment Industry | 16 |
| | *Chapter Review Questions* | 19 |
| | *Answers* | 21 |
| **Module 2** | **Introduction to Ethics and Regulation** | **23** |
| **Chapter 2** | **Ethics and Investment Professionalism** | **27** |
| | Learning Outcomes | 28 |
| | Introduction | 29 |
| | Investment Industry, Ethical Standards, and Trust | 30 |
| | Obligations of the Investment Professional | 31 |
| | Ethical Standards | 36 |
| | Benefits of Ethical Conduct and Consequences of Unethical Conduct | 40 |
| | Framework for Ethical Decision Making | 44 |
| | *Chapter Review Questions* | 50 |
| | *Answers* | 52 |
| **Chapter 3** | **Regulation and Supervision** | **55** |
| | Learning Outcomes | 56 |
| | Introduction | 57 |
| | Objectives of Regulation | 58 |
| | A Basic Regulatory Process | 59 |
| | Specific Types of Regulation | 64 |
| | Corporate Policies and Procedures | 71 |
| | Consequences of Regulatory Failures | 73 |
| | *Chapter Review Questions* | 75 |
| | *Answers* | 77 |
| **Module 3** | **Introduction to Tools and Inputs** | **79** |
| **Chapter 4** | **Financial Statements** | **81** |
| | Learning Outcomes | 82 |
| | Introduction | 83 |
| | Financial Statements | 84 |
| | Financial Statement Analysis | 94 |

| | | |
|---|---|---:|
| | *Chapter Review Questions* | 104 |
| | *Answers* | 107 |
| **Chapter 5** | **Quantitative Concepts** | **109** |
| | Learning Outcomes | 110 |
| | Introduction | 111 |
| | Time Value of Money | 111 |
| | Descriptive Statistics | 121 |
| | *Chapter Review Questions* | 139 |
| | *Answers* | 141 |
| **Chapter 6** | **Microeconomics** | **143** |
| | Learning Outcomes | 144 |
| | Introduction | 145 |
| | Demand and Supply | 146 |
| | Elasticities of Demand | 154 |
| | Profits and Costs of Production | 159 |
| | Pricing | 161 |
| | Industry Structure | 162 |
| | *Chapter Review Questions* | 167 |
| | *Answers* | 171 |
| **Chapter 7** | **Macroeconomics** | **175** |
| | Learning Outcomes | 176 |
| | Introduction | 177 |
| | Gross Domestic Product and the Business Cycle | 177 |
| | Inflation | 188 |
| | Monetary and Fiscal Policies | 193 |
| | *Chapter Review Questions* | 201 |
| | *Answers* | 204 |
| **Chapter 8** | **International Trade and Foreign Exchange** | **207** |
| | Learning Outcomes | 208 |
| | Introduction | 209 |
| | International Trade | 210 |
| | Balance of Payments | 214 |
| | Foreign Exchange Rate Systems | 221 |
| | Foreign Exchange Market | 223 |
| | Factors Influencing Exchange Rates | 226 |
| | *Chapter Review Questions* | 234 |
| | *Answers* | 237 |
| **Module 4** | **Introduction to Investment Instruments** | **239** |
| **Chapter 9** | **Equity Securities** | **241** |
| | Learning Outcomes | 242 |
| | Introduction | 243 |
| | Capital Structure and Priority of Claims | 243 |
| | Types and Characteristics of Equity Securities | 248 |
| | Valuation of Common Shares | 254 |

| | | |
|---|---|---|
| | Special Issues: Corporate Actions that Affect Equity Outstanding | 258 |
| | *Chapter Review Questions* | 265 |
| | *Answers* | 268 |

## Chapter 10  Debt Securities  271

| | |
|---|---|
| Learning Outcomes | 272 |
| Introduction | 273 |
| Types and Characteristics of Debt Securities | 273 |
| Bonds with Embedded Provisions | 280 |
| Risks of Investing in Debt Securities | 283 |
| Valuation of Debt Securities | 286 |
| *Chapter Review Questions* | 294 |
| *Answers* | 297 |

## Chapter 11  Derivatives  301

| | |
|---|---|
| Learning Outcomes | 302 |
| Introduction | 303 |
| Characteristics of Derivatives Contracts | 304 |
| Forward and Futures Contracts | 307 |
| Option Contracts | 314 |
| Swap Contracts | 320 |
| Uses of and Growth in Derivatives Contracts | 324 |
| *Chapter Review Questions* | 328 |
| *Answers* | 332 |

## Chapter 12  Alternative Investments  335

| | |
|---|---|
| Learning Outcomes | 336 |
| Introduction | 337 |
| Characteristics of Alternative Investments | 337 |
| Private Equity | 340 |
| Real Estate | 344 |
| Commodities | 348 |
| Concluding Thoughts | 349 |
| *Chapter Review Questions* | 351 |
| *Answers* | 353 |

# Volume 2

## Module 5  Introduction to Industry Structure  355

## Chapter 13  Structure of the Investment Industry  359

| | |
|---|---|
| Learning Outcomes | 360 |
| Introduction | 361 |
| Investors | 362 |
| How the Investment Industry Promotes Successful Investing | 369 |
| Financial Planning Services | 370 |
| Investment Management Services | 371 |
| Investment Information Services | 375 |
| Trading Services | 380 |
| Custodians and Depositories | 385 |

|  |  |  |
|---|---|---|
|  | Financial Intermediaries | 386 |
|  | Organization of Firms in the Investment Industry | 390 |
|  | Institutional Investment Management Processes | 393 |
|  | *Chapter Review Questions* | 398 |
|  | *Answers* | 402 |

### Chapter 14 — Investment Vehicles and Structures — 405

| | |
|---|---|
| Learning Outcomes | 406 |
| Introduction | 407 |
| Security Market Indices | 407 |
| Investment Vehicles and Structures | 412 |
| Structured Investment Products | 414 |
| Investment Companies | 416 |
| Hedge Funds | 424 |
| Funds of Funds | 426 |
| Managed Accounts | 427 |
| Tax-Advantaged Accounts | 428 |
| Pension Plans | 430 |
| *Chapter Review Questions* | 435 |
| *Answers* | 438 |

### Chapter 15 — Investment Market Characteristics — 441

| | |
|---|---|
| Learning Outcomes | 442 |
| Introduction | 443 |
| Primary Security Markets | 443 |
| Trading Service Providers | 447 |
| Structure of Secondary Security Markets and of Contract Markets | 450 |
| Positions | 456 |
| Orders | 458 |
| Settlement and Custodial Services | 465 |
| Transaction Costs | 467 |
| Efficient Financial Markets | 468 |
| *Chapter Review Questions* | 472 |
| *Answers* | 475 |

### Module 6 — Introduction to Industry Controls — 479

### Chapter 16 — Investment Industry Documentation — 483

| | |
|---|---|
| Learning Outcomes | 484 |
| Introduction | 485 |
| Objectives and Classification of Documentation | 485 |
| Internal Documentation | 487 |
| External Documentation | 493 |
| Document Management | 498 |
| *Chapter Review Questions* | 502 |
| *Answers* | 505 |

### Chapter 17 — Risk Management — 507

| | |
|---|---|
| Learning Outcomes | 508 |
| Introduction | 509 |

# Contents

|  |  |  |
|---|---|---|
|  | Definition and Classification of Risks | 510 |
|  | Risk Management | 512 |
|  | Risk Measurement | 520 |
|  | Operational Risks and Their Management | 522 |
|  | Compliance Risks and Their Management | 527 |
|  | Investment Risks and Their Management | 532 |
|  | Conclusion | 535 |
|  | *Chapter Review Questions* | 537 |
|  | *Answers* | 540 |
| **Chapter 18** | **Performance Evaluation** | **543** |
|  | Learning Outcomes | 544 |
|  | Introduction | 545 |
|  | Measuring Absolute Returns | 545 |
|  | Adjusting Returns for Risk | 552 |
|  | Measuring Relative Returns | 558 |
|  | Attributing Performance | 563 |
|  | *Chapter Review Questions* | 569 |
|  | *Answers* | 572 |
| **Module 7** | **Introduction to Serving Client Needs** | **575** |
| **Chapter 19** | **Investor Needs and Investment Policy** | **579** |
|  | Learning Outcomes | 580 |
|  | Introduction | 581 |
|  | Types and Characteristics of Investors | 581 |
|  | Investors' Needs | 586 |
|  | The Investment Policy Statement | 590 |
|  | *Chapter Review Questions* | 593 |
|  | *Answers* | 595 |
| **Chapter 20** | **Asset Allocation** | **597** |
|  | Learning Outcomes | 598 |
|  | Introduction | 599 |
|  | Systematic Risk, Specific Risk, and Diversification | 599 |
|  | Asset Allocation and Portfolio Construction/Management | 602 |
|  | *Chapter Review Questions* | 607 |
|  | *Answers* | 609 |
| **Chapter 21** | **Active and Passive Investment Management** | **611** |
|  | Learning Outcomes | 612 |
|  | Introduction | 613 |
|  | Market Efficiency | 613 |
|  | Active and Passive Management | 614 |
|  | *Chapter Review Questions* | 619 |
|  | *Answers* | 620 |
| **Glossary** |  | **G-1** |

# Module 5
# Introduction to Industry Structure

Watch an introductory video at cfainstitute.org/claritasstudy.

To work effectively in organizations that manage, sponsor, or trade investments, you must be familiar with how the investment industry serves its clients. You must be aware of who the clients are, what products and services investment managers provide to their clients, and how investment managers produce and sell these products and services. With this knowledge, you can better appreciate how the investment industry ultimately produces value for the individuals and institutions that the industry serves.

In Chapter 13, you will learn about the various organizations that use and provide investment services. Investment industry clients include retail, high-net-worth, and ultra-high-net-worth individuals; foundations and endowments; pension funds; and governments and their sovereign wealth funds. These clients hire investment managers to help them manage their investments. Investment managers provide investment advice and related financial planning services to their clients. Implementation of their advice requires trades that financial intermediaries help arrange. These financial intermediaries include brokers, exchanges, dealers, arbitrageurs, commercial and investment banks, and insurance companies that either directly or indirectly match buyers with sellers. Finally, transfer agents and custodians ensure that the investment assets are properly accounted for and not stolen or misplaced.

Investment managers serve their clients by creating investment products and providing investment services. Chapter 14 describes these products and services. The products include pooled investment vehicles, such as mutual funds and hedge funds, that represent ownership in professionally managed portfolios. The investment services include advisory services that managers provide to individual clients or to clients who have pooled their money together for common management. Investors obtain these services directly by contracting with financial advisers to manage their investments in individual or commingled (pooled) accounts or indirectly by buying pooled investment securities managed by investment managers.

Chapter 15 introduces you to the markets in which traders implement investment decisions. You will learn how firms issue securities in primary markets and how they subsequently trade these securities in secondary markets. The chapter identifies the types of positions that investors take and considers how investors specify trade orders to create and adjust these positions. You will learn how brokers, dealers, and exchanges arrange trades and how these and other intermediaries settle trades.

The chapter also discusses the benefits that everyone gains from having efficient markets that produce informative prices and that allow investors to trade at low cost. Everyone in the economy benefits when investors can cheaply and efficiently allocate their investable funds (capital) to the skilled entrepreneurs with the best ideas about how to use these funds. When investment markets work well, new capital will flow to the most promising projects and the most productive executives will manage companies that use existing capital. Everyone in the investment management industry who works on behalf of their clients to identify and purchase valuable investment assets contributes, directly or indirectly, to creating value for the economy as a whole.

Investment managers and financial intermediaries accomplish seemingly similar objectives in many different ways. It is important to understand the advantages and disadvantages associated with the various alternative approaches and products. The

Written by Larry Harris, PhD, CFA.
Copyright © 2012 CFA Institute

differences are almost always related to the various needs that different investors or their investment managers have. Members of the investment industry create value for their clients by providing products and services tailored to address the specific needs of diverse investors.

It is also important to understand the ways in which investment processes are structured to protect investors. Investors entrust enormous wealth to the investment managers, brokers, and custodians who control their funds. Professional investment management is possible only because various systems ensure that all traders settle their contracts and nobody takes what is not theirs. Everyone who works in the investment industry must be aware of the trust that investors place in them. As a participant in this industry, you must know why that trust is important and you must always act to preserve that trust.

# CHAPTER 13

## STRUCTURE OF THE INVESTMENT INDUSTRY

by Larry Harris, PhD, CFA

# LEARNING OUTCOMES

After completing this chapter, you should be able to do the following:

**a** Identify and describe types of individual and institutional investors;

**b** Describe needs served by the investment industry;

**c** Describe services provided by the investment industry, including financial planning, investment management, investment information, trading, and custodial and depository services;

**d** Compare passive and active management, and describe approaches used by active investment managers to design their investment strategies;

**e** Identify types of financial intermediaries, including deposit-taking institutions, finance corporations, securitizers, and insurance companies, and explain their role in the investment industry;

**f** Distinguish between buy- and sell-side firms in the investment industry;

**g** Distinguish between front-, middle-, and back-office functions in the investment industry;

**h** Identify positions and responsibilities for firms in the investment industry;

**i** Describe aspects of institutional investment management processes.

# INTRODUCTION

The investment industry helps individuals, companies, and governments save money for the future. The most common reasons individuals save are to ensure that money will be available for unforeseen circumstances, to buy a house, to cover their living expenses during retirement, to pay for college or university tuition, to fund travel and charitable gifts, and to pass wealth on to the next generation. Companies save to invest in future projects and to pay future taxes, payrolls, and other expenses. Governments save when they collect tax revenues or receive the proceeds of bond sales before these funds are spent.

The investment industry also facilitates borrowing by individuals, companies, and governments that need to spend money that they do not currently have. Individuals often borrow money to pay for houses, tuition, and unforeseen expenses. Companies borrow money to invest in new products and markets or to make acquisitions. Governments borrow when their current tax receipts are insufficient to fund their current spending plans.

Borrowers obtain money from investors by promising to make interest and principal repayments when due. The promises that borrowers make to return money in the future allow investors to save for the future. Successful investing is only possible when borrowers make the payments that investors expect to receive.

Companies can also issue shares of stock to raise funds. Investors who provide these funds receive shares that represent partial ownership of the company's assets and future profits. The investment industry helps arrange these equity transactions between companies and investors.

Investments work well when they preserve and grow wealth and when they generate income. Successful investments provide financial security and comfort to investors. Investments are unsuccessful when they lose value or fail to produce income during the period of the investment and thereby disappoint investors and reduce their wealth. Perhaps no financial activity promotes human welfare as much as successful investing.

The investment industry provides many services to facilitate successful investing. Investment advisers and managers recommend investments and oversee investment funds. Financial intermediaries create investment products that investors use to meet their financial goals. Brokers, dealers, exchanges, clearing and settlement agents, and custodians help investors buy, sell, and safeguard investment products.

This chapter describes the structure of the investment industry. It discusses how investment professionals organize their efforts to help their clients meet their financial goals. It also describes how their efforts help ensure that only the individuals, companies, and governments with the best value-enhancing plans for using capital receive funding.

# 2 INVESTORS

The investment industry serves various types of individual and institutional investors. This section identifies the major types of investors and discusses how they obtain investment services.

## 2.1 Individual Investors

Investment industry practitioners distinguish among individual investors according to their total investment assets. There is no universal standard to classify individual investors; the distinction between categories of individual investors varies across countries, currencies, and investment management firms. **Retail investors** have the fewest assets. **High-net-worth investors** have more investable assets. Finally, ultra-high-net-worth investors have the most investable assets of all individuals.

The services that the investment industry provides to individual investors differ depending on the investor's wealth and level of investment knowledge and expertise, as well as the regulatory environment. Retail investors tend to receive standardized services, whereas wealthier investors often receive services specially tailored to their needs.

### 2.1.1 Retail Investors

Retail investors are individuals who

- buy and sell relatively small amounts of securities and assets for their personal accounts,

- may select investments themselves or may hire professional managers to help them make investment decisions, and

- may invest indirectly by buying pooled investment products, such as mutual fund shares or insurance contracts.

The investment industry provides mostly standardized services to retail investors because retail investors are by far the most numerous, and because they generate the least revenue per investor. Many retail investment services are delivered over the internet or through customer service representatives working at call centers.

### 2.1.2 High-Net-Worth Investors

Wealthier investors generally receive more personal attention from more knowledgeable personnel. Their investment problems often involve tax and estate (i.e., inheritance) planning issues that require special attention. They either pay directly for these services on a fee-for-service basis or indirectly through commissions and other transaction costs (which are described more thoroughly in Chapter 15).

### 2.1.3 *Ultra-High-Net-Worth Investors and Family Offices*

Very wealthy individuals usually employ professionals who help them manage their investments, future estates, and legal affairs. These professionals often work out of a **family office**, which is a private company that manages the financial affairs of one or more members of a family or of multiple families. Many family offices serve the heirs of large family fortunes that have been accumulated over generations. In addition to investment services, family offices may also provide personal services to the family members, such as bookkeeping, tax planning, managing household employees, making travel arrangements, and planning social affairs.

Wealthy families often have substantial real estate holdings and very large investment portfolios. The investment professionals who work in family offices generally manage these investments using the same methods and systems that institutional investors use. They pay especially close attention to personal and estate tax issues that may significantly affect the family's wealth and its ability to pass wealth on to future generations or charitable institutions.

## 2.2 Institutional Investors

**Institutional investors** include companies, trusts, and governments that invest to advance their missions or to provide financial services to their clients. A trust is created by a grantor (also called creator or settlor), who transfers assets to the trust. The trust is managed by a trustee for the benefit of a designated party (or parties) known as the beneficiary (or beneficiaries). For example, a parent may create a trust to hold a portfolio of real estate properties for the benefit of their children. Institutions that invest to advance their missions include pension funds, endowments and foundations, governments and sovereign wealth funds, and non-financial companies. Those institutions that invest to provide financial services to their clients include investment companies, banks, and insurance companies.

Institutional investors have grown in importance over the last few decades, mainly as a result of increased prosperity and the growth of pension funds. They now are the dominant investors in most markets throughout the world. The funds in which institutional investors invest are often very large. Institutional investors may hire professional investment managers to manage their investments, or they may manage them in-house.

### 2.2.1 *Pension Funds*

**Pension funds** hold investment portfolios for the benefit of future and current retirees, called beneficiaries. The companies and governments that sponsor these plans are called pension sponsors or plan sponsors.

Pension plans differ by whether they are organized as defined benefit or defined contribution plans. **Defined benefit pension plans** promise a certain annual amount to their beneficiaries during their retirement. Defined benefit pension funds are among the largest institutional investors. They may invest in equity securities, fixed-income (debt) securities, real estate, precious metals, and commodities. As of September 2011, the Government Pension Investment Fund in Japan was the largest defined benefit pension fund in the world; it held US$1.43 trillion in assets on behalf of its beneficiaries.

In contrast, in a **defined contribution pension plan**, participants contribute to their own retirement plan accounts, usually through employee payroll deductions. In some cases, the pension sponsor also contributes an agreed-on amount (i.e., the defined contribution) to the participant's account. The participants choose how to invest their funds by picking investment products from a list of one or more approved products that the pension sponsor makes available to them. The sponsor generally limits the choices to a set of mutual funds sponsored by approved investment managers.

In the past, most pension plans were defined benefit pension plans. Because these plans promise benefits to their beneficiaries, they are expensive obligations for the sponsor. Many sponsors are no longer offering defined benefit pension plans, which explains the growth in defined contribution pension plans in most countries. Chapter 14 offers a detailed comparison of defined benefit and defined contribution pension plans.

### 2.2.2 Endowments and Foundations

**Endowment funds** are long-term funds of non-profit institutions, such as universities, colleges, and schools; museums, theaters, and opera companies; and hospitals and clinics. These organizations generally provide services to their students, patrons, and patients. **Foundations** are grant-making institutions funded by gifts and by the investment income that they produce. Most foundations do not directly provide services. Instead, they fund institutions that provide services in such areas as the arts or charities. Foundations often own endowment funds.

Endowment funds and foundations receive gifts from donors interested in supporting their activities. They typically have a charitable or philanthropic purpose for which money has been gifted or raised. Donors give funds for current or for future use. The gifts, such as cash or shares of stock, may have restrictions on how they can be used, or they may be unrestricted, in which case they usually fund operating expenses or special projects undertaken at the discretion of the recipient organization. In many countries, donations to these organizations are tax deductible for the donors—that is, donations reduce the income on which the donors have to pay taxes. Investment income and capital gains that these organizations receive from investing these funds may also be tax exempt.

Gifts given to provide long-term support include donations intended to provide income indefinitely (perpetual endowments) and those intended for use during a fixed term (term gifts). Both types of gifts are placed into endowment funds. Institutions manage perpetual endowment funds to maintain the real purchasing power of the funds, which is the principal value adjusted for inflation, while producing income to fund current spending. They generally invest endowment funds in equities, long-term bonds, real estate, and commodities. Many institutions also often receive gifts intended to support current programs. These institutions invest these current funds in short-term instruments until they need to use the money.

Most organizations with endowment funds hire professional investment managers to manage their funds. Some may manage portions of their funds internally, in some cases through an investment management company that they own and of which they are the only client.

As of September 2011, Harvard Management Company was the largest university-owned investment management company; the university had US$32 billion in endowment funds. Harvard Management Company manages the university's endowment funds using both internal and external managers. Examples of multi-billion-dollar foundations that successful business people have set up to provide funding for charitable purposes include the Bill & Melinda Gates Foundation in the United States, the Li Ka Shing Foundation in China, and Stichting INGKA in the Netherlands.

### 2.2.3 Governments and Sovereign Wealth Funds

Governments receive revenues from collecting taxes or selling bonds. When they do not have to spend these revenues immediately, they usually invest. Some governments have accumulated enormous surpluses from selling natural resources that they control or from financing the trade of goods and services. They have created **sovereign wealth funds** to invest these surpluses for the benefit of current and future generations of their citizens. Sovereign wealth funds invest in long-term securities and assets. They also may purchase companies. Sovereign wealth funds either manage their investments in-house or hire investment managers to manage their funds.

Abu Dhabi Investment Authority was created to manage the United Arab Emirates' funds from oil revenues; the fund receives the surplus wealth from petroleum production. It is an example of a very large sovereign wealth fund. Another example of a sovereign wealth fund is the State Administration of Foreign Exchange (SAFE) in China, which manages the country's foreign exchange reserves.

### 2.2.4 Non-Financial Companies

Analysts often identify companies as either financial companies or non-financial companies. Financial companies include investment companies, banks and other lenders, and insurance companies. These companies provide financial services to their clients. In contrast, non-financial companies produce goods and non-financial services for their customers.

Non-financial companies invest funds that they do not presently require to run their businesses. These may be short-term, mid-term, or long-term funds. The corporate treasurer usually manages the short-term investments. These funds typically include cash that the company soon will need to pay wages and accounts payable. Companies generally invest these short-term funds in instruments that are safe and liquid. These instruments include demand deposits (checking accounts) at banks, money market funds, and short-term debt securities issued by governments or other companies. Examples of short-term debt securities include short-term government bonds, certificates of deposit issued by banks, and commercial paper issued by financial and non-financial companies.

Long-term investments are usually managed under the direction of the chief financial officer or the chief investment officer, if the company has one. Companies often hold long-term funds to finance future research, investments, and acquisitions of companies and products. Companies may invest their long-term funds directly, or they may hire investment managers to invest on their behalf.

Many companies invest directly in the equities and bonds of their suppliers and in the equities of potential merger partners to strengthen their relationships with them. Practitioners call these investments "strategic investments." These types of investments are common in Asian countries, such as Japan and South Korea, and in European countries, such as France, Germany, and Italy.

### 2.2.5 Investment Companies

**Investment companies** include mutual funds, hedge funds, private equity funds, and investment trusts. These companies exist solely to hold investments on behalf of their shareholders, partners, or unit holders—units refer to shares and bonds for equity and debt securities, respectively. The shares or partnership interests of these companies are called **pooled investment vehicles** because investors in these companies pool their funds for common management. Investment companies are managed by professional investment managers who work for investment management companies. These management companies often organize and market the investment companies that they manage, and thus are their investment sponsors.

Fidelity Investments is an example of a company that organizes and manages mutual funds. Its subsidiary Fidelity Management & Research Company manages 424 mutual funds with a total of US$1.5 trillion in assets as of year-end 2011.

### 2.2.6 Finance Companies

Finance companies, such as banks, leasing companies, payday advance lenders, and factors (i.e., companies that provide funds to other companies by buying their accounts receivable), all hold investment portfolios that represent substantial portions of their balance sheets. The investments of those companies whose primary business is to lend money consist of the loans that they write. The investments of leasing companies consist of the plants and equipment that they lease, and the investments of factors consist of the accounts receivable that they buy.

### 2.2.7 Insurance Companies

Insurance companies collect premiums from the individuals and companies they insure. Premiums are payments that insurance companies require to provide insurance coverage. These premiums are put into reserve funds from which insurance companies pay out claims. Insurance companies invest their reserve funds in highly diversified portfolios of securities and assets to ensure that sufficient funds are always available to satisfy all claims. Regulators often set requirements to restrict the types of investments insurance companies can hold. Insurance companies profit from income that they can earn on the float, which is the amount of money they have available to use after receiving premiums and before paying claims.

Insurance companies write annuity contracts and life insurance policies. As described in Chapter 5, somebody investing in an annuity makes an initial payment of a sum to the insurance company in exchange for a fixed number of future payments of a certain amount. Insurance companies invest the sums received from the sale of annuity contracts and life insurance policies into long-term funds from which they pay annuity payments and life insurance claims. They invest these funds, which often are very large, in securities, commodities, real estate, and other real assets. Insurance companies that write property and casualty policies generally invest their reserve funds in shorter-term investments that are more conservative and liquid.

Insurance companies try to match their investments to their liabilities. For example, if they expect to make fixed annuity payments in the distant future, they may invest in long-term fixed-income securities to match the interest rate risk of their investments to the interest rate risk of their liabilities. This strategy of matching investment assets to liabilities, called asset/liability matching, reduces the risk that the company will fail to pay its claims when due if interest rates change substantially.

# Investors

Most large insurance companies manage their investments in-house. They also may contract with specialty investment managers to manage investments in industries, asset classes, or geographical regions where they lack expertise or access.

## 2.3 Comparison of the Types of Investors

**Individual Investors**

| | |
|---|---|
| Retail Investors | ■ Individuals who buy and sell relatively small amounts of securities and assets for their personal accounts. |
| | ■ Select investments themselves, hire professional managers to help them, and/or invest indirectly by buying pooled investment products. |
| | ■ Receive mostly standardized services because they are the most numerous and generate the least revenue per investor. |
| High-Net-Worth Investors | ■ Receive more personal attention from more knowledgeable personnel. |
| | ■ May have investment problems that involve tax and estate planning issues. |
| | ■ Pay directly for services on a fee-for-service basis or indirectly through commission and other transaction costs. |
| Ultra-High-Net-Worth Investors | ■ Usually employ professionals who work out of a family office to help them manage their investments, future estates, and legal affairs. |
| | ■ Often have substantial real estate holdings and very large investment portfolios. |
| | ■ Generally have their investments managed using the same methods and systems that institutional investors use. |
| | ■ Must pay especially close attention to personal and estate tax issues. |

**Institutional Investors**

| | |
|---|---|
| Pension Funds | ■ Hold investment portfolios for the benefit of future and current retirees (beneficiaries). |
| | ■ Defined benefit pension plans promise a certain annual amount to their beneficiaries during their retirement. |
| | ■ In defined contribution pension plans, participants contribute to their own retirement plan accounts, usually through employee payroll deductions. |

*(continued)*

| **Institutional Investors** | |
|---|---|
| Endowments and Foundations | ■ Endowment funds are long-term funds for non-profit institutions. |
| | ■ Foundations are grant-making institutions funded by gifts and by the investment income they produce. |
| | ■ Foundations often own endowment funds. |
| | ■ Both receive gifts from donors interested in supporting their activities. |
| Governments and Sovereign Wealth Funds | ■ Governments receive revenues from collecting taxes and selling bonds. When they do not have to spend these revenues immediately, they usually invest. |
| | ■ Governments create sovereign wealth funds to invest their surpluses for the benefit of current and future generations of their citizens. |
| Non-Financial Companies | ■ Produce goods and non-financial services for their customers. |
| | ■ Invest funds that they do not presently require to run their businesses. These may be short-term, mid-term, or long-term investments. |
| Investment Companies | ■ Include mutual funds, hedge funds, private equity funds, and investment trusts. |
| | ■ Exist solely to hold investments on behalf of their shareholders, partners, or unit holders. |
| | ■ The shares or partnership interests of these companies are called pooled investment vehicles because investors in these companies pool their funds for common management. |
| Finance Companies | ■ Hold investment portfolios that represent substantial portions of their balance sheets. |
| Insurance Companies | ■ Collect premiums from the individuals and companies they insure. |
| | ■ Premiums are put into reserve funds from which they pay out claims. |
| | ■ Invest their reserve funds in highly diversified portfolios of securities and assets to ensure that sufficient funds are always available to satisfy all claims. |

# HOW THE INVESTMENT INDUSTRY PROMOTES SUCCESSFUL INVESTING

Investing involves many activities that most individual and institutional investors cannot do themselves. Investors must

- determine how much money they will need to invest for future uses and how much money they can withdraw over time while still maintaining their investment objectives;

- identify potential investments;

- evaluate the risk and return prospects of potential investments;

- trade investment securities and assets; and

- hold, manage, and account for investment securities and assets during the periods of the investments.

These processes generally require information, expertise, systems, and contact with potential borrowers and equity issuers that few individual and institutional investors have. Investors obtain assistance with these processes from investment professionals, either directly by hiring investment managers or indirectly by investing in investment products that professional investment managers create and oversee, such as mutual funds, insurance contracts, and securitized assets. Recall from Chapter 10 that securitization refers to the creation and issuance of new debt securities that are backed (secured) by a pool of other debt securities, such as mortgage-backed securities. Securitization is further discussed in Section 9.2.

Raising debt also involves activities that many individuals and institutions cannot easily do themselves. Borrowers must

- determine how much money they are capable of repaying;

- decide how to structure their borrowing to obtain funds on the best possible terms;

- find investors willing to lend money or purchase their debt securities (bills, notes, and bonds); and

- when required, register their securities and provide current, timely, and audited financial reports.

Companies issuing equity likewise must

- determine how much money they are capable of raising;

- decide how best to structure their business plans, corporate governance, and equity issues to obtain funds at the lowest cost;

- find investors willing to purchase their shares of stock; and

- when required, register their securities and provide current, timely, and audited financial reports.

These funding processes also require information, expertise, systems, and contact with potential investors that few individuals, companies, and governments have on their own. Borrowers and issuers of equity obtain assistance with these processes from investment professionals who provide consulting and brokerage services. **Brokerage services** are the services provided to clients who want to buy and sell securities; they include not only execution services (i.e., processing orders on behalf of clients) but also investment advice or research. Investment professionals also may fund loans or purchase the bonds and equities issued by the companies and governments they advise.

Some firms and professionals working in the investment industry specialize in providing a single service or product. Others provide a broad spectrum of investment services. For the sake of clarity, this discussion considers each service separately, even though most firms and professionals provide multiple services. For example, many financial planners also provide investment advice, as do many brokers. Likewise, most commercial banks sell loans as well as certificates of deposit.

## 4  FINANCIAL PLANNING SERVICES

Investment clients often need advice about how much money they should save for future expenses or how much they can spend for current expenses while still preserving their capital. **Financial planners** provide answers to these questions for their clients. Financial planners help their clients understand their future financial needs, the risks that they face when investing, their ability to tolerate investment risks, and their preferences for capital preservation versus capital growth.

Financial planners also create savings and payout plans appropriate for their clients' needs. The plans often require complex analyses that depend on expected rates of return and risks for various asset classes, the investors' capacity and tolerance for bearing risk, tax issues, and projections of future expenses. Future expenses are often particularly hard to forecast. They may depend on inflation, and in the case of retirement expenses, uncertain longevity and uncertain future healthcare expenses. Analyses related to healthcare and pensions are typically done by actuaries—professionals who specialize in assessing insurance risks using statistical models.

Financial planners often suggest asset allocations that are intended to help investors meet their financial goals. Asset allocations indicate what fraction of total investable funds the client should invest in various asset classes, such as domestic equity, fixed income, real estate, foreign equity, and commodities. Financial planners may work for investment management firms as employees, contractors, or agents. They may also be self-employed brokers who arrange trades for their clients and earn income from the commissions on these trades.

Most financial planners serving retail clients are also **investment advisers** who recommend investment strategies and suggest trades. The fees that retail clients pay investment advisers may cover financial planning services, or the investment advisers may charge for these services separately.

Many investment management firms, such as those that manage mutual funds and pension funds, also employ financial planners to help shareholders and pension beneficiaries make better savings decisions. Some employers also contract with financial planning consultants to make financial planning services available to their employees and retirees. Increasingly, financial planners serving these clientele use automated electronic systems to provide financial planning advice over the internet.

Foundations and endowment funds sometimes hire financial planners to help them create their payout policies. **Payout policies** specify how much money the institution can take from long-term funds to use for current spending. A typical payout policy may state that the fund can pay out 5% of its average net asset value measured over the last three years. Because prospective donors frequently request information about investments and payout policies, foundations and endowment funds often establish these policies based on carefully prepared and well-articulated analyses. Financial planners who help write these policies typically work for investment consulting firms. The payout policies depend on the assumptions the financial planners make about future expected investment returns. Assuming high future expected returns allows for more current spending. But if these assumptions prove to be overly optimistic, payouts will exceed the returns generated by the fund, and the value of the fund will decrease over time.

## INVESTMENT MANAGEMENT SERVICES

Many investors rely on investment advisers for advice about the investments they should hold. They often give their advisers authority to trade securities and assets on their behalf. Advisers who have such discretionary authority are often called **investment managers** or **asset managers**. Investment managers who manage funds are also often called **fund managers**. Depending on the context, these terms may refer to the individuals who make investment decisions or to the companies for which they work.

The investment advisers who advise institutional investors typically work for investment management firms. Their clients may include mutual funds (which are typically founded by the investment management firm itself), pension funds, foundations, endowment funds, and family offices.

Many retail clients obtain investment advice from investment advisers who work for retail brokerage companies or for the investment management subsidiaries of these brokerages—more information about brokerages is provided in Section 7.1. Retail clients may also obtain investment advice from independent investment advisers, many of whom are brokers or agents who receive commissions from the companies that sell mutual funds and life insurance policies for the trades that they recommend. Retail clients also indirectly obtain advisory services when they invest in pooled investment products, such as mutual funds and pension funds that are managed by professional investment managers.

Investment advisers who accept payments only from their clients are called fee-only advisers. Unlike brokers and agents who are paid commissions on the trades that they recommend, fee-only advisers do not have incentives to generate commissions by recommending specific products, making excessive trades, or suggesting sales of real estate and collectibles to free up capital to purchase commissionable securities.

Clients pay management fees to their investment managers for their advisory services. The fees typically depend on the total assets under management. Clients may also pay incentive fees that depend on the investment performance of the portfolio.

## 5.1 Passive and Active Management

Investment advisers may provide passive or active investment advice, or both. **Passive investment managers** seek to match the return and risk of an appropriate benchmark. Benchmarks include broad market indices, indices for a specific market segment, and specifically constructed benchmarks. Index investing is the most important type of passive investing. Index investment managers buy and hold securities that they believe will produce portfolio returns that replicate closely the returns of an index. A fund designed to replicate the returns of a securities index is called an **index fund**.

Investors use passive investment strategies when they are willing to accept market rates of returns on their investments (minus the costs associated with investing). Passive investment strategies are the least costly strategies to implement because they only involve buying and holding securities based on their characteristics rather than on analyses of their future return prospects.

In contrast, **active investment managers** try to predict which securities and assets will outperform or underperform comparable securities and assets. They then act on their opinions by buying the securities and assets that they expect will outperform and selling (or simply not buying) those that they expect will underperform. Investors use active strategies when they believe that they can identify advisers whose advice will allow them to outperform the market after taking into consideration all fees and commissions.

When seeking excess performance, active managers may focus on individual securities, industries, sectors, or markets. Those that focus on individual securities are sometimes called stock pickers. Those that focus on industries, sectors, or markets are called tactical asset allocators.

Active investment managers collect and analyze as much relevant information as they can reasonably obtain in their efforts to predict which securities and assets will outperform or underperform their peers in the future. To this end, active managers employ research assistants to collect data and expert analysts to analyze data. Those analysts who primarily rely on mathematical and statistical models are called quantitative analysts or quants.

# Investment Management Services

Active investment managers differ in the methods that they use to identify future performance. Fundamental managers focus on macroeconomic, industry-specific, and company-specific factors that make securities and assets valuable. Other managers use technical or behavioral models to predict how trading by other market participants may change future market prices.

## 5.2 Fundamental Managers

As explained in Chapters 9 and 10, the value of a security can be viewed as the present value of all the cash flows the security will generate in the future. For example, recall from the Volkswagen example in Chapter 9 that an investor can estimate the value of a stock by discounting all the dividends she expects to receive while she holds the stock plus the proceeds from selling the stock. Value that is estimated this way is called the stock's **fundamental value** or **intrinsic value**. Although fundamental values are never observed, many investment managers work very hard to accurately estimate them. To do so, they must forecast future cash flows and estimate the rates at which these cash flows are discounted.

**Fundamental Management**   Fundamental managers operate on the premise that securities market prices tend to move toward their estimates of fundamental values. Their advice can produce exceptional returns when they accurately estimate values and make the appropriate investments before other market participants eventually concur with their opinions.

Fundamental managers pay attention to many issues when forming investment opinions. The issues most important to their opinions vary according to whether they are analyzing fixed-income securities or equities. When analyzing fixed-income securities (bonds, notes, and bills) or securities that share many common features with fixed-income securities (such as preferred stocks), they consider the borrowers' ability and willingness to pay their debts—that is, the borrower's creditworthiness and trustworthiness. Lenders consider borrowers to be creditworthy if they expect that the borrowers will be able to pay interest, principal, and preferred dividends when due. They consider borrowers to be trustworthy if they expect that borrowers will arrange their affairs to ensure that they can and will make these payments. Fundamental managers analyze financial data and past borrowing histories to determine whether borrowers are creditworthy and trustworthy.

When analyzing equities (and the debt securities of all but the most financially strong companies), fundamental managers pay close attention to the issuer's future prospects for earning money and producing valuable assets. Among many other issues, they consider the following:

- demand for the company's products;

- cost of producing those products;

- profit margins of the company, and whether these margins are sustainable;

- competitiveness of the company, and whether it can remain competitive;

- quality, stability, and security of the company's management, workforce, and physical and intellectual assets;

- productivity of its research and development efforts;

- amount of debt the company uses to fund its operations and investments;

- value of options to suspend or expand operations or to engage in new initiatives;

- prospects for disruptive technological innovations, the imposition or removal of significant regulatory constraints, and legal or extralegal expropriations that may affect the company's viability;

- macroeconomic issues, such as prospects for inflation, national economic growth, and unemployment;

- legal and regulatory environment the company operates within, and whether any major changes are planned; and

- corporate governance problems that may allow corporate managers to waste or misuse corporate earnings that otherwise could be distributed to shareholders or be retained to pay off debt holders.

**Valuation Analysis** Good fundamental valuation analyses require excellent information about markets, technologies, politics, and governance. The information must be relevant, detailed, and current. Sound analyses also require financial, economic, technical, and political experts who can reliably draw the proper inferences from relevant information. Managers who can obtain and correctly analyze information before others can produce the most valuable advice. Accordingly, fundamental managers devote considerable resources to acquiring information and to obtaining the services of expert analysts. They may organize these resources internally or contract to obtain them from companies that provide professional research.

**Specialization** Fundamental managers generally specialize in different analytical approaches. For example, managers using the top-down approach first examine general economic conditions to determine which industries or asset classes will most likely outperform in the future. They then select securities in those industries or asset classes for their portfolios. In contrast, managers using the bottom-up approach look for companies that they expect will outperform their peers regardless of industry or macroeconomic conditions.

Many fundamental managers also specialize in different market sectors. For example, some managers specialize in particular industries, whereas others consider the broad market. Likewise, value managers specialize in securities issued by well-established companies that have strong current revenues, whereas growth managers focus on securities issued by generally younger companies with substantial prospects for future revenue growth.

## 5.3 Technical and Behavioral Managers

Investment managers who use technical and behavioral approaches try to buy a particular security or asset before an increase in buyer interest or a decrease in seller interest causes the price of the security to rise. Recall from the discussion about supply and demand in Chapter 6 that an increase in demand (which occurs when there is either an increase in buyer interest or a decrease in seller interest) has a positive effect on price. Technical and behavioral managers likewise try to sell before an increase in seller interest or a decrease in buyer interest causes the price of the security to fall. Their advice is valuable when they can predict the trades that large traders, or large numbers of small traders, will make.

To anticipate these trades, technical managers study market information, including price patterns and trading volumes, whereas behavioral managers focus on indicators of market sentiment, such as manufacturers' new orders or indices of consumer expectations.

## 5.4 The Challenge of Active Management

Accurately predicting future security and asset returns is very difficult because prices generally already reflect most publicly available information about fundamental values. Accordingly, even well-informed analysts cannot predict most price changes. The competition among investors ensures that almost everyone obtains only market rates of returns, on average, when investing. Much academic and practitioner research has shown that most active managers do not consistently outperform the market over long time periods, after accounting for fees and expenses. Unfortunately, identifying those active managers who will outperform the market in the future is generally as difficult as identifying those assets that will outperform the market.

The investment research necessary to predict future prices and the active trading necessary to profit from these insights make active investment management costly. Concerns about the costs, the average or below-average performance of most active managers, and the difficulties of identifying active investment managers who will outperform in the future have made passive investment strategies increasingly popular over time. Despite these concerns, active management still remains popular because many investors want to beat the market—especially when interest rates are low, as they have been following the global financial crisis of 2008.

# INVESTMENT INFORMATION SERVICES 6

Many investors and their investment managers obtain investment research, financial data, and investment consulting services from companies that specialize in providing these services. These companies include investment research providers, credit rating agencies, financial news services, financial data vendors, and investment consultants. This section introduces these companies and discusses the various business models that they use to generate revenue.

## 6.1 Investment Research Providers

Many investors use investment research reports when making investment decisions. These reports often help them obtain deeper insights into investment values, credit risks, and investment strategies.

The firms that provide investment research assemble information and opinions that most investors cannot easily produce themselves. To produce their research, these companies employ data collectors, financial reporters, and expert analysts. Investment research reports can be particularly valuable when they are written by industry experts who understand the financial implications of new industrial technologies—for example, the fracking technologies that oil and gas drillers now increasingly use to extract hydrocarbons.

Most investment reports are largely based on the publicly available financial disclosures made by issuers. These reports summarize information from these lengthy disclosures that would otherwise be very time consuming for investors to assemble themselves. Many reports also present financial analyses that estimate the values of an issuer's securities. The authors of these reports usually identify and discuss the assumptions on which they base their valuation estimates.

Investors often get research reports from their brokers, who purchase research reports (or produce them internally in their research departments) to distribute to their clients. Brokers give research to their clients to better serve them, to attract new clients, and to encourage their clients to trade. Investors may also purchase reports directly from independent research companies, or they may obtain reports from research companies that issuers pay to produce investment reports about their securities.

Some institutional investors, such as mutual funds, pay soft commissions to their brokers when trading. **Soft commissions** (also called soft dollar commissions or arrangements) refer to the use of commissions to buy services other than execution services. Brokers add a fee to execution-only trading services, and this fee is used to pay for investment research that the institutional investor's hired managers use in their decision-making processes. Rather than paying for the research services directly in cash (i.e., hard currency), institutional investors pay for them indirectly through the trading commissions that they pay their brokers.

Soft commissions are controversial because they make expenses less transparent by hiding some of the costs of managing funds. If the investment managers had to pay for the research services with cash, their management fees would be higher and the additional cost would be reported to investors as an expense in the fund accounting statements. Instead, soft commissions are hidden in brokerage commissions, which do not appear as expenses in fund accounting statements. Like all other expenses, soft commissions reduce fund performance, but they are less transparent than if they were reported as a separate expense in the accounts. In many countries, regulators restrict the use of soft commissions. Client commission arrangements and commission sharing arrangements have become increasingly popular between institutional investors and their brokers to clearly separate payments for trading execution from payments for research services.

Many companies that provide investment research disseminate their reports through investment newsletters that they distribute regularly to their paying subscribers. To speed distribution, many research providers now distribute their newsletters over the internet. Some research providers support their operations by selling advertising in their newsletters. They also may supplement their revenues by selling their mailing lists, if their privacy policies permit them to do that.

The benefits for investors from using high-quality research reports depend on how many other investors receive the same information and on how quickly the investors receive and act on the information. When research services have many clients, the first investors to receive information or analyses generally benefit the most from that information. Trading by early recipients often causes security prices to change, which makes the information less valuable to later recipients. Accordingly, investment research providers may charge higher fees to those clients who receive their reports first.

## 6.2 Credit Rating Agencies

**Credit rating agencies** are investment research providers who specialize in providing opinions about the credit quality of bonds and of their issuers. A high bond rating indicates that the rating agency believes that the issuer, for example a company, has a high probability of making all future payments of principal and interest when due. Among other factors, a bond's rating depends on the financial strength of the issuer and on the value of any collateral or third-party guarantees, such as bond insurance, that support the bond.

As discussed in Chapter 10, investors generally consider investment-grade bonds that Fitch Ratings or Standard & Poor's rate as BBB– and above (or that Moody's Investors Service rates as Baa3 and above) to be lower-risk investment-grade securities. Bonds rated below BBB– are called high-yield, speculative, or junk bonds and are considered to be higher-risk securities. Many institutional investors and investment managers have investment policies that restrict or even prevent them from investing in high-yield-grade securities to reduce the chance of losing invested capital.

Most rating agencies do not charge investors for their ratings, although they may charge them for the detailed reports on which the ratings are based. Instead, corporate issuers pay rating agencies to rate their securities because ratings generally make securities more marketable. An obvious conflict of interest thus arises because issuers are likely to direct their business to those agencies that will provide high ratings. But credit rating agencies should recognize that if they lose their independence, investors may no longer respect their ratings.

Some rating agencies also sell their research to investors on a subscription basis or on a fee-for-report basis. The purchasers must promise not to further disseminate the ratings and research reports because such dissemination would make it harder for the agency to sell its products to other investors.

## 6.3 Data Vendors

To invest and trade successfully, investors—especially active investors—need current and accurate information about company fundamentals and market conditions. Many **data vendors** provide these information resources.

The data that interest investors include historical data and real-time data. Exhibit 1 shows the types of historical data that may be of interest to investors, and how investors may use these data to make decisions.

**Exhibit 1   Types, Examples, and Potential Uses of Historical Data**

| Type of Data | Examples | Potential Uses |
|---|---|---|
| Reference data | Information about assets, securities, and financial contracts, including their key characteristics. For example, for a bond, the database will mention the issuer, maturity date, par value, number of units, coupon (interest) rate, and so on. | Investors and financial analysts use reference data to identify information that determines or affects the value of assets, securities, and financial contracts. |
| Macroeconomic data | ■ Information about economic activity, such as production, trade flows, and labor utilization.<br>■ Information about government revenues and expenses, interest rates, and exchange rates. | Fundamental analysts use macroeconomic data to better understand the environment in which companies operate and compete. |
| Financial data | ■ Accounting information, such as a company's financial statements, including the balance sheet, income statement, and cash flow statement, as well as the footnotes to these financial statements.<br>■ Information about dividends and share repurchases. | Fundamental analysts use financial and corporate earnings and price forecast data to estimate the fundamental value of securities, such as stocks and determine whether they want to buy, hold, or sell these stocks. |
| Corporate earnings and price forecasts data | Information about corporate earnings and price forecasts that analysts make. | |
| Historical market data | Information about past market prices and trading volumes. | ■ Fundamental analysts use historical market data to understand past price changes.<br>■ Technical analysts use historical market data to identify patterns in market prices and trading volumes that they believe will help them predict future price changes. |
| Corporate governance data | Information about corporate governance structures, such as the number of independent (i.e., outside) directors and whether the chief executive officer is also the chairman of the board of directors. | Investors and financial analysts use corporate governance data to better understand the control mechanisms at a company, how value is created by management, and whether the value will accrue to the benefit of shareholders and bondholders (as opposed to managers or their associates). |
| Insider holdings and trading data | Information about the positions and trades of corporate insiders, such as senior executives or board members. | Investors and financial analysts use insider holdings and trading data to assess insiders' sentiments and to determine whether insiders have a strong incentive to work hard and to increase shareholder value. |
| Large investor holdings data | Information about the positions and trades of large investors, such as institutional investors. | Investors and financial analysts use large investor holdings data to better understand institutional investors' strategies. |

## Exhibit 1  (Continued)

| Type of Data | Examples | Potential Uses |
|---|---|---|
| Benchmark data | Information about securities market indices for various markets and asset classes. | Financial analysts use benchmark data to evaluate the performance of their investments and investment managers. |

The following are the most important real-time data resources:

- Market data feeds. Market data feeds provide traders with current information about market quotes, orders, and recent trades. Traders need this information to effectively arrange their trades. Managers of large mutual funds pay particular attention to this information because their trades can move markets. If markets are not sufficiently liquid to accommodate their desired trades, fund managers cannot fully achieve their objectives.

- Newsfeeds. Newsfeeds provide current news about company and market fundamentals that investors need to know when valuing securities. Poorly informed traders risk trading on stale information and losing to better-informed traders. Financial news services employ reporters to collect and distribute information about companies. They also receive and immediately redistribute press releases that companies distribute electronically. Vendors allow their customers to filter these newsfeeds to receive only news about companies that interest them and to make keyword queries for stories.

Data vendors may provide many or all of these services (and more), or they may specialize in providing information in a narrow niche. Bloomberg and Thomson Reuters are examples of large, full-service data vendors. In contrast, some specialty data vendors collect information, such as product inventory on hand, on a confidential basis from many companies in an industry. They then sell summaries of this information to analysts.

Access to investment data was once very expensive and thus restricted to institutional investors and broker/dealers. The growth of information technologies, particularly those involving the internet, has substantially reduced the cost of accessing data, so more investment data are now widely available to the general public. Some data, such as regulatory disclosures by issuers, can be freely accessed over the internet. Other data are only available on a subscription basis from vendors. Although these services are often very expensive, the scope and depth of the information resources that they provide have grown substantially over time.

The widespread availability of investment data has greatly changed the investment industry landscape. Access to data used to be a key driver of investment profits, but now investment profits increasingly depend on the ability to analyze data.

### 6.4 Investment Industry Consultants

Although they are not formally considered providers of investment information, investment industry consultants provide various information services that help institutional investors and sophisticated retail investors improve their investment processes. These services include transaction cost estimation, risk estimation, manager selection, and performance evaluation. These services often require technical expertise and access to databases that are not widely available. Investment consultants may charge their clients by the hour for these services, or they may charge annual fees for access to their systems.

Aon Hewitt, Mercer, Russell Investments, and Towers Watson are examples of large investment consultants with global operations. These firms offer a wide range of services in human resources and talent management, pensions, insurance, and risk management.

Some consultants also provide consulting services to exchanges and investment managers seeking to create new products. These consultants may be paid by the project, or they may license the investment products that they create for their clients.

## 7 TRADING SERVICES

Brokers, dealers, arbitrageurs, and exchanges provide various services that facilitate investment by helping buyers and sellers of investment securities and assets arrange trades with each other.

### 7.1 Brokers

**Brokers** are agents who arrange trades for their clients. They generally provide many different trading services. First and foremost, brokers find sellers for their clients who want to buy as well as buyers for their clients who want to sell. For highly liquid securities, the search usually only involves routing (directing) a client's order to an exchange or to a dealer. For less liquid securities and investment assets, brokers may spend substantial resources looking for suitable counterparties. For complex trades, such as real estate transactions, for which effective negotiation is essential to successful investment, brokers often serve as professional negotiators. In such transactions, skilled negotiators can increase the probability of arranging trades on favorable terms.

Brokers often also ensure that their clients will settle their trades. Such assurances are essential when public exchanges arrange trades between strangers who do not have credit arrangements with each other. For such trades, brokers guarantee settlement of their clients' trades.

Clients pay commissions to their brokers for arranging their trades. The commissions vary widely but typically depend on the values or quantities traded. It is worth noting that commissions have decreased over the past 30 years, primarily because of deregulation, technological progress, and increased competition among brokers.

**Investment banks** provide important brokerage services by helping their clients arrange trades. They also organize fund raising for their corporate and government clients. Their corporate finance divisions help companies raise money by selling newly issued equities, bonds, and warrants to the public or by brokering bank loans. Their public finance divisions help governments raise money by selling bonds and notes. The investment bankers who provide these services are specialists in matching investors with companies and governments seeking capital. They pay close attention to the types of investments that investors most want so that they can help companies and governments seeking capital to design securities that will suit their needs and appeal to investors. By offering securities that investors want to purchase, these companies and governments are able to obtain funds at a lower cost.

The merger and acquisition (M&A) divisions of investment banks help companies identify and acquire other companies or sell off one or more divisions within the companies. The investment bankers who provide these services must understand the potential values and costs of various business combinations. Many mergers, acquisitions, and divestments occur when bankers recognize potentially value-enhancing transactions and bring them to the attention of corporate managers. The investment bankers are rewarded by commissions, underwriting fees, and profits from trades they may make in anticipation of the deals that they hope to arrange.

In addition to brokering many types of transactions, most investment banks act as dealers in many securities. Investment banks also commonly offer strategic advice to their corporate clients and research to their brokerage clients. Although no universal organizational structure exists, most investment banks consist of three distinct but related businesses: traditional investment banking (i.e., capital raising and strategic advisory services), sales and trading (i.e., brokerage and dealing), and research.

Barclays Capital, Deutsche Bank, Goldman Sachs, and Standard Chartered Bank are a few examples of very large global investment banks.

## 7.2 Exchanges and Alternative Trading Systems

Exchanges and most alternative trading systems arrange trades by matching buy and sell orders submitted by authorized participants. Authorized participants are brokers, dealers, and other traders to whom these trading systems permit access. The participants may trade for their own accounts, or they may act as brokers to arrange trades on behalf of other traders.

**Exchanges** organize auction markets to which buyers and sellers submit orders for matching. In an auction market, a set of rules is used to match buy and sell orders to arrange trades. All traders can participate, either directly or with the assistance of brokers who are authorized participants. Most exchanges now use electronic systems to conduct their auctions, although some exchanges still organize their trading on floors where brokers and dealers interact with each other in person.

**Alternative trading systems**, known in Europe as multilateral trading facilities, are designed to meet the special needs of various traders. Many of these systems permit only certain types of traders to use their facilities. For example, **crossing networks** arrange trades between large traders who are unwilling to expose their orders at exchange markets for fear of information leaks. The customers obtain low-cost trades arranged on a confidential basis, but only if buyers and sellers are present on both sides of the market.

Exchanges charge fees for their services. They may charge the buyer, the seller, or both parties a small transaction fee, which is essentially a commission. Increasingly, many exchanges have adopted the maker/taker pricing model, in which the trader who initiates a trade (the market taker) pays an access fee to the exchange. The exchange rebates a portion of this fee to the trader whose order was taken (the maker) and who thus provided liquidity. The difference between the access fee and the liquidity rebate is the net fee that the exchange receives for arranging the trade.

## 7.3 Dealers

**Dealers** make it possible for their clients to trade when they want to trade; they are ready to buy from their clients when their clients want to sell and to sell to their clients when other clients want to buy. Dealers thus participate in their clients' trades. In contrast, brokers only arrange trades on behalf of their clients.

Dealers profit when they can buy securities for less than they sell them. The price at which they buy securities (called the bid price) is lower than the price at which they sell them (called the ask price or offer price). If by chance dealers can arrange trades simultaneously with buyers and sellers, they will make risk-free profits. Otherwise, dealers risk losses that can occur if prices fall after they purchase but before they can sell, or if prices rise after they sell but before they can repurchase.

Dealers provide liquidity to their clients by allowing them to buy and sell when they want to trade. In effect, dealers match buyers and sellers who want to trade the same instrument but who arrive at different times, and so are unable to trade directly with each other. In contrast, brokers must bring a buyer and a seller together to trade at the same time and place. Dealers are often called **market makers** because they are willing to make a market (i.e., trade on demand) in specified securities at their bid and ask prices.

## 7.4 Arbitrageurs

**Arbitrageurs** simultaneously buy and sell identical (or similar) securities, assets, financial contracts, or portfolios of these instruments in two or more markets. In the case of identical instruments, they trade when they can buy in one market at a lower price than they can sell in another market. If the price difference is greater than their costs of trading plus their costs of transferring the instrument from one market to the other, then the arbitrageurs will profit.

For example, when the price of gold in London is higher than the price of gold in New York, arbitrageurs will buy gold in New York and sell gold in London. They will profit if the price difference covers the cost of shipping gold from New York to London or if they can reverse their transactions at a profit before shipping the gold.

Arbitrageurs provide liquidity to traders by, in essence, matching buyers and sellers who want to trade similar risks at the same time but who are unable to trade directly with each other because they are in different markets. In the gold arbitrage example, arbitrageurs who buy from New York gold sellers and who sell to London gold buyers effectively allow the London buyers to buy from the New York sellers through their intermediation.

Because dealers and arbitrageurs both provide liquidity to other traders, they often compete with each other. The dealers connect buyers and sellers who arrive in the same market at different times, whereas the arbitrageurs connect buyers and sellers who arrive at the same time in different markets.

Dealers and arbitrageurs are examples of proprietary traders. **Proprietary traders** trade for the house account, which may be their own account or their firm's account. Like all other traders, they profit when they buy at lower prices than those at which they sell. Dealing and arbitrage are the most common proprietary trading strategies. Proprietary trading—most of which is now entirely electronic—provides much of the liquidity present in organized exchange markets throughout the world. Those that trade very quickly using computer programs are called **high-frequency traders**.

## 7.5 Clearing and Settlement Agents

Clearing and settlement agents settle trades after they have been arranged. In a process called confirmation, they first confirm that both sides agreed to the same terms. This process is straightforward in electronic trading systems but is important in floor-based systems in which records of trades are more prone to error. The agents then later settle the trades in a process called delivery versus payment, in which they simultaneously exchange securities for cash. The delivery-versus-payment mechanism eliminates the losses that would occur if one party arranges to settle and the other does not.

In futures markets, **clearinghouses** guarantee contract performance. They act as the seller for every buyer and the buyer for every seller. Only broker/dealers who are members of the clearinghouse (clearing members) can introduce contracts to the clearinghouse. Brokers who are not clearing members must arrange to have a clearing member introduce their clients' trades to the clearinghouse. Such brokers are called "introducing brokers." The clearing members are responsible for the performance of all contracts that they introduce.

To ensure that their members settle the trades that they present to the clearinghouse, clearinghouses require that their members have adequate capital and that they post margins. **Margins** are cash or securities that are pledged as collateral. Clearinghouses also may limit the aggregate net (i.e., buy minus sell) quantities that their members can settle. Similarly, clearing members require that their customers have adequate capital and post margins, and they monitor their customers' trading to ensure that they do not arrange trades that they cannot settle.

A hierarchical system of responsibility thus ensures that traders settle their trades. Brokers guarantee settlement of the trades they arrange for their individual and institutional customers. Clearing members guarantee settlement of the trades that their clearing customers present to them, and clearinghouses guarantee settlement of all trades presented to them by their clearing members. If a clearing member fails to settle a trade, the clearinghouse settles the trade using its own capital or capital drafted from the other members of the clearinghouse.

Reliable settlement of all trades promotes liquidity because it allows strangers to confidently contract with each other without worrying much about **settlement risk**—the risk that their counterparties will not settle their trades. A secure clearing system thus greatly increases the number of counterparties with whom a trader can safely arrange a trade.

LCH.Clearnet is a very large European clearinghouse that, as of June 2011, clears approximately 50% of the US$442 trillion global interest rate swap market, among many other contracts.

## 7.6 Comparison of Groups that Facilitate Investment

| | |
|---|---|
| Brokers | ■ Find sellers for their clients who want to buy as well as buyers for their clients who want to sell |
| | ■ Serve as professional negotiators |
| | ■ Ensure their clients will settle their trades |
| Investment banks | ■ Help clients arrange trades |
| | ■ Organize fund raising for their corporate and government clients |
| | ■ Help companies identify and acquire other companies or sell off one or more divisions within the companies |
| | ■ Act as dealers in many securities |
| | ■ Offer strategic advice to their corporate clients and research to their brokerage clients |
| Exchanges | ■ Organize auction markets to which buyers and sellers submit orders for matching |
| Alternative trading systems | ■ Meet the special needs of various traders, permitting only certain types of traders to use their facilities |
| Dealers | ■ Allow their clients to trade when they want to trade by being ready to buy from their clients when their clients want to sell and to sell when their clients want to buy |
| | ■ Participate in their clients' trades |
| | ■ Provide liquidity to their clients by allowing them to buy and sell when they want to trade |
| | ■ Called market makers because they are willing to trade on demand |
| | ■ Are proprietary traders |
| Arbitrageurs | ■ Simultaneously buy and sell identical (or similar) securities, assets, financial contracts, or portfolios of these instruments in two or more markets |
| | ■ Provide liquidity to traders by matching buyers and sellers who want to trade similar risks at the same time but who are unable to trade directly with each other because they are in different markets |
| | ■ Are proprietary traders |

| | |
|---|---|
| Clearing and settlement agents | ■ Settle trades after they have been arranged |
| | ■ Clearinghouses guarantee contract performance, act as the seller for every buyer and the buyer for ever seller and require that their members have adequate capital and post margins |

## CUSTODIANS AND DEPOSITORIES

**Custodians** play a very important role in the investment industry. They hold money and securities on behalf of their customers, help arrange trade settlements, and collect interest and dividends for their customers. These services help prevent the loss of securities and payments through fraud, oversight, or natural disaster. They also ensure that securities cannot be pledged more than once by the same borrower as collateral for loans. Banks and brokerage firms provide most custodial services.

Custodians ensure that securities said to be purchased are actually purchased. Having reputable third-party custodians hold all assets managed by an investment manager helps prevent investment fraud, such as Ponzi schemes that use funds contributed by new investors to pay purported returns to existing investors rather than to purchase additional securities.

Security ownership records were once commonly held as actual paper certificates in secure vaults. Now, through the use of depositories, securities are almost exclusively held in book-entry form as secure computer records. A **depository** is an organization that holds securities on behalf of customers whose ownership is recorded as a book entry. The conversion of evidence of security ownership from physical certificates (called immobilization) or from electronic corporate ownership records (called dematerialization) into standardized book-entry records greatly reduces the costs of clearing and settling trades.

The Depository Trust Company, a subsidiary of the Depository Trust & Clearing Corporation, is the largest depository in the world. As of year-end 2011, it held custody of more than 3.6 million securities worth US$36.5 trillion, including securities issued in the United States and in more than 120 foreign countries and territories.

Most individual and many smaller institutional investors hold securities in brokerage accounts that provide them with custodial services. Their brokers, in turn, hold the securities with custodian banks and depositories for safekeeping.

# 9 FINANCIAL INTERMEDIARIES

**Financial intermediaries** connect investors with borrowers (or with equity issuers). The connections often are quite indirect. For example, a commercial bank connects investors with borrowers when it uses funds obtained from accepting deposits and from selling its bonds and stocks to loan money to borrowers.

Financial intermediaries create new instruments that depend on the cash flows and associated risks of other instruments. The instruments that they create are more attractive to their clients than the instruments that they are based on. The appeal often is because of the value that financial intermediaries add when they check or guarantee credit, combine large numbers of positions into pools or split large projects into shares, and create differentiated investment products to appeal to diverse clientele.

## 9.1 Deposit-Taking Institutions and Other Financial Companies

**Deposit-taking institutions** (or **depository institutions**) are institutions that obtain funds primarily from depositors and lend them to borrowers. They pay their depositors interest and offer transaction services, such as check writing and check cashing, in exchange for using their money. They may also raise funds by issuing and selling bonds or stocks.

Deposit-taking institutions differ in whom they serve and how they are organized. They also may have different names in different countries. Savings and loan banks specialize in financing long-term residential mortgages. Retail banks provide banking products and services to individuals and small businesses. These products and services include checking and savings accounts, debit and credit cards, and mortgage and personal loans. An increasing number of retail banking transactions are now performed either electronically via automated teller machines (ATMs) or over the internet. Commercial banks provide a wide range of products and services to companies and other financial institutions. Savings and loan, retail, and commercial banks are organized as companies.

In contrast, cooperative banks and mutual banks are financial institutions that their members own and sometimes run. Credit unions and building societies specialize in providing mortgages. Other mutual banks may offer a much wider range of products and services, similar to those offered by commercial banks.

In practice, and in the rest of this section, the terms bank and deposit-taking institution will be used interchangeably and will also include cooperative banks.

Banks are financial intermediaries because they transfer funds from their depositors and investors to their borrowers. The depositors and investors benefit because they earn a return (in interest, transaction services, dividends, or capital appreciation) on their capital without having to locate the borrowers, check their credit, contract with them, and manage their loans. In many countries, the depositors also benefit from government-guaranteed deposit insurance. The borrowers likewise benefit because they obtain the funds they need without having to search for investors who will trust them to repay their loans.

Many other financial companies provide similar services. For example, various finance companies, such as the ones mentioned in Section 2.2.6, provide credit to borrowers by lending them money secured by such assets as consumer loans, machinery, future paychecks, or accounts receivables. They finance these loans by selling commercial paper, bonds, and stocks to investors. These companies are financial intermediaries because they connect investors with borrowers. The investors obtain investments secured by a diversified portfolio of loans, whereas the borrowers obtain funds without having to search for investors.

Brokers also act as financial intermediaries when they lend money or securities to clients. Clients may use the borrowed money to buy securities or use the borrowed securities to sell securities short. Short-selling is used by investors who believe that a security's price will decrease and they want to benefit from it. An investor may borrow securities, for example 1,000 shares of Apple, from a broker and sell these shares in the market. The investor then needs to buy back 1,000 shares of Apple and return them to the broker. If Apple's share price has decreased between the time the investor sold the shares and the time she bought them back, she will have made a profit. Brokers obtain funds and securities either from other clients who deposit them in their accounts or from commercial banks and other brokers who, in turn, obtain them from their depositors and investors.

**Prime brokers** help their clients finance their positions and clear and settle trades. Although other brokers often arrange the trades, prime brokers clear and settle them. The other brokers are said to "give up" these trades. Prime brokerage allows investors to net their collateral requirements across all deals that they do, thereby lowering the costs of financing their positions.

Banks and brokers can raise money from depositors and other lenders only because their owners retain residual interests in the performance of the loans that they make. If the borrowers default, banks and brokers still must pay their depositors and other lenders. If they cannot collect sufficient money from their borrowers, they will have to use the owners' capital to pay their debts. The risk of losing capital should focus their attention so that they do not offer credit foolishly. However, notable lapses occasionally occur, such as in the run-up to the financial crisis of 2008 when investors too often were not aware of, ignored, or could not control the risks that their managers were taking.

## 9.2 Securitizers

Banks and investment companies create new financial products when they repackage securities or other assets in a process called **securitization**. The resulting securities generally are have a greater aggregate value to investors than the securities and assets from which they are constructed because the new securities have attributes that are more attractive to investors.

For example, mortgage banks commonly originate thousands of residential mortgages (also called home loans) by lending money to homeowners. They then place them in a pool and sell shares of the pool to investors as mortgage pass-through securities, which are also known as mortgage-backed securities. All payments of principal and interest are passed through to the investors each month, after deducting the costs of servicing the mortgages. Investors who purchase these pass-through securities obtain securities that in aggregate have the same net cash flows and associated risks as the pool of mortgages.

Mortgage-backed securities have the advantage that default losses and early repayments are much more predictable for a diversified portfolio of mortgages than they are for individual mortgages, which makes them less risky than individual mortgages. They also are attractive to the vast majority of investors who cannot service mortgages efficiently and who generally cannot evaluate the creditworthiness of individual mortgages. By securitizing mortgage pools, mortgage banks allow investors who are not large enough to buy hundreds of mortgages to gain the benefits of diversification, economies of scale in loan servicing, and professional credit screening.

Besides mortgages, investment banks and other finance companies also securitize other assets, such as car loans, credit card receivables, bank loans, and airplane leases. Collectively, the securities that they create are called **asset-backed securities**.

Securitizers are financial intermediaries because they help connect investors who want to lend money with those who want to borrower money. These connections are often made with the assistance of other financial intermediaries that create the assets that become securitized. For example, lenders and leasers (also called lessors) create loans and leases when they lend money to borrowers and lease equipment to companies. These assets are often securitized.

Securitization greatly improves liquidity in the underlying asset markets because it allows investors in pass-through securities to indirectly buy assets that they otherwise would not or could not buy directly. Because the financial risks associated with security pools are much more predictable than the risks of the individual assets, asset-backed securities are easier to price and, therefore, easier to sell when investors need to raise cash. These characteristics make the markets for asset-backed securities more liquid than the markets for the underlying assets. Because investors value liquidity, they may pay more for securitized assets than for the individual underlying assets. The creators of these assets—homeowners, in the case of mortgages—benefit because higher asset prices imply lower interest rates.

When financial intermediaries securitize assets, they often create several different classes of securities with various rights to the cash flows from the asset pool. The different classes are called tranches, and they typically have different credit ratings. The tranches are structured so that some produce more predictable cash flows than others.

Consider the following simplified example. Suppose that the cash flows from a mortgage pool are allocated to two security tranches: a senior tranche and a junior tranche. The senior tranche has first rights to the cash flows from the mortgage pool. The junior tranche then receives all remaining cash flows from the mortgage pool. The senior tranche has the most predictable and secure cash flows. Thus, it has a lower risk than the junior tranche, which bears most of the credit and early repayment risks associated with the mortgage pool. If some borrowers default on their mortgages or decide to prepay their mortgages, the cash flows from the pool of mortgages will decrease, and investors in the junior tranche will be affected first. Because the junior tranche bears a disproportionately greater share of the risk of the pool, investors in the junior tranche expect higher returns than investors in the senior tranche.

Cutting a pool into tranches can increase the total value of the pool by creating instruments that appeal to different types of investors. Investors (such as insurance companies) that seek secure and predictable returns buy the senior tranches, whereas those willing to bear more risk (such as hedge funds) buy the junior tranches.

The complexity associated with slicing asset pools into tranches can make the various security tranches difficult to value. Mistakes in valuing these securities and the failure of credit rating agencies to fully appreciate their associated risks contributed to the global financial crisis of 2008.

Investment companies create securities, such as mutual funds and exchange-traded funds, that represent investments in portfolios of securities and assets. Although not normally considered asset-backed securities, these structures create similar benefits for their shareholders. The shareholders of these funds benefit from securitization because they can buy or sell shares in professionally managed, diversified portfolios with single transactions. The shareholders also benefit because they can cheaply invest in any of the large number of market segments in which various mutual funds specialize.

## 9.3 Insurance Companies

**Insurance companies** help individuals and companies offset risks that concern them. To hedge against a potential loss, their clients buy insurance contracts (also known as policies) that provide payments in the event that losses occur. Common examples of insurance contracts include auto, fire, life, liability, medical, theft, and disaster. Japan Post Holdings, Swiss Life, and Principal Financial Group are examples of large life insurers. Allianz, GEICO, and Allstate are examples of large property and casualty insurers.

Insurance contracts transfer risks from those who buy the contracts to those who sell them. Although insurance companies occasionally broker trades between the insured and the insurer, they more commonly provide the insurance themselves. In this case, the insurance company's owners and creditors become the indirect bearers of the risks that the insurance company assumes.

Insurance companies also often transfer risks that they do not want to bear by buying reinsurance policies from reinsurers. Munich Re, Swiss Re, and Lloyd's are among the world's largest reinsurance companies. Insurance companies also issue catastrophe bonds (often referred to as cat bonds) to transfer a specified set of risks (such as earthquake or hurricane casualty loss risk) to investors who purchase the bonds.

Insurers are financial intermediaries because they connect buyers of their insurance contracts with investors, creditors, and reinsurers who are willing to bear the insured risks. The buyers benefit because they can easily obtain the risk transfers that they seek without searching for entities that would be willing to assume those risks.

The owners, debt holders, and reinsurers of the insurance company benefit because the company allows them to earn a return for taking on these risks without having to manage the insurance contracts. Instead, the company manages the relationships with the insured—primarily collections and claims—and hopefully controls the various problems—for example, fraud, moral hazard, and adverse selection—that often plague insurance markets. **Fraud** occurs when people deliberately cause or falsely report losses to collect insurance settlements. **Moral hazard** occurs when people are less careful about avoiding losses once they have purchased insurance, potentially leading to losses occurring more often when they are insured than when they are not. **Adverse selection** occurs when only those who are most at risk buy insurance, causing insured losses to be greater than average losses.

Everyone benefits because insurance companies hold large, diversified portfolios of policies. Loss rates for well-diversified portfolios of insurance contracts are much more predictable than for single contracts. For contracts, such as auto insurance, for which losses are almost uncorrelated across policies, diversification ensures that the financial performance of a large portfolio of contracts will be quite predictable, thus making the portfolio less risky. The insured clients benefit because they do not have to pay the insurers much to compensate them for bearing diversifiable risk. Instead, their insurance premiums primarily reflect the expected loss rate in the portfolio plus the costs of running and financing the company.

## 10 ORGANIZATION OF FIRMS IN THE INVESTMENT INDUSTRY

Practitioners classify many firms in the investment industry by whether they are on the sell side or the buy side. **Sell-side firms**—investment banks, brokers, and dealers—primarily provide transaction services and investment products. **Buy-side firms**—investment managers—purchase these services and products. This classification scheme is generally not applied to independent firms that sell investment data, research, and consulting.

The buy-side/sell-side classification scheme is somewhat arbitrary and not easily applied to many large integrated firms. For example, many investment banks have divisions or wholly owned subsidiaries that provide asset management services. These functions are on the buy-side, even though investment banks are sell-side firms.

Practitioners also use the term "buy side" to refer to the investors who purchase investment services and products from the sell side. For example, mutual funds, pension funds, hedge funds, and insurance companies are all considered buy-side entities. Practitioners also sometimes use the term to refer to consultants who provide services only to buy-side entities. For example, many buy-side consultants help buy-side institutions measure and evaluate investment performance.

### 10.1 Firm Organization

Most sell-side firms organize their activities along similar lines. Activities are classified by whether they are in the front office, the middle office, or the back office. Note that the classification of activities varies among practitioners, especially with respect to what this chapter calls middle-office activities, which some practitioners may consider to be either front- or back-office activities.

The **front office** consists of client-facing activities that provide direct revenue generation. The sales, marketing, and customer service departments are the most important front-office activities. Some practitioners also consider the trading department to be a front-office activity, especially if the traders regularly interact with clients. Others also consider research to be a front-office activity because it generates revenue.

The **middle office** includes the core activities of the firm. Risk management, information technology (IT), corporate finance, portfolio management, and research are generally considered middle-office activities, especially if these departments do not

# Organization of Firms in the Investment Industry

interact directly with clients. The IT systems are particularly important because most investment industry firms need to process and retrieve vast quantities of data efficiently and accurately. The risk management department is also critical because it is responsible for ensuring that the firm and its clients are not intentionally, inadvertently, or fraudulently exposed to excessive risk.

The **back office** houses the administrative and support functions necessary to run the firm. These functions include accounting, human resources, payroll, and operations. For brokerages and banks that provide custodial services, the accounting department is especially important because it is responsible for clearing and settling trades and for keeping track of who owns what.

Some activities are not easily classified as front, middle, or back office. For example, compliance activities are relevant to the entire organization. A firm's compliance department ensures that the firm and its customers comply with the many rules and regulations that govern the investment management and trading industries. The chief compliance officer must ensure that:

- All personnel are appropriately registered with regulatory authorities if so required.

- Securities sold to clients are suitable for those clients.

- No investment management decision would lead to the violation of a covenant or constraint.

- All clients are treated equally, fairly, and appropriately.

- All mandated reports are completed when due.

- In general, all behavior within the organization meets the company's standards of conduct.

The terms front office, middle office, and back office are generally not used when describing buy-side firms. However, the main departments of buy-side investment management firms are similar to those of sell-side firms. These departments are sales and client relations, investment research and portfolio management, trading, compliance, accounting, and administration.

## 10.2 Leadership Titles and Responsibilities

Exhibit 2 identifies the major leadership titles and responsibilities in the investment industry.

### Exhibit 2   Leadership Titles and Responsibilities

| Title | Responsibility |
| --- | --- |
| Chief executive officer (CEO) | Manages the firm. |
| Chief financial officer (CFO) | Responsible for financing the firm and for financial reporting. |
| Chief operating officer (COO) | Responsible for the day-to-day management of the firm. |
| Chief investment officer (CIO) | Responsible for any investment advice that the firm provides to its clients, and for the investment decisions that the firm makes for itself and on behalf of its clients. |
| Head trader | Responsible for all trading operations. At firms that engage in proprietary trading, the head trader is responsible for all positions, risk, and profits. |
| Chief accountant (also known as finance controller) | Responsible for the accounting and financial systems. |
| Treasurer | Responsible for cash management, including the investment of receipts and payment of bills. |
| Chief risk officer | Responsible for identifying and managing the risks to which either the firm or its clients are exposed. |
| Chief compliance officer | Responsible for ensuring that the firm complies with all constraints placed on it by laws, regulations, exchanges, clearinghouses, and clients. |
| Chief audit executive | Leads the internal audit department, which is responsible for providing independent assessments of the firm's operational systems along with suggestions for improvement. |
| General counsel | Leads the legal department, which reviews and helps write contracts, responds to or initiates lawsuits, and interprets regulations, among many other activities. |

At many firms, especially smaller ones, some people hold multiple titles. For example, the chief investment officer of many investment management companies may also be the chief executive officer.

### 10.3 Other Positions

Firms in the investment industry employ many types of investment professionals.

- Portfolio managers at buy-side firms make investment decisions for one or more portfolios.

- Buy-side, sell-side, and independent research analysts produce the investment research portfolio managers use to make decisions. They also write the research reports that some firms sell.

- Research assistants assist the research analysts with the collection and analysis of investment information.

- Buy-side traders interact with sell-side firms to trade orders created by their portfolio managers.

- Sales traders at sell-side firms help arrange trades for their buy-side customers.

- Sales managers manage all sales for regions, products, or customer types.

- Salespeople identify potential clients and sell them the firm's products and services.

- Sales assistants provide administrative and creative support to the salespeople.

- Client service agents and their assistants answer client questions and help clients open, close, and manage their accounts.

The investment professionals who interact with clients also may be known as account executives and account managers at many firms.

A research assistant is very often the entry level position for investment professionals interested in becoming portfolio managers. Assistants who acquire strong expertise in a particular area and who can write well may be promoted to research analysts. Those analysts who demonstrate excellent investment judgment often become portfolio managers. Likewise, sales assistants and account services assistants are entry-level positions for investment professionals interested in sales or account services.

Companies that provide investment management services also employ many other types of professionals besides investment professionals. These include professionals working in accounting, information services, marketing, and legal services.

# INSTITUTIONAL INVESTMENT MANAGEMENT PROCESSES — 11

Most institutional investors organize their investment processes along similar lines. This section describes their general organization, how they select new managers, and how they review performance.

## 11.1 General Organization

All institutional investors have leaders responsible for their investment programs. The leaders may include the chief executive officer, chief financial officer, chief investment officer, or members of an investment committee appointed by the board of directors. These leaders may delegate some of their responsibility and authority for investment decisions to professional investment staff that the institution employs. Institutions may also contract with outside firms to help manage their investments.

All institutional investors create and adopt an overall investment policy statement. Most investment policy statements specify many of the following points:

- the general objectives (including return objectives) of the investment program and their relationship to the mission of the institution;

- the risk tolerance of the organization and its capacity for bearing risk;

- all economic and operational constraints, such as tax considerations, legal and regulatory circumstances, and any other special circumstances;

- the time horizon over which funds are to be invested;

- the importance of capital preservation versus capital growth;

- the classes of securities and assets in which the institution is allowed to invest;

- a target asset allocation that indicates how much of the total investment funds will be invested in each asset class;

- whether leverage (use of debt) may be used or short positions taken;

- how actively the institution will trade; and

- the benchmarks against which the institution will measure overall investment returns.

The board of the institution or its senior leadership formally adopts the investment and payout policies.

The investment leaders decide whether to manage investments in-house or to contract with one or more investment managers. Institutions that manage their investments in-house build a team of investment professionals to manage their investments.

Institutions that use outside investment managers may use one manager to manage all investments or multiple managers. Institutions often use multiple managers to reduce the risk of substantial loss as a result of the poor performance of one specific manager. Many institutions also use different managers for each asset class in which they invest. By hiring managers who specialize in particular asset classes, the institutions gain investment expertise and access to investments that a generalist might not have.

## 11.2 Selecting New Investment Managers

Institutions seeking new investment managers first identify prospective candidates. Many institutions contract with investment consultants for this purpose. The consultants provide information about various managers that includes characterizations of their investment philosophies, styles, resources, and past performance. Some institutions—including many governments—must publish a request for proposal (RFP) when seeking new managers. The request for proposal process fosters competition among bidders, usually leading to the best pricing. It also provides transparency and helps reduce the possibility that the institution will improperly award investment management contracts to cronies (friends) of the institution's investment leadership.

In the course of conducting its due diligence, the investment leadership or its consultants may also talk with current and previous clients of the candidates and conduct background checks of the key personnel working for the candidate managers.

Finally, the investment leadership chooses the new manager, and if necessary, obtains confirmation from its board of directors or senior executives.

The new manager and the institution then establish an investment contract that will govern their relationship. In addition to specifying compensation and assets under management, the contract will incorporate the institution's investment policy statement. It also may specify additional investment policies specific to the asset classes in which the manager will recommend investments.

If the new manager will hold the institution's assets in its accounts, as is generally the case for real estate, venture capital, and hedge fund investments, the institution then transfers funds to the manager to invest. Otherwise, it gives authority to the new manager to order security trades on its behalf. In the latter case, the institution notifies the institution's brokers, clearing agents, and custodians of the changes and provides them with parameters that limit the authority of the manager.

## 11.3 Monitoring Performance

Institutions receive regular reports from their brokers of the trades that their outside and inside investment managers arrange on their behalf. Their brokers generally transmit these trade reports at the end of the day, but they also may send the reports in real time. The institutions' investment professionals review these trade reports to confirm that the trades arranged by their managers conform to their investment mandates.

Institutional investors also receive periodic account statements from their investment managers. These statements indicate what investments are on account with the manager or under the manager's control. They also summarize transactions over the period and provide measures of investment performance. The institutions' investment professionals review these statements carefully.

Many large institutions also produce their own analyses of the investment performance of their managers. They produce and review these reports at least annually—and generally more often. The investment staff may conduct these analyses internally, or they may contract with investment consultants to perform these analyses for them. Performance analyses indicate how the investments of the institution are performing overall and relative to various benchmarks. Attribution analyses identify the factors that contributed to the performance. For example, an attribution analysis will show whether strong performance was attributable to market timing (i.e., being invested in a rising asset class) or whether it was attributable to security selection (i.e., being invested in those securities within an asset class that outperformed). Generally, the institution obtains separate analyses for each of its investment managers and often for each asset class in which it invests. Performance and attribution analyses are discussed more thoroughly in Chapter 18.

The institutions' investment professionals review these analyses for several reasons. First, to identify managers who are performing well and those who may need more attention; second, to ensure that their managers are doing what they promised to do; and third, to determine whether they need to reallocate funds from one manager to another to improve performance or to rebalance their asset allocation among asset classes.

Institutions rarely terminate managers for poor performance over intervals of less than three to five years. Over such intervals, even the best managers will occasionally underperform. Reallocating funds from one manager to another could thus be unproductive. The high transaction costs associated with reallocations—old investments have to be sold and new investments bought—also discourage reallocations among managers.

The members of the investment staff pay particular attention to whether their managers' performance is abnormal. They consider whether the managers' decisions are consistent with their stated investment processes and whether the managers are reporting performance improperly.

Large institutions may also conduct transaction cost analyses to evaluate the effectiveness of the brokers who execute their trades. These analyses indicate how much impact on price the institutions experienced when trading and whether they lost value because they could not complete a trade or because they did not trade sooner. Many investment managers also contract for these analyses to help them determine whether they should trade more aggressively or less aggressively. Consultants who have many clients generally do these analyses because they can provide meaningful performance benchmarks based on the trades of all their clients.

## SUMMARY

- The investment industry helps connect those who require financing with those who can provide it.

- The investment industry serves various types of individual and institutional investors. Practitioners distinguish among retail, high-net-worth, and ultra-high-net-worth investors depending on the investor's total investment assets. Institutional investors include pension funds, endowments and foundations, governments and sovereign wealth funds, non-financial companies, investment companies, finance companies, and insurance companies.

- The main services that the industry provides include the following:

  - Financial planning—consulting to help investors better understand their needs;

  - Investment management—assistance with selecting investments;

  - Investment information—providing investment research and financial data necessary to make decisions;

- Brokerage—assistance with the search for suitable counterparties;
- Liquidity—the ability to buy or sell in a timely fashion at a price close to fair market value;
- Trading support—assistance provided by clearing and settlement agents, custodians, and depositories; and
- Securitization and financial intermediation—the creation of investment products that best serve investors and the transformation of those products into vehicles that best serve borrowers and equity issuers.

■ To provide their investment services, participants in the investment industry must assemble and analyze data that address

- their clients' financial situations,
- the creditworthiness and trustworthiness of their clients and of their clients' counterparties,
- who would be willing to take the other side of their clients' trades,
- the probability that debtors will be able and willing to repay their loans,
- the business prospects of companies, and
- how companies might be reorganized to operate more effectively.

■ The tasks associated with the investment industry require experts who can ask the right questions, acquire the necessary data, and process the data to obtain useful information. The end products are high-quality investment services and products that benefit retail and institutional investors who could not produce them on their own.

# CHAPTER REVIEW QUESTIONS

Test your knowledge of this chapter at **cfainstitute.org/claritasstudy**.

1 Which of the following types of investors is *most likely* to receive standardized services from the investment industry?

   A  Retail investors

   B  High-net-worth investors

   C  Endowments and foundations

2 An endowment fund is *best* described as a long-term fund invested:

   A  to provide income to current and future retirees.

   B  to provide benefits to current and future citizens.

   C  to support the mission of a non-profit or not-for-profit institution.

3 Which of the following investors hold investments on behalf of their clients?

   A  Foundations

   B  Insurance companies

   C  Investment companies

4 A company issuing debt or equity securities would *most likely* require assistance from an investment professional to:

   A  prepare audited financial statements.

   B  identify potential investments for the proceeds.

   C  find investors willing to purchase the securities.

Copyright © 2012 CFA Institute

# Chapter Review Questions

**5** An investor concerned about retirement would *least likely* hire an investment professional to:

   **A** determine the level of assets required to cover living expenses after retirement.

   **B** identify potential investments and analyze associated risk and return characteristics.

   **C** determine how to structure his mortgage or other debt to obtain the best possible terms.

**6** Financial planners help clients by:

   **A** holding securities on behalf of customers whose ownership is recorded as a book entry.

   **B** suggesting asset allocations that are intended to help investors meet their financial goals.

   **C** providing investment research to help clients assess fundamental values, risks, and strategies.

**7** Investment professionals who create savings plans and recommend investment strategies are *most likely*:

   **A** dealers.

   **B** investment advisers.

   **C** investment research providers.

**8** Which of the following is *least likely* to be a service provided by financial custodians?

   **A** Collecting interest and dividends for clients

   **B** Holding money and securities on behalf of clients

   **C** Helping clients arrange investment trades with one another

**9** Passive managers will *most likely* sell securities when the:

   **A** securities are expected to outperform.

   **B** securities are expected to underperform.

   **C** composition of an index benchmark changes.

**10** Securitization is the process of:

　**A** lending money or securities to clients.

　**B** connecting buyers of insurance contracts with those who are willing to bear the insured risks.

　**C** creating new products by financial intermediaries who repackage securities or other assets.

**11** Sell-side firms are *best* described as firms that:

　**A** sell insurance products to retail clients.

　**B** sell investment data, research, and consulting.

　**C** provide transaction services and investment products.

**12** Practitioners *most likely* use the term "buy side" to refer to:

　**A** dealers who provide transaction services and investment products.

　**B** investors who purchase investment services and products from the sell-side.

　**C** independent firms that provide investment data, research, and consulting services.

**13** The department *least likely* to be classified as middle office is:

　**A** sales.

　**B** risk management.

　**C** information technology.

**14** The chief investment officer of an investment firm is *least likely* responsible for:

　**A** investment advice that the firm provides its clients.

　**B** investment decisions that the firm makes for itself and its clients.

　**C** trading operations, including positions taken, risk, and profits.

**15** An investment firm searching for a new investment manager would *least likely*:

　**A** conduct a transaction cost analysis.

　**B** perform background checks of key personnel.

　**C** contract with investment consultants to suggest candidates.

# Chapter Review Questions

**16** The investment policy statement for an institutional investor *most likely* specifies the:

   **A** assets under management.

   **B** individuals on the board of the institution and their positions.

   **C** general objectives of the investment program as it relates to the institution's mission.

# ANSWERS

1. A is correct. Retail investors, compared with high-net-worth and ultra-high-net-worth investors, are more numerous, have lower levels of assets, and generate the least revenue per investor. As a result, the investment industry primarily provides standardized services to retail investors. B is incorrect because high-net-worth investors generally receive more personal attention from investment professionals. C is incorrect because endowments and foundations require specialized services and, in some cases, will establish their own investment management firms.

2. C is correct. Endowment funds are long-term funds of non-profit and not-for-profit institutions that are invested to provide support for the institutions' activities. A is incorrect because pension funds hold investment portfolios for the benefit of future and current retires. B is incorrect because sovereign wealth funds have been established by some governments to invest their country's surplus for the benefit of current and future citizens.

3. C is correct. Investment companies, such as mutual funds, hedge funds, private equity funds, and investment trusts, exist solely to hold investments on behalf of their clients. A is incorrect because foundations are grant-making institutions funded by gifts and by the investment income that they produce. Foundations have endowment funds to invest. B is incorrect because insurance companies provide insurance coverage to their clients in exchange for premiums that are used to pay out claims. Insurance companies invest their reserves accounts.

4. C is correct. Issuers of securities may need assistance finding investors willing to purchase the securities. Investment professionals, such as investment banks, specialize in matching issuers with investors and helping clients structure investment products that the market demands. A is incorrect because investment professionals do not prepare audited financial statements; audit companies do. B is incorrect because it is individual investors, not issuing companies, who often need assistance from investment professionals, such as financial advisers, to identify potential investments. Issuing companies are likely to be raising funds to finance already identified investments.

5. C is correct. An investor concerned about retirement will likely hire an investment professional to advise him specifically about matters related to his retirement. Although mortgage or other debt may be considered in establishing investment objectives for a retirement portfolio, the individual investor will not necessarily require assistance with his mortgage or other debt from investment professionals. A is incorrect because an investor concerned about retirement will likely need assistance from an investment professional to help determine how much money to save to cover living expenses during retirement. B is incorrect because investors need to obtain assistance with retirement planning from an investment professional who can identify potential investments and analyze associated risk and return characteristics.

**Answers**

**6** B is correct. Financial planners help clients by suggesting asset allocations that are intended to help investors meet their financial goals. They identify the various asset classes, such as fixed income, equities, real estate, and commodities, and the percentage of total assets that should be invested in each asset class. A is incorrect because depositories hold securities on behalf of customers whose ownership is recorded as a book entry. C is incorrect because investors and investment managers obtain research reports from investment research providers to help inform their investment decisions.

**7** B is correct. Investment advisers are investment professionals who may provide both financial planning and investment advisory services. Financial planning services include the creation of savings plans, identification of asset allocations, and other services that assist clients in assessing their investment objectives, risk profiles, and other preferences. Investment advisers will also recommend investment strategies and suggest potential investments to their clients. A is incorrect because dealers are agents who provide services for their clients by participating directly in each trade. C is incorrect because investment research providers research and compile data about industries, companies, and technologies and document the results in investment reports. Investment research providers do not interact with clients on their investment planning needs.

**8** C is correct. Helping buyers and sellers arrange trades with each other is a trading service provided by brokers, dealers, arbitrageurs, and exchange providers, but not by financial custodians. A and B are incorrect because collecting interest and dividends for clients and holding money and securities on behalf of clients are services provided by custodians. Custodians also process trade settlements and confirm trade transactions for their clients.

**9** C is correct. Passive managers seek to match the return and risk of an appropriate benchmark. Thus, they trade when the composition of the index benchmark changes. A and B are incorrect because it is active, not passive, managers who trade securities to beat the benchmark. Note that active managers will *buy* securities that are expected to *outperform* and *sell* securities that are expected to *underperform*.

**10** C is correct. Securitization refers to the process of financial intermediaries' creating new products when they repackage securities or other assets. For example, financial intermediaries repackage mortgages into diversified pools and sell shares in the form of mortgage-backed securities. A is incorrect because lending money or securities to clients is part of brokerage services, not securitization. B is incorrect because connecting buyers of insurance contracts with investors, creditors, and reinsurers who are willing to bear the insured risks is part of insurance services, not securitization.

**11** C is correct. Sell-side firms provide transaction services and investment products. Brokers, dealers, and investment banks that provide trading services and investment vehicles to their customers are considered sell-side firms. A is incorrect because insurance companies or financial advisers sell insurance products to retail investors, but these insurance companies and investments professionals are not considered sell-side firms. B is incorrect because independent firms sell investment data, research, and consulting and are considered to be in the investment information services business. This category includes investment consultants and financial data vendors.

**12** B is correct. Practitioners typically use the term buy side to refer to investors who purchase investment services and products from the sell side. A is incorrect because sell-side firms provide transaction services and investment products. C is incorrect because independent firms sell investment data, research, and consulting services. The classifications of buy side and sell side are not usually applied to independent firms.

**13** A is correct. Sales is usually classified as front office, not middle office. The front office consists of client-facing activities that provide direct revenue generation, such as sales, marketing, and customer service departments. B and C are incorrect because risk management and information technology are typically classified as middle office, which includes the core activities of the firm.

**14** C is correct. Supervising trading operations, including positions taken, risk, and profits, is the responsibility of the head trader, not the chief investment officer. A and B are incorrect because the chief investment officer of an investment firm is responsible for any investment advice the firm provides its clients and has ultimate responsibility for the investment decisions the firm makes for itself and on behalf of its clients.

**15** A is correct. Transaction cost analysis is used by large institutions to evaluate the effectiveness of the brokers who execute their trades. B is incorrect because an investment firm should conduct background checks of key personnel as a part of conducting due diligence. C is incorrect because an investment firm may contract with investment consultants to provide possible candidates.

**16** C is correct. The investment policy statement for most institutional investors specifies the general objectives of the investment program and how they relate to the mission of the institution. A is incorrect because such information as assets under managements is not included in the investment policy statement. B is incorrect because although the board of the institution or its senior leadership formally adopts the investment and payout policy, there is no indication that the individuals are specified in the investment policy statement for institutional investors.

# CHAPTER 14

## INVESTMENT VEHICLES AND STRUCTURES

by Larry Harris, PhD, CFA

# LEARNING OUTCOMES

After completing this chapter, you should be able to do the following:

a   Explain the purpose of security market indices, identify their types, and describe uses of security market indices in the investment industry;

b   Compare investing through direct investments in securities and assets with investing through indirect investments;

c   Describe structured investment products, including equity-linked annuities and exchange-traded notes;

d   Distinguish among closed-end funds, open-end funds, exchange-traded funds, and unit investment trusts and identify their relative advantages and limitations;

e   Describe characteristics of hedge funds;

f   Describe characteristics of funds of funds;

g   Explain the differences between separate accounts and commingled accounts;

h   Compare investment in taxable and tax-advantaged accounts;

i   Compare defined contribution and defined benefit pension plans.

# INTRODUCTION

Investment professionals have created numerous financial products and services to help their clients address their investment and risk management problems. The large variety of products and services reflects the many different problems their clients face. Understanding these products and how they are structured is necessary to appreciate how the investment industry creates value for its clients.

This chapter is about investment vehicles and structures. **Investment vehicles** or **investment products** are the assets that investors use to move money from the present to the future. These assets include securities, such as stocks, bonds, and warrants; real assets, such as gold; and real estate. Many investment vehicles are entities that own other investment vehicles. For example, an equity mutual fund is an investment company that owns stocks.

**Investment structure** refers to how investors hold their investments and how those investments are managed. A mutual fund represents one type of investment structure discussed in this chapter: an investment in which investors pool their assets for joint management by a professional investment manager. A separate account is another type of investment structure: an investment account that serves a single entity, which may be self-directed or professionally managed. Practitioners have developed many types of investment structures to serve investors with various needs. They use these structures to create functional investment vehicles, many of which are constructed from other vehicles.

This chapter introduces the most important investment products and explains how they are structured and how those structures serve investors. Understanding these products and how they benefit clients will help you support investment professionals and contribute to the value creation process.

# SECURITY MARKET INDICES

If you want to assess how a stock market performed this week, you could look at the performance of every single security listed on the market. Alternatively, you may prefer to use a single measure that is representative of the stock market performance. If you are located in the United States, you can look at Standard & Poor's (S&P) 500 Index; if you are in France, you can look at the CAC 40 Index; or if you are in South Korea, you can look at the Korea Stock Price Index (KOSPI). These are stock market indices that are widely used to reflect the performance of national equity markets.

Copyright © 2012 CFA Institute

A **security market index** is a group of securities representing a given security market, market segment, or asset class. Examples of such indices (sometimes referred to as indexes) include the following:

- FTSE 100—an index that includes the stocks of 100 large companies listed on the London Stock Exchange. Practitioners commonly pronounce FTSE as "footsie."

- Dow Jones Industrial Average (DJIA)—an index that includes the stocks of 30 large companies based in the United States. It is sometimes simply called the Dow 30.

- Nikkei 225—an index that includes the stocks of 225 large companies based in Japan.

These and many other indices are widely published. Practitioners also have created many indices for private use. The percentage change in the value of an index over some time interval is the index return. Analysts focus more on index returns than on index values because index levels are arbitrary. For example, the value of the FTSE 100 was arbitrarily set to a base value of 1,000 on 3 January 1984, when the *Financial Times* and the London Stock Exchange created the index.

## 2.1 How to Compute the Value of Indices

The value of an index is computed from the prices of the securities that are included in the index. Two important elements affect the value of an index:

- the list of the securities included in the index, and

- the weight assigned to each security in the index.

Some indices include a small number of securities from one national market or one particular sector. For example, the DJIA includes only 30 large U.S. company stocks or the Dow Jones Utilities includes only 15 large U.S. company stocks from utility companies. Other indices try to capture a larger share of the securities market and include hundreds or thousands of securities from around the world. For example, the Morgan Stanley Capital International (MSCI) World Index includes more than 6,000 stocks from 24 developed markets. Note that the list of securities included in an index may change from time to time. The process of adding and removing securities included in the index is called **index reconstitution**.

There are different approaches used to assign weights to the securities included in the index: price-weighted, capitalization-weighted, or equal-weighted.

A **price-weighted index** is an index in which the weight assigned to each security is determined by dividing the price of the security by the sum of all the prices of the securities. As a consequence, high-priced securities have a greater weighting and more of an effect on the value of the index than low-priced stocks. The DJIA and the Nikkei 225 are examples of price-weighted indices.

Many indices are **capitalization-weighted indices** (also known as **cap-weighted**, **market-weighted**, or **value-weighted** indices). The weight assigned to each security depends on the security's market capitalization. The market capitalization or capitalization of a security is the market price of the security multiplied by the number of units outstanding of the security. For example, as of October 2012, Apple's stock price is $628 and there are 937 million shares. Thus, Apple's market capitalization is $588 billion. Securities included in capitalization-weighted indices are given weights in the proportion of their market capitalizations. The Hang Seng Index in Hong Kong, FTSE 100 in the United Kingdom, and S&P 500 Market Weight Index are examples of capitalization-weighted indices.

**Equal-weighted** indices show what returns would be made if an equal value were invested in each security included in the index. The prices of these securities change continuously. Thus, to maintain the equal weights between securities, regular **index rebalancing** is necessary. That is, the weights given to securities whose prices have risen must be decreased, and the weights given to securities whose prices have fallen must be increased. The S&P 500 Equal Weight Index is an example of equal-weighted index.

The fact that different indices include different securities and use different approaches to assign weights to the securities explains why the changes in values of indices vary, even when focusing on one national market or sector. For example, as of October 2012, Apple is the largest company by market capitalization. Apple stock is not included in the DJIA but is included in both the S&P 500 Equal Weight and Market Weight Indices. Because the S&P 500 Equal Weight Index assigns the same weights to all the stocks it includes, Apple represents only 0.2% (1/500th) of the S&P 500 Equal Weight Index. Because the S&P 500 Market Weight Index assigns to each stock a weight that reflects the company's market capitalization, Apple represents 4.3% of the S&P 500 Market Weight Index. A change in the price of Apple's stock will not affect the DJIA, will have a small effect on the S&P 500 Equal Weighted Index, and will have a much larger effect on the S&P 500 Market Weight Index. Knowing which securities are included in an index and how much weight is assigned to each is very important information for people using the index.

## 2.2 Index Funds

The investment industry creates many investment products based on security market indices. Examples of these products include index funds, index futures contracts, and index-linked variable annuities.

Index funds are the most important of these products. An **index fund** is a portfolio of securities structured to track the returns of a specific index, called the benchmark index. Index funds are popular among individual and institutional investors because they generally are broadly diversified and highly transparent, with very low management and trading costs. They are tax-efficient because they do not do a lot of trading that can generate taxable capital gains. Also, the lack of trading keeps trading costs low. Most individual investors and many institutional investors invest in index funds by buying mutual funds that hold index portfolios. Mutual funds are discussed further in Section 5. Many large institutions also hold index portfolios in their investment accounts.

Chapter 13 introduced the distinction between passive and active investment strategies. Passive managers seek to match the return and risk of a benchmark, and active managers try to outperform (beat) the benchmark. Indices are very often used as benchmarks. Index funds represent a passive investment strategy because index fund managers aim to replicate the benchmark index; they simply buy and hold the securities included in the index.

Index fund managers may invest in every security in the index, a strategy known as full replication. Some index funds may find it difficult to buy and hold all of the securities included in the benchmark index. The securities may not be easily available or the transaction costs of acquiring and holding all the securities included in the benchmark index may be very high. If full replication is difficult or too costly, index fund managers may invest in only a representative sample of the index securities, a strategy called sampling replication. Managers of small funds that track indices with many securities often use the sampling replication strategy to reduce costs.

Once set up, index funds only trade if the weightings need to be adjusted (e.g., in the case of index reconstitution when securities are added or deleted from the list of index securities). All index funds are affected by index reconstitution, but equal-weighted index funds are most affected by a need to change weightings. The equal-weighted index fund has to trade to maintain the equal weighting. The capitalization-weighted index fund only needs to rebalance if corporate actions, such as mergers and acquisitions, affect weightings. Index funds sometimes trade securities to invest or generate cash when cash inflows are received. Cash inflows include receipt of dividends and/or interest. They also include additional net cash inflows from investors—that is, additional investments from investors that exceed withdrawal requests by investors. Index funds may have to sell securities if withdrawal (redemption) requests from investors exceed additional investment from investors.

Many investors like passive investment strategies because they generate minimal transaction costs, are inexpensive to implement, and produce returns that closely track market returns.

## 2.3 Common Analyses that Depend on Indices

To evaluate investment managers, investors need benchmarks against which to measure portfolio performance. As mentioned earlier, they often use indices as benchmarks, particularly when investing in passively managed index funds.

More generally, practitioners use indices to attribute portfolio performance to various factors. For example, suppose that an equity portfolio outperformed the market by holding financial stocks when financial stocks performed well. By using an established index of financial stocks, an analyst can determine to what extent the outperformance of the portfolio was attributable to exposure to the broader financial sector as opposed to selection of specific stocks within the financial sector. Answers to performance attribution questions such as these can help investors identify the strengths of their investment managers. Performance attribution will be discussed more thoroughly in Chapter 18.

# Security Market Indices

Practitioners also analyze indices to characterize the risks associated with securities and portfolios. The returns of most securities are correlated with the returns of indices of similar securities. Risk analysts use these relationships to predict how security and portfolio values will change when market or sector valuations change.

Indices may measure price returns or total returns. A **price index** (not to be confused with a price-weighted index) only measures changes in security prices. The indices discussed earlier are price indices. In contrast, practitioners use **total return indices** to measure the total returns that investors would get if they bought and held the index securities. The difference between price and total return indices is because of the income (e.g., dividends and interest) received by security holders. Price indices ignore current income, but total return indices reflect these payments. In particular, the return to a total return index is equal to the price index return plus the income yield (percentage of total value returned as income) of the index securities. Total return indices thus have higher returns when compared with the returns of an equivalent price index.

Analysts generally use total return indices for performance evaluation, attribution, and risk management analysis because investors receive investment income in addition to price returns from their investments.

## 2.4 The Index Universe

Analysts have created indices to measure the values of almost every existing market, asset class, country, and sector:

- Broad market indices cover an entire asset class—for example, stocks or bonds—generally within a single country or region.

- Multi-market indices cover an asset class across many countries or regions.

- Industry indices cover single industries.

- Sector indices cover broad economic sectors—sets of industries related by common products or common customers, such as health care, energy, or transportation.

- Style indices provide benchmarks for common styles of investment management. Examples of equity style indices include indices of value and growth stocks; of small-, mid-, and large-capitalization stocks; and of combinations of these classifications, such as small growth.

- Fixed-income indices cover debt securities and vary by characteristics of the underlying securities and by characteristics of the issuers. For example, separate indices are available for government (sovereign) and corporate credits; short-, mid- (intermediate-), and long-term bonds; investment-grade and junk bonds; inflation-protected and convertible bonds; and asset-backed securities.

- Other indices track the performance of such alternative investments as hedge funds, real estate investment trusts (REITs), and commodities. As discussed in Chapter 12, real estate investment trusts are public companies that mainly own, and in most cases operate, income-producing real estate.

### 2.5 Other Index-Related Products and Strategies

In addition to index funds, indices play important roles in many other investment and risk management products. For example, the values of many futures, options, and swap contracts depend on index values.

The widespread availability of these financial products makes it easy for investors to use tactical asset allocation strategies, in which they shift risk between asset classes, markets, sectors, or countries based on their expectations of future returns. In many cases, they form their expectations by analyzing the relationships among various indices or the dynamics of particular markets.

## 3  INVESTMENT VEHICLES AND STRUCTURES

### 3.1 Direct and Indirect Investments

Investors make **direct investments** when they buy securities issued by companies, governments, and individuals and when they buy real assets, such as real estate, art, or timber.

Investors make **indirect investments** when they buy the securities of companies, trusts, and partnerships that make direct investments. Examples of indirect investment vehicles include

- shares in mutual funds, exchange-traded funds (ETFs), and real estate investment trusts;

- limited partnership interests in hedge funds, oil wells, and leasing companies;

- asset-backed securities, such as mortgage-backed securities and student loan asset-backed securities; and

- interests in pension funds, foundation funds, and endowment funds.

Most indirect investment vehicles are **pooled investments** (also known as collective investment schemes) in which investors pool their money together to gain the advantages of working together as part of a large group. The resulting economies of scale often significantly improve investment returns.

Indirect investment vehicles provide many advantages to investors in comparison with direct investments:

- They are professionally managed. Professional management is particularly important when direct investments are hard to find and must be managed.

- They allow small investors to use the services of professional managers, whom they otherwise could not afford to hire.

- They allow investors to share in the purchase and ownership of large assets, such as skyscrapers. This advantage is especially important to small investors who cannot afford to buy large assets themselves.

- They allow investors to own diversified pools of risks and thereby obtain more predictable, although not necessarily better, returns. Many indirect investment vehicles represent ownership in many different assets, each of which typically is subject to some specific risks not shared by the others. For example, an important risk of owning a home mortgage is that the homeowner may default on the mortgage. Defaults on individual mortgages are highly unpredictable, which makes holding an individual mortgage quite risky. In contrast, the average default rate among a large set of mortgages is much more predictable: Investing the same dollar amount in shares of a large mortgage pool is much less risky than investing that same amount in a single mortgage.

- Finally, they are often substantially less expensive to trade than the underlying assets. This cost advantage is especially significant for publicly traded investment vehicles that own highly illiquid assets; recall from Chapter 12 that this is one of the benefits of real estate investment trusts compared with real estate limited partnerships or real estate equity funds. Although the assets in which traded investment vehicles invest may be very difficult to buy and sell, ownership shares in these vehicles may trade in liquid markets.

Indirect investments also present some disadvantages to investors compared with direct investments:

- Direct investors can exercise more control over their investments than investors who hold indirect investments. The latter generally must accept all decisions made by the investment managers, and they often cannot provide input into those decisions.

- Direct investors can choose when to buy or sell their investments to minimize their tax liabilities. In contrast, although the managers of indirect investments often try to minimize the collective tax liabilities of their investors, they cannot simultaneously best serve all investors when those investors have diverse tax situations.

- Direct investors can choose not to invest in certain securities, for example, in securities of companies that sell tobacco or alcohol. In contrast, indirect investors concerned about such issues must seek investments with investment policies that include these restrictions.

- Large investors often can obtain high-quality investment advice at a lower cost when investing directly rather than indirectly.

## 3.2 Investment Control Problems

Investors may prefer direct or indirect investments based on how well they can oversee their investment managers. Unfortunately, although the majority of investment managers work faithfully to serve their clients, some managers are not always careful, conscientious, or honest, which can lead to investment losses from poor research, missed opportunities, self-serving advice, or outright fraud. Consider some examples:

- Investment managers who cut corners on research may suggest inappropriate securities. They also may fail to identify attractive investment opportunities.

- Investment managers who receive commissions on trades that they recommend may recommend too many trades. Practitioners commonly call this problem churning.

- Investment managers may favor themselves or their preferred clients over other clients when allocating among accounts trades that have been, or are expected to be, profitable. This practice is known as fraudulent trade assignment.

To successfully use the services of professional investment managers, investors must control these problems. Investors who cannot easily deal with these issues often invest in indirect vehicles, such as public mutual funds, for which a board of directors (or trustees) has primary responsibility for monitoring the performance of the professional investment managers. Unfortunately, although board members generally work conscientiously on behalf of their shareholders, some may be more loyal to the managers that they monitor than to the shareholders that they represent. Regardless, the managers of public mutual funds generally work hard for their investors because they usually are paid in proportion to their total assets under management. Because good performance tends to attract additional investments, mutual fund managers generally work to produce the good investment returns that attract new investments and thus increase their fees.

In contrast, large institutional investors often are direct investors who hire and oversee investment managers. These institutional investors generally devote substantial resources to monitoring and evaluating their managers.

# 4  STRUCTURED INVESTMENT PRODUCTS

**Structured investment products** are special purpose securities that investment banks and other large, creditworthy financial institutions, such as insurance companies, issue. These instruments encompass a wide variety of features and are designed to provide returns with various properties that investors cannot easily obtain from direct investments in other securities or contracts.

Most structured products are securities whose returns replicate the returns of complex combinations of financial instruments that may include stocks, bonds, futures contracts, options contracts, and swap contracts. The issuers structure these products to meet the needs of particular investors. Many structured products are mass produced on a regular calendar offering cycle and distributed through broker–dealers or registered investment advisers to serve a broad audience of investors. Other structured products are crafted on a one-off basis and individually customized to the risk–return preferences of individual retail or institutional investors.

## 4.1 Equity-Linked Securities

An equity-linked note is an example of a structured product. Despite the term "equity" in the name, **equity-linked notes** are bonds. They are linked to equity because the final payout of these bonds depends on the performance of an underlying equity or equity pool, which may be a stock, a stock portfolio, or a stock index.

Some equity-linked notes are principal protected. A principal-protected note is a note that, at maturity, will return to the investor at least the original amount invested, regardless of market conditions. In particular, if the linked equity drops in value, the equity-linked note will simply return the original principal to the investor when the note matures, assuming, of course, that the issuer does not default.

If the market rises during the life of the note, at maturity the investor will receive the principal plus a participation rate (specified in the note) multiplied by the equity return multiplied by the original principal. For example, if the participation rate is 80% and the equity return during the investment period is 50%, at maturity the note will pay 1 + (0.80 × 0.50) = 1.4 times its original principal amount.

Equity-linked notes that feature some degree of partial or full principal protection are attractive to risk-averse investors who want exposure to the stock market but are unwilling to lose money. The investors give up interest income in exchange for principal-protected equity upside.

Another popular example of a structured investment product is the **equity-linked annuity**, which is also known as an **equity-indexed annuity**. These securities earn interest at rates that depend on the performance of a stock or a stock index. Similar to equity-linked notes, they usually are principal protected. Insurance companies are the most common issuers of equity-linked annuities.

Equity-linked annuities are popular with investors who are saving for retirement or who have recently retired. In comparison with fixed annuities, they provide exposure to equity risk, but the investors give up interest income if the linked equity returns are low. In some countries, these annuities provide a means of deferring taxes on investment income similar to standard annuities.

## 4.2 Exchange-Traded Notes

**Exchange-traded notes** are another structured investment product, although they are rarely recognized as such. Exchange-traded notes are debt securities issued by investment banks that pay the value of an index when they mature, minus fees paid to the bank. The notes thus closely replicate the returns to the index. Exchange-traded notes are listed on many exchanges and tend to be very liquid securities.

### 4.3 Advantages and Disadvantages of Structured Products

In addition to providing risk and return profiles that appeal to certain investors, structured products may also provide tax benefits to these investors that would be unavailable if the investors constructed the products themselves. Any such benefits depend on the local tax regime and, in particular, on how returns of the structured products are taxed relative to returns on the contracts and other securities involved. Alternatively, tax advantages may accrue to the investment bank that creates the product. In either case, in competitive markets, the products will be priced so that both sides share any tax benefits.

Structured investment products have several significant disadvantages for investors:

- With the exception of exchange-traded notes, many structured investment products do not trade in secondary markets and thus are illiquid. They cannot easily be sold to others, and market prices may be difficult to obtain for these products.

- Structured investment products are hard to value. At best, analysts can value these products by identifying the portfolio of instruments that produce the same returns, assuming, of course, that values for these instruments are available. At worst, valuation of the structured investment product requires detailed information on product specifications and analysis of complex financial engineering models. These valuation methods are beyond the abilities of almost all retail investors and most institutional investors. Investors thus risk overpaying for these products, especially if they cannot easily comparison shop, which is generally the case.

- Structured products have credit risk. If the issuer that offers the product fails, investors will become general creditors of the issuer and may lose much or all of their investments. This situation happened in September 2008 when Lehman Brothers filed for bankruptcy, thereby defaulting on its corporate bonds and all of its structured note offerings.

## 5 INVESTMENT COMPANIES

Investment companies include closed-end funds, which may be called investment trusts in some countries, open-end mutual funds, exchange-traded funds, and unit investment trusts. An exhibit is included at the end of this section that summarizes characteristics, advantages, and disadvantages of each of these forms of investment companies. The sole purpose of these companies is to own investment securities and assets. The investment companies, in turn, are owned by their investors, who share in the companies' profits and losses in proportion to their ownership. Ownership in investment companies is one of the most common indirect pooled investment vehicles.

Investors in an investment company do not share ownership of the investment securities and assets held by the investment company. Instead, they share in the ownership of the investment company that owns these securities and assets. They are the beneficial owners of the investment company's assets but not the legal owners.

Banks, insurance companies, and investment management firms organize most investment companies. The organizer is often called the sponsor. Sponsors may organize investment companies as business trusts, limited partnerships, or limited liability companies. Depending on the form of the organization, ownership shares are known as shares, units, or partnership interests. Large sponsors may organize hundreds of different investment companies.

A board of directors, a board of trustees, a general partner, or a single trustee oversees every investment company; the governance structure depends on the form of legal organization. In some countries, investment company directors must be independent of the sponsor. In other countries, employees or directors of the sponsor may also serve as directors of its associated investment companies. The investment company or the sponsor pays fees to the directors for their service.

The directors appoint a professional investment manager, who is almost always an affiliate of the sponsor. The manager works for the investment company on a contractual basis in exchange for a management fee paid by the investment company from its assets. The amount of the management fee varies among types of investment companies. The investment manager—or hired sub-adviser—chooses the securities held by the investment company, distributes securities issued by the investment company, and keeps track of its accounts. Most investment companies have no employees. Instead, contractors do all the work.

Many investors confuse investment companies with the firms that sponsor them. The shares of an investment company derive their value from the assets held by the investment company and the expenses of managing them. The securities that an investment company issues represent ownership only of the assets held by the investment company. They are not liabilities of the sponsor. The confusion comes from the fact that sponsors often heavily promote the investment companies that they create and manage. Sponsors thus become closely identified with the investment companies that they sponsor.

The four main types of investment companies (closed-end funds, open-end mutual funds, exchange-traded funds, and unit investment trusts) differ primarily in how investors trade them, how they are managed, and the level of management fees. Closed-end funds, exchange-traded funds, and unit investment trusts trade in organized secondary markets just like common stocks. Open-end mutual funds are continuously offered and continuously redeemable securities that the funds sell to and redeem from their investors. exchange-traded funds are also redeemable securities, but only authorized participants can purchase or redeem these securities directly from the investment companies. Everyone else must trade them on exchanges or with dealers.

Investment companies vary by whether their managers use active or passive investment strategies. Almost all closed-end funds use active management strategies. In contrast, unit investment trusts are not managed at all. They simply hold a fixed portfolio of securities that the sponsor chooses when it organizes and funds the trust. Open-end mutual funds may use active or passive investment strategies, depending on the fund.

Most exchange-traded funds use passive indexing strategies, but some are actively managed. Fees are generally higher if managers use an active management strategy than if managers use a passive investment strategy.

All investment companies disclose their investment policies, deposit and redemption procedures, fees and expenses, and past performance statistics in an official offering document called a **prospectus**. Investors use this information to evaluate potential investments. Funds may disclose additional information through other mandated regulatory filings, on their websites, or in marketing materials.

### 5.1 Closed-End Funds

**Closed-end funds** sell shares to the public in initial public offerings (IPOs), as described in Chapter 9, soon after they are first organized. They then use the proceeds from the initial public offering to purchase investment securities or other assets. They may issue additional shares in secondary offerings or through rights offerings or they may repurchase shares, but these events are uncommon. Accordingly, the total number of shares outstanding for most closed-end funds rarely changes.

After the initial public offering, investors who want to buy or sell a closed-end fund do so through exchanges and dealers. The closed-end fund does not participate in these transactions aside from registering the resulting ownership changes. Investors buy and sell the shares at whatever prices they can obtain in the market.

Closed-end funds are actively managed and generally trade at values different from their **net asset value (NAV)**. The net asset value of a fund is computed by dividing the total net value of the fund (the value of all assets minus the value of all liabilities) by the current total number of fund shares outstanding. A closed-end fund is said to trade at a discount if the trading price is lower than the fund's net asset value or at a premium if the trading price is greater than its net asset value.

Discounts are more common than premiums because many closed-end fund investment managers have been unable to add more value to their funds than the funds lose through their various operational costs. The investment management fee typically is the largest of these costs. Other costs include portfolio transaction costs and fees for accounting and other administrative services.

### 5.2 Open-End Mutual Funds

**Open-end mutual funds** can issue and redeem shares as necessary. When investors want to invest, the fund issues new shares in exchange for cash that the investors deposit. When existing investors want to withdraw money, the fund redeems (repurchases) their shares and pays the investors cash. From the fund's point of view, investor purchases and sales are deposits and redemptions, respectively.

The administrator of an open-end mutual fund determines the prices at which deposits and redemptions occur. No-load funds, which do not collect deposit or redemption fees, set the same price for deposits and redemptions on any given day. This price is the net asset value of the fund. Managers compute the fund's net asset value each day following the normal close of exchange market trading. They use last reported trade prices to value their portfolio securities. They usually publish their net asset values a few hours after the market closes.

Investors may pay **sales loads** when buying or selling open-end mutual funds. A sales or front-end load is a fee paid to buy a fund. It is computed as a percentage of the sales price. The percentage is usually around 3% but may be as high as 9%. The investor may pay the load at the time of purchase, at the time of redemption, or over time. Typically, the fund distributor, who markets the fund, receives the load. It pays part of it to the investment manager and part of it to anybody who helped arrange the trade, except where legally restricted from doing so. Some distributors also collect contingent deferred sales charges, which are also known as back-end loads. Back-end loads are fees that investors may have to pay when they sell a fund that they have not held for more than some pre-specified period, typically a year or more.

Some funds also charge purchase or redemption fees. Investors pay these fees to the fund as opposed to paying them to the distributor as in a front-end or back-end load. These fees help compensate existing shareholders for costs imposed on the fund when other shareholders buy and sell their shares. These costs primarily consist of the costs of trading portfolio securities incurred when making purchases to invest the cash received from investors or when making sales to raise cash for redemptions.

Open-end mutual funds may be passively or actively managed. The index funds discussed in Section 2.2 are passively managed open-end mutual funds. Passively managed funds typically have much lower fees than actively managed funds.

A mutual fund complex is a set of mutual funds managed and distributed by the same sponsor. The manager, or one or more designated sub-advisers, chooses the securities in which the various funds invest. The same set of directors (or trustees) usually serves on the boards of each mutual fund in the complex, and each fund in the complex typically uses the same fund distributor and transfer agent. The transfer agent keeps track of share ownership. Although each fund in the complex is a separate investment company, their common relationship with the sponsor and the sponsor's investment management, fund distribution, and transfer agent subsidiaries makes the funds in the complex similar in many operational aspects. Fund complexes generally permit investors to exchange funds within the complex. In an exchange, the investor sells shares in one fund and with the proceeds buys shares in another. Most exchanges are exempt from further sales loads so that once an investor has paid a sales load to buy one fund in a complex, all subsequent transfers among funds in the complex are not subject to further load payments. In effect, investors pay loads only when moving money into the complex.

**Money market funds** are a special class of open-end mutual funds that investors consider uninsured interest-paying bank accounts. Unlike other open-end mutual funds, regulators permit money market funds to accept deposits and satisfy redemptions at a constant price per share (typically one unit of the local currency—for example, a euro per share in the eurozone) if they meet certain conditions. In particular, they may only hold money market securities—that is, generally very short-term, low-risk bills and notes issued by entities with very high-quality credit. In that case, regulators allow the funds to pay daily income distributions to their shareholders, which they typically distribute at the end of the month. These arrangements ensure that money market funds' net asset values remain very close to their constant reported values.

Money market funds are vulnerable to a run on assets. In particular, if investors expect that the value of their money market funds will decline in the near future, they may rush to redeem their shares before the net asset value falls. These actions can be very destabilizing because they force funds to sell portfolio securities when the market is weakest.

## 5.3 Exchange-Traded Funds

**Exchange-traded funds** are pooled investment vehicles that are typically passively managed to track a particular index, sector, or group. Exchange-traded funds generally are organized by investment managers who provide investment managerial and administrative services. The fees for these services and trading costs are low because exchange-traded funds are typically passively managed. Most of them are structured as trusts so that their ownership interests are known formally as trust units, but in practice, they are generally referred to as shares.

Similar to closed-end funds, shares of exchange-traded funds trade continuously in organized markets where traders determine trade prices. Usually, the market price is close to the net asset value because exchange-traded funds allow certain qualified financial institutions, called authorized participants, to deposit and redeem shares in-kind rather than in cash. By allowing depositors to deliver a portfolio of securities and redeemers to receive a portfolio of securities that matches the portfolio held by the exchange-traded fund, the price of an exchange-traded fund's share has to be close to its net asset value. Otherwise, the authorized participants would have an arbitrage opportunity—that is, an opportunity to earn profits without risk by taking advantage of differences in prices on the same assets in different markets or forms. However, market prices may occasionally deviate significantly from the exchange-traded fund's net asset values.

Some exchange-traded fund sponsors design leveraged exchange-traded funds by using debt and derivative instruments to magnify the return of an index and provide leveraged returns, inverse returns, or leveraged inverse returns to their investors. In the case of leveraged returns, when the return of the index is positive, the return of the exchange-traded fund is higher. In the case of inverse returns or leveraged inverse returns, when the return of the index is positive, the return of the exchange-traded fund is negative. Thus, inverse and leveraged inverse returns allow investors to benefit when market prices are falling. In absolute value, the return of the exchange-traded fund is the same as the return of the index in the case of inverse returns, but magnified in the case of leveraged returns. The use of leverage, either through the use of debt or derivatives, thus makes these investment companies risky.

## 5.4 Unit Investment Trusts

**Unit investment trusts** are funds that are not actively managed.[1] Instead, unit investment trusts simply hold a fixed portfolio of securities or assets until the trust expires. At expiration, the trust liquidates any remaining positions and distributes the proceeds to its unit holders in proportion to their ownership.

Unit investment trusts are typically set up by large investment managers who sell them to the public through brokerage firms in an initial public offering. Some unit investment trusts will redeem their units from investors at the net asset value. Sponsors often are willing to buy their sponsored trust units and resell them to other investors. Unlike other investment companies, unit investment trusts do not have boards of directors, officers, or investment advisers. The lack of trading and management results in very low fees and costs.

## 5.5 Advantages and Disadvantages of Investment Company Structures

Each investment company structure has some advantages and disadvantages for investors. The main differences involve management accountability, costs, taxes, and risks.

### 5.5.1 Management Accountability

Because all investment companies are indirect investment vehicles, investors cannot directly choose who will manage their investments. They can, however, choose the funds in which they invest and thus can invest in funds run by managers that they trust and sell funds run by managers they no longer have confidence in.

Among the various investment company structures, management issues are of the least concern for the unit investment trusts that hold unmanaged portfolios. Concerns are also small for exchange-traded funds and open-end mutual funds that use passive investing strategies because their managers have little effect on portfolio performance in comparison with active portfolio managers.

The managers of actively managed open-end mutual funds and exchange-traded funds are particularly sensitive to shareholder concerns because shareholders will withdraw their money from these funds if they are unhappy with the management. When shareholders redeem shares of an open-end mutual fund, the fund assets under management decrease, which reduces the management fee paid to the investment manager.

The managers of closed-end funds are largely insulated from their shareholders. Shareholders can sell their shares to new investors, but the assets under management remain the same. The managers are accountable to their boards, but board members may be more loyal to their managers than to their shareholders. This problem often causes closed-end funds to trade at substantial discounts to their net asset value. In extreme cases, when a discount becomes very large, arbitrageurs may attempt to take control of the fund with the objective of liquidating it to realize the value of the discount. Such efforts are very costly and thus are uncommon.

---

1 Unit investment trusts should not be confused with investment trusts in the United Kingdom. Unit investment trusts are closed-end funds, although a different name is used. Similar to the closed-end funds discussed earlier, they are typically actively managed.

### 5.5.2 Managerial and Administrative Costs

The costs that investment companies incur are deducted from their assets and thus reduce their performance. The most important costs are those associated with management, distribution, and account maintenance.

Management fees depend primarily on the style of asset management and the type of assets managed. Investors in passively managed funds generally pay lower management fees regardless of their organizational structure. Management fees for actively managed funds are higher.

### 5.5.3 Liquidity and Trading Costs

Investors can trade a closed-end fund, exchange-traded fund, or unit investment trust at any time that they can find a counterparty willing to take the other side of their trade. In contrast, investors in open-end mutual funds can trade only at the end of the day. They can place their orders at any time but settlement occurs after close when the net asset value is determined.

Investors who trade exchange-traded products generally know the prices at which their trades take place because they or their brokers arrange their trades. Investors trading exchange-traded products generally must pay commissions to their brokers to arrange trades. Open-end mutual fund investors must accept the net asset value determined by their funds, and they must commit to trading before they know these prices.

### 5.5.4 Distributions and Taxes

Investment companies generally distribute the income (typically interest and dividends) that they receive from holding securities as cash dividends to their investors. They also distribute any short- and long-term capital gains realized on their portfolio security trades as cash dividends. Distributions (expressed on a per-share basis) are the same for all investors, regardless of how long the shares have been held. Investors may choose, if the investment company allows it, to reinvest these distributions rather than receive them. They should be aware that doing so does not generally eliminate any tax liability associated with the distribution.

### 5.5.5 Risks

The risks of holding investment companies mainly depend on the investment securities and assets that they hold in their portfolios. These risks vary much more by fund than by how the funds are organized. In general, index funds are less risky than actively managed funds that invest in the same asset class because investors in actively managed funds risk that their managers will underperform the market for that asset class.

Closed-end funds generally are riskier than similar open-end mutual funds because the discounts and occasional premiums to their net asset values at which closed-end funds trade vary over time. Uncertainty in the variation of these discounts and premiums increases the risk of holding closed-end funds.

Exchange-traded funds sometimes also trade at discounts and premiums to their net asset values, but these variations tend to be small because these securities are redeemable. If the discounts or premiums grow large, authorized participants create or redeem shares while taking offsetting positions in the portfolio securities. Their trading keeps discounts and premiums from growing large.

# Investment Companies

Investors in funds that trade in organized secondary markets face the risk that the costs of arranging secondary market trades in their funds will increase and, in particular, that they will not be able to easily find buyers when they want to sell their shares. This risk is greatest for smaller closed-end funds in which few other investors may have any interest.

## 5.6 Comparison of Investment Company Structures

Exhibit 1 offers a summary table of characteristics, advantages, and disadvantages of closed-end funds, open-end mutual funds, exchange-traded funds, and unit investment trusts.

**Exhibit 1  Comparison of Closed-End Funds, Open-End Mutual Funds, Exchange-Traded Funds, and Unit Investment Trusts**

|  | Closed-End Funds | Open-End Mutual Funds, Including Money Market Funds | Exchange-Traded Funds | Unit Investment Trusts |
|---|---|---|---|---|
| Managed | Yes, primarily actively | Yes, actively or passively | Yes, primarily passively | Not managed after inception |
| Exchange traded | Yes, but not traded continuously | No | Yes, traded continuously | Yes |
| If exchange traded, size of the gap between the price and the net asset value | Can be large, usually trade at a discount to the net asset value |  | Small, usually trade at close to the net asset value | Small, usually trade at close to the net asset value |
| Redeemable | No | Yes, by all participants, after the close of the market each day, in cash, at the net asset value | Yes, but only by authorized participants, in kind, at the net asset value | No, theoretically. In practice, sponsors may accept redemptions |
| Liquidity | Yes | No | Yes | Yes |
| Fund management's accountability | Management not particularly responsive to shareholders' concerns | Issues with management are limited, in particular for passively managed funds | Issues with management are limited, in particular for passively managed funds | Not applicable because there is no management |
| Managerial and administrative costs | Limited | Yes, because of the fees to distributors and transfer agents | Limited | Limited |
| Relative level of fees and costs | Higher because of active management | Higher if actively managed, lower if passively managed | Lower because of passive management | Very low because it holds a fixed portfolio of securities or assets until the trust expires |

*(continued)*

**Exhibit 1** (Continued)

|  | Closed-End Funds | Open-End Mutual Funds, Including Money Market Funds | Exchange-Traded Funds | Unit Investment Trusts |
|---|---|---|---|---|
| Risky | Yes, more than open-end mutual fund | Yes, more so for actively managed funds | Yes, more so for actively managed funds and for leveraged exchange-traded funds | Yes |

## 6. HEDGE FUNDS

**Hedge funds** are private investment pools that investment managers organize and manage. As a group, hedge funds pursue very diverse strategies. Most funds, however, only use a single strategy.

The term "hedge" once referred to the practice of buying one asset and selling a correlated asset to take advantage of the difference in their values without taking much risk—thus the term hedge because it refers to a reduction or elimination of risk. Although many hedge funds do engage in some hedging, it is no longer the distinguishing characteristic of hedge funds, if it ever was.

Hedge funds are distinguished from other pooled investment products primarily by

- their availability to only a limited number of select investors,
- agreements that lock up the investors' capital for fixed periods, and
- their managers' performance-based compensation.

They may also be distinguished by their use of strategies beyond the scope of traditional mutual funds.

### 6.1 Availability

Hedge funds are private investment pools available only to some investors, who usually meet various wealth, income, and investment knowledge criteria that regulators set. The criteria are designed to ensure that these lightly regulated investment products are suitable for their investors. Most money invested in hedge funds comes from such large institutions as pension funds, university endowments, and sovereign wealth funds and from high-net-worth individuals.

## 6.2 Agreements

Most hedge funds lock up their investors' capital for various periods, the length of which depends on how much time the managers expect that they will need to successfully implement their strategies. Funds that engage in high-frequency strategies generally have shorter lock-up periods than funds that engage in strategies that may take much more time to realize their expected returns, such as strategies that involve reforming corporate governance.

## 6.3 Compensation and Performance Fees

Perhaps the most distinguishing characteristic of hedge funds is the managerial compensation scheme that they use. Hedge fund managers generally receive an annual management fee plus a performance fee that is a specified percentage of the returns that they produce in excess of a hurdle rate. For example, a manager who receives "2 and 20" compensation will receive 2% of the fund assets in management fees every year plus 20% of the return on the fund assets that exceeds a specified target as a performance fee.

Absolute return funds are hedge funds that strive to produce the highest possible return to investors without much correlation with any other asset classes. The performance target for these funds typically is a short-term interest rate.

Hedge fund managers earn the performance fee only if the fund is above its current high-water mark. The **high-water mark** is the maximum level of the fund on which performance fees were paid in the past. The high-water mark provision ensures that investors pay the managers only for net returns calculated from the initial investment and not for returns that recoup previous losses. This provision is also called the loss-carryback provision. High-water marks are tracked for every new investment in a hedge fund. In any given year, managers may receive performance fees from some investors but not others depending on when each investor first invested in the fund.

The loss-carryback provision causes many managers to terminate their funds and start over when they have significant losses. Restarting gives them a new high-water mark. Otherwise, they would receive no performance fee until they raised the value of the fund over the previous high-water mark. Of course, managers who have performed poorly often have difficulty raising new funds.

Investors pay high performance fees in the belief that the fees provide strong incentives to managers to perform well. These incentives work when the fund is near its high-water mark. They are much less powerful when the fund has performed poorly.

## 6.4 Risk

Although many hedge funds are not particularly risky, the high performance fees may encourage some fund managers to take substantial risks. Hedge funds typically increase their risk exposure through leverage. Such increased leverage can be achieved through the use of borrowed funds or through the use of derivatives. If their investments are successful, the performance fee can make the managers extremely wealthy.

But if the hedge fund has poor returns, the investors lose their whole investment, and the managers lose only the opportunity to stay in business. This asymmetry in their compensation encourages risk taking.

Hedge fund investment managers often also participate as investors in their hedge funds. Their co-investments help assure their investors that the managers' interests are well aligned with theirs. Such assurances help managers raise funds.

Most hedge funds are open-end investment vehicles that allow new investors to buy-in and existing investors to leave at the net asset value. But most funds only allow investors to withdraw funds following a lock-up period and then only on specific dates.

## 6.5 Legal Structure and Taxes

The legal structure and legal domicile of hedge funds generally depend on their managers' and investors' tax situations. For example, most hedge funds serving U.S. investors are organized as domestic limited partnerships in which the manager is the general partner and the investors are the limited partners. This structure, which is very similar to the structure of private equity funds described in Chapter 12, allows for some of the fees to be treated as capital gain rather than ordinary income. Some hedge funds are domiciled in offshore financial centers where tax rates may be lower. The Cayman Islands are a popular domicile for hedge funds because of favorable laws and regulations for investors and investment managers and the tax advantages this location offers.

# 7 FUNDS OF FUNDS

**Funds of funds** are investment vehicles that invest in other funds. Most are organized as hedge funds that invest primarily in other hedge funds. Funds of funds may be actively managed or passively managed.

Two main investment strategies characterize most actively managed funds of funds. Some managers try to identify funds with managers they believe will outperform the market. They then invest in funds managed by those managers. Others use various proprietary models to predict which investment strategies are most likely to be successful in the future and then invest in funds that implement those strategies. Both types of managers try to hold well-diversified portfolios of funds to reduce the overall risk of their funds.

The costs of investing in actively managed funds of funds can be very high. Investors pay management and performance fees directly to their managers, and they also indirectly pay these fees to the managers of the funds in which their funds of funds invest. Funds-of-funds investors thus pay these fees twice.

Investors in well-diversified funds of hedge funds may pay particularly high management fees because of the performance fees paid to hedge fund managers. In a well-diversified fund of funds, investment gains in some funds are often offset by losses in the other funds. The fund of funds pays performance fees to the winning hedge fund managers and thus shares its gains in these funds with those managers. But losing hedge managers do not share in the losses of their hedge funds. If the gains and losses are of equal size, fund-of-hedge-funds investors will not profit on net, but they will pay substantial performance fees to the winning managers.

# MANAGED ACCOUNTS    8

Many investors contract with investment advisers to help manage their investments. The advisers generally promise to implement specific strategies in exchange for an advisory fee or for commissions on the trades that they recommend. Investors increasingly are using fee-based advisers to ensure that their advisers will not profit from recommending excessive trading.

Institutional investors that do not manage investments in-house use fee-based advisers. Retail investors often obtain the services of fee-based investment advisers through wrap accounts. In a **wrap account**, the charges for investment services, such as brokerage, investment advice, financial planning, and investment accounting, are all wrapped into a single flat fee. The fee typically ranges between 1% and 3% of total assets per year and usually is paid quarterly or annually.

Investment advisers may hold their institutional clients' investments in separate accounts or in commingled accounts. In a **commingled account**, the capital of two or more investors are pooled together and jointly managed. In contrast, funds and securities in a separate account are always kept separate from those of other investors, even if the manager uses identical investment strategies for several such accounts.

When funds are commingled, the advisers must keep track of the ownership interests of each investor. They account for ownership using the same methods as open-end mutual funds. In particular, they divide ownership of the account into shares. Whenever investors contribute cash or securities to the commingled account, the advisers compute the net asset value of the account and allocate new shares to the investors in proportion to the current market values of their contributions. They do similar calculations when investors withdraw cash or securities.

A commingled account solves a serious problem that arises when many separate accounts are under common management and using a common investment strategy. The adviser must allocate all trades fairly to every account. This objective can be difficult to achieve when accounts have insufficient funds to pay for a purchase or when the allocation would result in fractional shares, which can occur frequently with many small adjustments. These issues cause performance to vary among separate accounts that are all managed using the same strategy. In contrast, investors in a commingled account all obtain equal returns because they share ownership of the single account.

Although commingled accounts solve the allocation problem, they present other problems. In particular, they are not appropriate for investors with substantially different objectives or cash flow needs. The problem associated with different objectives is obvious: A single account cannot be managed to simultaneously meet multiple objectives.

Commingled accounts face the same cash flow problem as any vehicle that permits frequent trading. Unless investors compensate their co-investors for the portfolio costs associated with accommodating their cash flows, the co-investors will be harmed. Commingled accounts control these problems by imposing deposit and redemption fees, by requiring that deposits and redemptions be done in-kind, or by simply prohibiting frequent cash flows into and out of the account. They also may impose lock-up agreements that require investors to remain in the account for certain periods.

Another serious problem with commingled accounts involves tax issues. When investors leave a commingled account, they may impose tax liabilities on the remaining investors if the account must sell an appreciated asset to distribute cash to the departing investor. This tax liability problem can be mitigated if the account sells assets that have depreciated. But selling assets with a high bases lowers the tax basis of the account, which would mean the commingled accountholders would have to pay higher taxes in the future. The tax liability problem can be avoided if the departing shareholders receive in-kind distributions of securities instead of cash.

Accounts with unrealized capital gains are said to have tax overhangs—that is, a potential tax liability. Taxable investors should avoid buying into any pooled investments with substantial tax overhangs to avoid the risk of paying higher taxes in the future on gains that they did not earn. Accordingly, commingled accounts work best when all investors are tax exempt or when all investors enter and exit the account at the same time. To avoid these problems, many investors prefer to hold separate accounts.

## 9 TAX-ADVANTAGED ACCOUNTS

To promote savings for retirement income, educational expenses, and health expenses, many countries give tax advantages to certain accounts. In general, **tax-advantaged accounts** allow investors to avoid paying taxes on investment income and capital gains as they earn them. In addition, contributions made to these accounts or distributions received from them may have tax advantages. In exchange for these privileges, investors must accept stringent restrictions on when the money can be withdrawn from the account and sometimes on how the money can be used.

Many countries allow contributions made to certain tax-advantaged accounts to be tax deductible, which means that they reduce the income on which taxes are paid. Tax-deductible contributions are common for retirement accounts. In most countries, contributions made to pension plans by employers or employees, as well as contributions made by individuals to specific types of retirement accounts, are tax deductible up to certain limits. These accounts are allowed to grow tax free so that any income or capital gains earned by the account will not be taxed if left in the account. But taxes may be due when the money is ultimately withdrawn. For most retirement accounts, all distributions from the account are taxed as ordinary income.

Some countries also allow investors to contribute after-tax funds to tax-advantaged accounts. After-tax funds are the amounts that remain after taxable income and gifts are received and taxed. When placed in tax-advantaged accounts, the funds grow tax free. When withdrawn, taxes, if any, are collected only on the accumulated investment income and capital gains earned during the period of the investment. The original principal, which was taxed once, is not taxed again.

Many countries allow all distributions from certain tax-advantaged accounts to be tax free if the money is used for higher education or for health care. Distributions from retirement accounts generally are taxed as ordinary income.

Governments usually prohibit early withdrawals or withdrawals for unauthorized purposes from tax-advantaged accounts. When such withdrawals are permitted, they generally incur penalties and immediate taxes. In some countries and for some accounts, investors can circumvent these restrictions by borrowing against the values of their accounts.

## 9.1 Advantages of Taxable Accounts

Saving in tax-advantaged accounts from which distributions are not taxed is unambiguously advantageous for investors if they are certain that they will ultimately use the money for its authorized purpose. For example, investors always will be better off saving in tax-advantaged accounts if the withdrawals used to fund educational expenses are not taxed. But if the money would be lost if not used for educational expenses, investors need to weigh the potential tax advantage against the probability of loss when deciding whether to use these accounts.

The benefits of deferring taxes are less obvious. Whether deferral is advantageous depends on the tax rates at which the principal and investment income would otherwise be taxed and on the rates at which the deferred income is taxed. If future tax rates will be lower or the same as current tax rates, deferral is advantageous.

Deferring taxes may not be beneficial if tax rates will be higher in the future. Future rates may be higher under a variety of circumstances: Tax rates may change during the period of the investment, the investor may be wealthier in the future and thus subject to higher tax rates, or the investor may pay ordinary income tax rates on distributions from a tax-advantaged account but would have paid lower rates on capital gains or investment income earned on the investment if the money was invested in a taxable account.

Whether investors should defer income depends on the tax regime, their expectations of future tax rates (including estate tax rates, which are imposed on the transfer of properties from the deceased to his or her heirs), and the probability that they will need money that they cannot access if placed in a tax-advantaged account. Financial planners help investors work through these issues.

## 9.2 Managing Taxable Accounts to Minimize Tax Liabilities

Investors in taxable accounts often can minimize their tax liabilities through careful investment management decisions. In particular, most countries do not tax capital gains until they are realized for tax purposes. Capital gains and losses generally are realized on the sale of a previously purchased security or asset. Investors who have unrealized capital gains because their purchases rose in value can avoid paying taxes by simply not selling their appreciated securities or assets. If they need cash, they can borrow money using their appreciated securities and assets as collateral instead of selling them.

Most countries allow taxpayers to offset their realized capital gains with realized capital losses so that they are taxed only on the net gain. Accordingly, investors frequently realize losses by selling losing positions so that they can use them to offset realized capital gains.

Many countries tax capital gains at lower rates than they tax investment income, such as interest and dividends. Taxpaying investors in these countries can minimize their taxes by holding securities that do not pay investment income. For example, many companies distribute cash by repurchasing shares on the open market instead of paying dividends. Share prices of these companies tend to rise over time as the share repurchases reduce the total number of shares. Investors who retain their shares thus earn long-term capital gains rather than current investment income. These companies provide more tax-efficient investments than do otherwise similar companies that pay dividends. Some countries, such as Hong Kong and Singapore, do not have capital gains taxes.

The mutual fund industry has created many funds to serve taxable investors seeking tax-efficient investments. These funds avoid realizing capital gains, realize losses to match any gains that they do realize, and avoid securities that produce investment income. Investors who hold these funds defer their taxes into the future and, in many cases, past their deaths.

Many countries provide similar tax advantages to such insurance products as annuities and life insurance policies that investors use to save for retirement. Investors who buy these tax-advantaged securities effectively obtain many of the same advantages that they could obtain using tax-advantaged accounts.

## 10 PENSION PLANS

In most countries, pension funds are the largest institutional investors. Worldwide, they collectively hold more than $20 trillion of assets, more than any other class of investor. Understanding pension funds is thus essential to understanding the investment industry, the financial markets in which pension funds operate, and the welfare of their beneficiaries. This section briefly examines the structure of pension investments.

Pension plans are vehicles that provide income to people in their retirement. Pension plans may be sponsored by companies that employ workers, by governments on behalf of their citizens, by labor unions on behalf of their members, or by individuals for their own benefit. The people who ultimately receive payments are called beneficiaries.

Some plans are **pay-as-you-go plans**, in which the sponsors pay pension benefits out of current revenues. Most company plans are **funded plans** to which the sponsors make periodic contributions long before the benefits are paid. The accumulation of these contributions is responsible for the enormous assets that pension funds hold.

Funded plans are much better for their beneficiaries than pay-as-you-go plans because payments from pay-as-you-go plans depend on the continued viability of their sponsors. Moreover, because pay-as-you-go sponsors do not fund their obligations up front, they have a tendency to promise more than they can afford in the future. Repeated problems with pay-as-you-go plans have caused many countries to require that employers fund their pension plans at regular intervals.

Pension funds differ by whether they are defined benefit plans or defined contribution plans. A defined benefit plan promises certain pension benefits to its beneficiaries. Defined benefit pension plan sponsors must pay those benefits. In contrast, the sponsors of defined contribution plans make certain contributions to their pension plans on behalf of their beneficiaries. The beneficiaries ultimately receive whatever benefits the accumulated contributions and associated investment returns can fund at retirement. The two different plan types have very different risk characteristics for sponsors and beneficiaries.

## 10.1 Defined Benefit Plans

A defined benefit plan promises certain benefits to its beneficiaries—for example, specified payments of real income (income adjusted for the effects of inflation) per year. These promises are called pension liabilities, and the pension sponsor is ultimately responsible for them.

The pension promises of most employer-sponsored defined benefit programs increase with the total time that the employee has worked for the company. They also are generally larger for high-salary employees than for low-wage workers.

The right to receive pension benefits often is not vested until an employee has worked for the company for some period specified by the pension plan. When their rights are vested, employees are entitled to receive benefits even if they do not continue to work for the company.

The sponsors of funded pension plans generally must make contributions to their plans soon after their pension liabilities are created and as these liabilities grow larger over time. A fully funded plan has sufficient assets to pay all currently vested pension liabilities when due.

Determining whether a plan is fully funded requires a very complex computation that depends on many factors. Pension actuaries are professionals who do these calculations.

To determine the funding status of a plan, pension actuaries first estimate the value of future pension benefits. These benefits depend on how long the beneficiaries will live, what fraction of the beneficiaries will quit before their benefits vest (and thus extinguish pension liabilities), and what fraction will quit before they retire (and thus qualify for less benefits).

Because the pension benefits all occur in the future, pension actuaries also must choose appropriate rates for discounting future payments to express them in present values; recall from Chapter 5 that a cash flow received in the future is worth less than a cash flow received today. Future cash flows must be discounted using a discount rate that reflects the riskiness of these future cash flows. Pension sponsors prefer high discount rates because there is an inverse relationship between the value of future cash flows today and the discount rate; that is, a high discount rate produces a low present value.

So discounting the future pension benefits at a high discount rate leads to a lower amount today and thus smaller current contributions. In contrast, beneficiaries prefer low discount rates. Low rates imply higher contributions that increase the probability that their plans will have the resources to pay their benefits when due.

The discount rate issue is very contentious because small differences in rates can imply large differences in contributions. Given the importance of the discount rate and the huge interests aligned on both sides of the issue, many governments have intervened to regulate these rates and associated funding requirements. However, the results may not always best serve the interests of the beneficiaries.

After pension actuaries estimate the present value of the plan's future liabilities, they compare them with the plan assets to determine whether the plan is fully funded, overfunded, or underfunded. Companies with underfunded plans generally must increase their contributions to catch up and eliminate the funding shortfall. Regulators set the rates at which sponsors must catch up as well as the length of time they have to cover the funding shortfall. In some countries, these rates are quite low.

## 10.2 Defined Contribution Plans

The problems and cost associated with defined benefit pension plans have led to substantial growth in defined contribution plans. The sponsors of defined contribution plans make defined (specified) contributions to their plans on a periodic basis. Employers with defined contribution plans usually contribute to their plans in proportion to the earnings of their employees. The plans or regulations may limit these contributions. Sometimes the employees also contribute to these plans.

The contributions go into separate accounts for each beneficiary. The beneficiaries of defined contribution plans generally are responsible for how their account balances are invested. Plan sponsors usually allow them to choose from a short list of investment managers who in turn allow the beneficiaries to choose among investments in a variety of mutual funds or annuities. When the beneficiaries retire, these accounts are used to fund their retirement. A major concern is the possibility of retirees not having enough saved and outliving their retirement accounts.

In many countries, workers can transfer the vested balances of their accounts to another plan if they quit working for their current employer or after they retire from the company.

## 10.3 Comparative Risks of the Two Pension Schemes

The primary risk that most defined benefit plan beneficiaries face is funding risk. Their pensions depend on the ability of their pension sponsors to pay all pension liabilities when due.

Beneficiaries of defined benefit plans whose promised benefits are not adjusted for inflation also face substantial risk that inflation will reduce the real value of their benefits. In contrast, beneficiaries of defined contribution plans can avoid much inflation risk if they do not invest too much of their funds in long-term fixed-rate bonds.

The primary risk that the sponsors face is investment risk. If their plan portfolio returns are lower than expected, then they will have to make greater future contributions.

Defined contribution plan beneficiaries also face investment risk as their primary risk. Their benefits ultimately depend on the investment performance of their accounts.

In many defined contribution plans, the beneficiaries are responsible for the asset mix in their accounts. The asset mix generally is the single most important determinant of investment performance in the long run. Unfortunately, many beneficiaries are poorly qualified to make well-informed asset allocation decisions.

Defined contribution plan sponsors increasingly provide financial guidance to their beneficiaries or arrange for financial planners to help guide them. Without such assistance, beneficiaries often choose very conservative asset allocations that can produce returns too low to fund their future retirement income needs. Beneficiaries also tend to equally allocate among the investment alternatives presented to them, especially when the list of alternatives is short.

## SUMMARY

Companies in the investment industry produce many products that help retail and institutional investors meet their investment goals. Investors use these products to reduce their costs of investing, control their risk exposure, and improve their returns. By pooling their investment funds, investors can gain access to skilled professional investment managers, substantial reductions in risk from diversified investments, and significant administrative economies of scale.

The great diversity in investment products is a result of differences in investor needs, preferences, and wealth. In their search for profits, investment companies create various products designed to appeal to diverse investors whose greatest concerns may be liquidity, tax efficiency, growth, security, confidentiality, or estate planning.

This chapter provided an overview of the investment vehicles and structures that investors commonly use. Some important points to remember include the following:

- Practitioners have created indices to track industries, markets, asset classes, and regions. In addition to being used for performance evaluation, these indices often serve as the basis for passive investment products.

- Price indices measure price appreciation only. Total return indices measure the total investment performance—price appreciation plus investment income.

- Passive investment products consist of buy-and-hold portfolios. Some investors like them because they generally have low management fees and little risk of loss from poor investment decisions.

- Investors who make direct investments by buying and holding investment securities and assets in their name benefit from the ability to time their trades to minimize their taxes.

- Investors who make indirect investments buy products that represent portfolios of investment securities and assets. They benefit from various services that the investment sponsor provides, such as the production of investment vehicles that are often highly liquid or that produce a payoff structure that an investor would have difficulty in replicating with direct investments.

- Structured investment products include linked notes, equity-linked annuities, and exchange-traded notes that provide, in a single instrument, risk–return trade-offs that appeal to certain types of investors. These risk–return trade-offs often can be constructed from other instruments, but most investors cannot produce them by themselves because they do not know how or because they are too costly to personally create and manage.

- Pooled investments, such as closed-end funds, open-end mutual funds, exchange-traded funds, and unit investment trusts, are often very liquid. Investors also like them because they allow them to cheaply invest in highly diversified portfolios in a single low-cost transaction.

- Hedge funds operate in almost every corner of the investment universe. Their defining characteristics include lock-up periods that give managers extraordinary control over invested assets and performance-based managerial compensation contracts that provide strong incentives to managers to work hard.

- Funds of funds are funds that invest in other funds. Fund-of-funds managers seek to add value by selecting managers who will outperform their peers rather than by selecting securities that will outperform other securities.

- Separate accounts are managed for the exclusive benefit of a single investor, but they can be expensive to manage. In contrast, commingled accounts provide investors the benefit of economies of scale in asset management. The managers of taxable accounts consider the tax consequences of all their decisions. In contrast, the managers of tax-advantaged accounts pay much less attention to tax issues. They often can profit from making investment decisions that do not appeal to taxable investors.

- Pension plans may have defined contributions or defined benefits. The sponsors of a defined contribution plan regularly contribute agreed-on amounts to the personal pension accounts of their beneficiaries, who then decide how to invest these funds. In contrast, the sponsors of a defined benefit plan promise to provide a certain level of benefits to their beneficiaries when they retire.

# CHAPTER REVIEW QUESTIONS

Test your knowledge of this chapter at **cfainstitute.org/claritasstudy**.

1 From the perspective of an investor, index funds are popular because they generally are:

   A diversified.

   B tax-free investments.

   C not subject to management costs.

2 Analysts would *least likely* use a security market index to assess:

   A the performance of a portfolio.

   B the factors that contributed to the performance of a portfolio.

   C the management and trading costs that reduced the performance of a portfolio.

3 The reason why individual investors find passive investment strategies appealing is *least likely* to be because:

   A they have low costs associated with them.

   B they do not require replication of a market index.

   C they produce returns that closely track market returns.

4 An index that measures income as well as changes in security prices is a:

   A price index.

   B total return index.

   C price-weighted index.

5 The investment *most likely* to be purchased by an investor with a preference for direct investments is a share in a:

   A company.

   B mutual fund.

   C real estate investment trust.

Copyright © 2012 CFA Institute

**6** Relative to indirect investments, direct investments:

  **A** are less expensive to trade.

  **B** offer more control to investors.

  **C** allow small investors to share in the purchase of large assets.

**7** Equity-linked notes are:

  **A** equity securities.

  **B** debt securities that can be converted into equity securities.

  **C** debt securities whose final payout depends on the performance of an equity security or a pool of equity securities.

**8** Compared with shares of closed-end funds, shares of open-end funds:

  **A** are exchange traded.

  **B** are generally more risky.

  **C** are redeemable at the fund's net asset value (NAV).

**9** Exchange-traded funds (ETFs) are *most likely* to:

  **A** be actively managed.

  **B** trade at close to their net asset value (NAV).

  **C** have relatively high trading costs and management fees.

**10** Unit investment trusts are *most likely* to:

  **A** be exchange traded.

  **B** be passively managed.

  **C** have investment advisers.

**11** Managers of hedge funds are *most likely* to:

  **A** impose capital lock-up periods.

  **B** raise capital from retail investors.

  **C** use investment strategies similar to traditional mutual funds.

## Chapter Review Questions

**12** Which of the following investment strategies is *least likely* to be used by an actively managed fund of funds?

  **A** Investing in index funds.

  **B** Identifying fund managers who will likely outperform the market.

  **C** Using models to predict which investment strategies will most likely be successful.

**13** Pooling the capital of two or more investors together and jointly managing them most likely describes a:

  **A** wrap account.

  **B** separate account.

  **C** commingled account.

**14** Investors in a commingled account will *most likely*:

  **A** own equal proportions of the fund.

  **B** earn returns that vary across investors.

  **C** have similar objectives and cash flow needs.

**15** The ability to defer taxes in tax-advantaged accounts will be *most* beneficial for investors who expect their tax rates in the future to:

  **A** increase.

  **B** decrease.

  **C** remain unchanged.

**16** A pension plan that promises specified payments to its beneficiaries is *most likely*:

  **A** a funded plan.

  **B** a defined benefit plan.

  **C** a defined contribution plan.

# ANSWERS

1. A is correct. Index funds are diversified. They are also transparent and tax efficient with very low management and trading costs. B is incorrect because index funds are tax-efficient investments but not tax-free investments. C is incorrect because index funds represent investments with very low but not zero management costs.

2. C is correct. Security market indices are not useful for assessing the management and trading costs that reduced the performance of a portfolio. Management and trading costs are separate from market performance. A and B are incorrect because security market indices are useful for assessing the performance of a portfolio (performance measurement) and the factors that contributed to the performance of a portfolio (performance attribution).

3. B is correct. Passive investment strategies do require replication of a market index. These strategies are designed to match the return and risk of a benchmark, and the benchmark is very often a market index. A is incorrect because an advantage of passive investment strategies is the low costs associated with them. C is incorrect because passive investment strategies, by seeking to replicate a market index, produce returns that closely track market returns.

4. B is correct. An index that measures income as well as changes in security prices is a total return index. A is incorrect because a price index only measures changes in security prices. C is incorrect because a price-weighted index is an index in which the weight assigned to each security is determined by dividing the price of the security by the sum of all the prices of the securities included in the index.

5. A is correct. Buying a share in a company is a direct investment. B and C are incorrect because shares in a mutual fund or real estate investment trust are indirect investments.

6. B is correct. Investors who hold direct investments can exercise more control over their investments than investors who hold indirect investments. Investors who hold indirect investments must accept all the decisions made by the investment managers, and they often cannot provide input into those decisions. A is incorrect because indirect investments often are substantially less expensive to trade than direct investments. C is incorrect because indirect investments, not direct investments, allow investors to share in the purchase of large assets. This advantage is important to small investors who cannot afford to purchase large assets by themselves.

7. C is correct. Equity-linked notes are debt securities whose final payout depends on the performance of an equity security or a pool of equity securities, such as a stock market index. A is incorrect because equity-linked notes are not equity securities, but they are debt securities. B is incorrect because convertible bonds, not equity-linked notes, are debt securities that can be converted into equity securities.

Answers

**8** C is correct. The shares of open-end funds are redeemable by all participants after the close of the market each day, in cash, at the fund's net asset value. In contrast, shares of closed-end funds are not redeemable. A is incorrect because it is the shares of closed-end not open-end funds that are exchange traded. B is incorrect because shares of closed-end funds are generally more risky than the shares of open-end funds, not the other way around.

**9** B is correct. Exchange-traded funds usually trade at close to their net asset value. A is incorrect because exchange-traded funds are usually passively managed. C is incorrect because, as a result of being primarily passively managed, exchange-traded funds do not trade frequently. Thus, they have relatively low trading costs and management fees.

**10** A is correct. Unit investment trusts are exchange traded. They are typically set up by large investment managers who sell them to the public through brokerage firms in an initial public offering. B is incorrect because unit investment trusts are not managed after inception; they simply hold a fixed portfolio of securities or assets until the trust expires. C is incorrect because unlike other investment companies, unit investment trusts do not have boards of directors, officers, or investment advisers.

**11** A is correct. Hedge funds impose capital lock-up periods, the length of which depends on how much time the managers expect they will need to successfully implement their strategies. Funds that engage in high-frequency strategies generally have shorter lock-up periods than funds that engage in strategies that may take much more time to realize their expected returns, such as strategies that involve reforming corporate governance. C is incorrect because hedge funds are distinguished by their use of investment strategies beyond the scope of traditional mutual funds. They are also distinguished by their availability to only a limited number of select investors, by agreements that lock up the investors' capital for fixed periods, and by their managers' performance-based compensation. B is incorrect because hedge funds are available only to some investors, who usually meet various wealth, income, and sophistication criteria that regulators set. The criteria are designed to ensure that these lightly regulated investment products are suitable for their investors. Most money invested in hedge funds comes from such large institutions as pension funds, university endowments, and sovereign wealth funds or from high-net-worth individuals.

**12** A is correct. Investing in index funds is a strategy used by passively managed rather than actively managed funds of funds. B and C are incorrect because identifying fund managers who will likely outperform the market and using proprietary models to predict which investment strategies will most likely be successful are two main investment strategies used by actively managed funds of funds.

**13** C is correct. In a commingled account, the capital of two or more investors is pooled together and jointly managed. A is incorrect because in a wrap account, the charges for such investment services as brokerage, investment advice, financial planning, and investment accounting are all wrapped into a single flat fee. The fee typically ranges between 1% and 3% of total assets per year and usually is paid quarterly or annually. B is incorrect because in a separate account, the capital of two or more investors remains separate and is managed separately.

**14** C is correct. Investors in a commingled account must have similar objectives and cash flow needs. In a commingled account, the capital of two or more investors is pooled together and jointly managed. A single account, such as a commingled account, cannot be managed to simultaneously meet multiple objectives. A is incorrect because commingled funds are not necessarily owned in equal proportions. When funds are commingled, the advisers must keep track of the ownership interests of each investor. They divide ownership of the account into shares. Whenever investors contribute cash or securities to the commingled account, the advisers compute the net asset value of the account and allocate new shares to the investors in proportion to the current market value of their contributions. B is incorrect because investors in a commingled account all receive equal returns because they share ownership of the single account.

**15** B is correct. Deferral is advantageous if future tax rates are expected to be lower than current tax rates. In this case, investors will be better off if they pay taxes at the lower future tax rate rather than at the higher current tax rate.

**16** B is correct. In a defined benefit plan, the sponsor promises specified payments to the pension plan's beneficiaries. A is incorrect because a funded plan refers to the timing of funding, not to the payments. In a funded plan, the sponsor makes periodic contributions long before the benefits are paid rather than when the benefits are paid. C is incorrect because in a defined contribution plan, the sponsor makes specified contributions to the pension plan but does not make any promises regarding the future payments to the pension plan's beneficiaries.

# CHAPTER 15

## INVESTMENT MARKET CHARACTERISTICS

by Larry Harris, PhD, CFA

## LEARNING OUTCOMES

After completing this chapter, you should be able to do the following:

**a** Distinguish between primary and secondary markets;

**b** Identify characteristics of quote-driven, order-driven, and brokered markets;

**c** Compare the roles of brokers and dealers;

**d** Explain the roles of exchanges and alternative trading systems;

**e** Compare long, short, and levered positions in terms of risk and potential return;

**f** Compare different orders and order instructions;

**g** Describe steps for clearing and settlement of trades;

**h** Identify types of transaction costs;

**i** Describe market efficiency in terms of operations, information, and allocation.

# 1. INTRODUCTION

Investors implement some of their investment decisions in financial markets. They buy and trade securities that are issued by companies and governments that need to raise capital. Investment banks help companies and governments seeking capital to design and issue securities that will suit their needs and appeal to investors. Investors also trade contracts, such as futures contracts and options. Trades in securities and contracts take place in markets that are organized by financial intermediaries. Financial intermediaries that specialize in trading services include brokers, dealers, exchanges, and alternative trading systems. These specialists perform a variety of tasks, including matching buyers and sellers, taking positions on trades, and executing orders. **Orders** are instructions that people who want to trade give to the brokers, dealers, and exchanges that arrange their trades. Orders typically specify the quantity the trader wants to buy or sell, and an order may also specify prices.

Well-functioning financial markets are very important for economic welfare. It is important that investment industry participants understand how markets work; this understanding will help them appreciate how the industry serves to connect investors (savers) with borrowers and investors with each other. In this chapter, you will learn how primary and secondary markets operate, how investors and traders use these markets, and what characterizes well-functioning financial markets.

# 2. PRIMARY SECURITY MARKETS

Primary markets are the markets in which issuers sell their securities to investors. **Issuers** are typically companies and governments; they issue (sell) securities, such as stocks and bonds, to raise money. As discussed in Chapter 9, an issuer that sells securities to the public for the first time makes an initial public offering (IPO), sometimes also called a placing or placement. In contrast, the selling of new shares by a publicly traded company subsequent to their initial public offering is referred to as a secondary or seasoned equity offering.

When a company sells shares to the public for the first time, practitioners say that the company is going public. The initial public offering (IPO) of a company's shares consists of new shares to be issued by the company. It also may include shares that the founders and other early investors in the company want to sell. The IPO provides these investors with a means of converting their investments into cash, a process known as monetizing.

Both initial public offerings and seasoned offerings occur in the primary market, which is the market in which new securities are issued and sold to investors in exchange for cash. Later, if investors trade these securities among themselves, they do so in the secondary market. Note that the issuer only receives additional capital when it issues new securities in the primary market. It will not receive any capital from the trading of its securities in the secondary market.

## 2.1 Public Offerings

Companies generally contract with investment banks (also called merchant banks) to help them sell their securities to the public. The investment banks identify investors who will buy the securities. These investors are known in the industry as subscribers. Investment bankers call this process book building. In London, the book builder is called the book runner. The investment bank tries to build a book of orders from clients or other interested buyers to whom they can sell the offering. When the issuer is in immediate need of financing, it may issue securities through an accelerated book build in which the investment bank arranges the offering in only one or two days. Such sales often occur at discounted prices.

Before the offering, the issuer makes a detailed disclosure of its business and inherent risks and the proposed uses for the funds. This information is offered as a prospectus to potential investors. Most stock exchanges and their regulators stipulate detailed rules regarding the format and content of the prospectus.

The most common offering type for initial public offerings and seasoned offerings is an **underwritten offering**. In an underwritten offering, the investment bank (underwriter) guarantees the sale of the issue at an offering price that is negotiated with the issuer. If there are not enough buyers for all the securities that are for sale, the issue is said to be undersubscribed. In this case, the underwriter will buy whatever securities it cannot sell to the public at the offering price. Alternatively, if there is more demand than there are securities for sale, the issue is said to be oversubscribed. In this case, some investors may receive fewer securities than they were willing to buy.

Large issues are usually organized by a syndicate that includes several investment banks. The syndicate helps the investment bank that leads the offering (lead underwriter) build the book. The issuer pays an underwriting fee for these various services. In the case of an initial public offering, the underwriter also usually promises to ensure that the secondary market will be liquid and to provide price support, if necessary, for about a month. Exhibit 1 summarizes the roles and responsibilities of those involved in a public offering.

# Primary Security Markets

| Exhibit 1 | Roles and Responsibilities of Those Involved in a Public Offering |
|---|---|
| **Role** | **Responsibility** |
| Investment bank (underwriter) | Identifies investors who will buy securities and help sell securities to the public.<br>In underwritten offerings, it guarantees the sale of the issue at an offering price that is negotiated with the issuer.<br>In an initial public offering, it promises to ensure that the secondary market will be liquid and to provide price support for a limited time. |
| Issuer | Makes a detailed disclosure of its business and inherent risks and the proposed uses for the funds. |
| Syndicate (other investment banks) | Helps the lead underwriter build the book of orders. |

In a best efforts offering, the investment bank acts only as a broker and does not take the risk of having to buy securities. If the offering is undersubscribed, the issuer will sell fewer securities and may not be able to raise as much capital as it had planned.

For both underwritten and best efforts offerings, the issuer and the investment bank usually negotiate the offering price. If they set a price that investors consider too high, the offering will be undersubscribed, and they will fail to sell the entire issue. If they set the price too low, the offering will be oversubscribed, in which case the securities will often be allocated to preferred clients or on a pro rata (proportionate) basis.

Investment banks have a conflict of interest with respect to the offering price in underwritten offerings. As agents for the issuers, investment banks should price the issue to raise the most money for the issuer. But as underwriters, they have strong incentives to choose a lower price. If the price is lower than it should be in theory, underwriters face a lower risk of having to buy some of the shares. They can also allocate essentially underpriced shares to benefit their clients, which indirectly benefits them.

In contrast, if the price is higher than it should be in theory, the issue is likely to be undersubscribed, and the underwriter will have to buy essentially overpriced shares. In addition, during the month following an initial public offering (IPO), the underwriter may have to buy shares to support the price in the secondary market. Both types of purchases are costly to investment banks. These considerations motivate underwriters to set initial offering prices so that prices in the secondary market often rise immediately following an IPO, although this is not always the case. For example, the price of Facebook's shares declined substantially in the weeks that followed the company's IPO in 2012 despite price support from the underwriters.

Price considerations are less important in a seasoned offering because the issuer's securities already trade in the secondary market. Thus, it is easier to identify an appropriate price for the offering.

First-time issuers may accept lower offering prices because they are concerned about the possibility of the issue being undersubscribed. Many believe that an undersubscribed initial public offering (IPO) conveys unfavorable information about a company's prospects at a time when the company is most vulnerable to public opinion about its future. The issuer may fear that an undersubscribed IPO will reduce the benefits of going public, such as the opportunity to raise capital in subsequent offerings and the positive publicity associated with a successful IPO.

Companies sometimes sell new issues of seasoned securities directly to the public on a piecemeal basis via a shelf registration. In a **shelf registration**, the company makes the same public disclosures that it would for a regular offering. However, in contrast to a seasoned offering in which all the shares are sold in a single transaction, a shelf registration allows the company to sell the shares directly into the secondary market over time and when it needs additional capital. The sale of the additional shares can be timed over several months or even years. Shelf registrations provide companies with flexibility on the timing of their capital transactions, and they can alleviate the downward pricing pressures often associated with large secondary offerings.

Many companies may also issue shares via dividend reinvestment plans that allow their shareholders to reinvest their dividends in newly issued shares of the corporation. Some companies have direct purchase plans that permit existing shareholders and other investors to periodically buy shares at a slight discount to current prices.

## 2.2 Private Placements

Companies sometimes issue their securities to select investors in private placements. In a **private placement**, companies sell securities directly to a small group of investors, usually with the assistance of an investment bank. These investors are expected to have sufficient knowledge and experience to recognize the risks that they assume and to have sufficient wealth to assume those risks responsibly. Most countries require less disclosure for a private placement than is required for public offerings. Compared with public offerings, private placements allow quicker access to capital with a lower level and cost of regulatory compliance. But because securities offered in a private placement do not trade in a secondary market, they are illiquid. To compensate for this illiquidity, private placement buyers generally require higher returns—that is, they are willing to pay less for securities offered in a private placement than in a public offering.

## 2.3 Rights Offerings

Companies also can raise capital and issue new shares via a rights offering. As discussed in Chapter 9, in a rights offering, a company distributes rights to existing shareholders to buy shares at a fixed price (exercise price) pro rata (in proportion) to their holdings. These rights are often known as pre-emptive rights because they give shareholders the right of first refusal on any new equity offerings. Without such rights, the issuing company's managers could dilute (reduce) the ownership interests of existing investors without their consent.

Because rights do not need to be exercised, they are options—one of the types of derivative instruments presented in Chapter 11. But the exercise price is typically set below the current market price of the shares so that buying shares by exercising rights is immediately profitable. Accordingly, most rights are exercised. Existing shareholders who do not want to exercise their rights can sell them to others who will exercise them and participate in the equity offering. In this case, the existing shareholders' proportional ownership decreases; it gets "diluted."

Shareholders generally dislike rights offerings because they must provide additional capital to avoid dilution losses or sell their rights.

## 2.4 Other Primary Market Transactions

The national governments of financially strong countries generally issue their debt securities in public auctions organized by a branch of the government, usually the finance ministry. These governments may also sell issues directly to dealers, who then resell them to their clients. Smaller and less financially secure national governments and other levels of government often contract with investment banks to help them sell and distribute their securities. Many governments' laws, however, require that they auction their securities.

## 2.5 Importance of Secondary Markets to Primary Markets

Liquidity is an important consideration for investors. In a liquid market, investors can buy or sell securities with low transaction costs and small price concessions when they want to trade. Investors value liquidity because they may need to sell their securities to raise cash. So, investors will pay more for securities that they can easily sell than for those that are costly, or even impossible, to sell. Higher prices translate into lower costs of capital for issuers. Thus, companies and governments can raise money in the primary markets at lower cost when their securities can be traded in liquid secondary markets.

# TRADING SERVICE PROVIDERS

In primary markets, securities essentially trade between the issuer and the investor. In secondary markets, securities trade among investors. This trading is facilitated by trading service providers who help arrange trades. These trading service providers include brokers, dealers, exchanges, and alternative trading systems.

Trading service providers are classified as agency traders when they trade on behalf of their clients and as proprietary traders when they trade for their organization's own accounts. Brokers are agency traders, and dealers are proprietary traders.

## 3.1 Brokers

Brokers are agents who fill orders for their clients. They do not trade with their clients. Instead, they search for traders who are willing to take the other side of their clients' orders. Individual brokers may work for large brokerage firms, the brokerage arms of banks, or at exchanges. Some brokers match clients personally. Others use specialized computer systems to identify potential trades and help their clients fill their orders. Many simply route their clients' orders to exchanges or to dealers. Brokers help their clients to trade by reducing the costs of finding counterparties for their trades.

**Block brokers** provide brokerage service to investors with large orders. Large orders are hard to fill because finding a counterparty willing to do a large trade is often quite difficult. A large buy order generally will trade at a premium to the current market price, and a large sell order generally will trade at a discount to the current market price. These price concessions encourage other traders to trade. But they also make investors with large orders reluctant to expose their orders to the public before their trades are arranged because these investors do not want to "move the market"—that is, to have too large an effect on price. Block brokers thus carefully manage the orders entrusted to them, which makes filling them difficult.

## 3.2 Dealers

Dealers are proprietary traders who fill their clients' orders by trading with them. Dealers buy from their clients when their clients want to sell securities. When their clients want to buy securities, the dealers sell them securities that they own or have borrowed. By allowing their clients to trade when they want to, dealers provide them with liquidity.

After completing transactions, dealers hope to reverse their transactions by trading with another client on the other side of the market. When dealers buy after they sell or sell after they buy, they effectively connect buyers who arrived at one point in time with sellers who arrived at another point in time. Dealers profit when they can buy at prices that on average are lower than the prices at which they sell.

Dealers may organize their operations within proprietary trading houses, investment banks, hedge funds, or sole proprietorships. Some dealers are traditional dealers in the sense that individuals make trading decisions. Others use computerized trading systems to make all trading decisions. Examples of companies with large dealing operations include Deutsche Securities (Germany), RBC Capital Markets (Canada), Nomura (Japan), Timber Hill (United States), Knight Securities (United States), Goldman Sachs (United States), and IG Group Plc (United Kingdom). Almost all investment banks and many commercial banks have large dealing operations in which traders stand ready to buy and sell currencies, bonds, stocks, and derivatives if nobody else does. These traders who offer to trade "make a market," which is the reason why dealers are also known as market makers. Traders who trade with them "take the market."

Many dealers also broker orders, and many brokers also deal to their clients in a process called internalization. Internalization is when brokers fill their clients' orders acting as proprietary traders rather than as agency traders—that is, by trading directly with their clients rather than by arranging trades with others on behalf of their clients. Because the distinction between broker and dealer is not always clear, many practitioners often use the term broker/dealer to refer to them jointly.

Broker/dealers have a conflict of interest with respect to how they fill their clients' orders. When acting as brokers, they must seek the best price for their clients' orders. When acting as dealers, however, they profit most when they sell to their clients at high prices or buy from their clients at low prices. This dual trading problem is most serious when clients allow their brokers to decide whether to trade their orders with other traders or to fill them internally. Consequently, when trading with broker/dealers, some clients may specify that they do not want their orders to be internalized. To avoid the dual trading problem, investors also may choose to trade only with pure agency brokers who do not also act as dealers.

**Primary dealers** are dealers with whom central banks trade when conducting monetary policy; recall from Chapter 7 that monetary policy refers to central bank activities that are directed toward influencing the money supply, interest rates, and credit in an economy. Primary dealers buy bills, notes, and bonds when the central banks sell such securities to decrease the money supply. They then sell these securities to their clients. Likewise, when the central banks want to increase the money supply, the primary dealers buy these securities from their clients and sell them to the central banks.

### 3.3 Exchanges

Exchanges provide places where traders can meet to arrange their trades. Historically, brokers and dealers met on an exchange floor to negotiate trades. Increasingly, exchanges now arrange trades based on orders that brokers and dealers submit to them. These exchanges essentially act as brokers, blurring the distinction between exchanges and brokers. Exchanges and brokers that use electronic order matching systems to arrange trades among their clients are functionally indistinguishable when arranging these trades. Examples of exchanges include the NYSE (New York Stock Exchange), NYSE Euronext, Eurex, Deutsche Börse AG, the Chicago Mercantile Exchange, the Tokyo Stock Exchange, and the Singapore Exchange.

Exchanges are most easily distinguished from brokers by their regulatory operations. Most exchanges regulate their members' behavior when trading on the exchange and sometimes also away from the exchange. Brokers generally regulate trading only in their brokerage systems.

Many securities exchanges also regulate the issuers that list on the exchange. Their regulations generally require timely financial reporting and disclosure. Financial analysts use this information to value the securities traded on the exchange. Without such information, valuing securities would be very difficult, and market prices might not reflect the fundamental values of the securities; recall from Chapter 13 that a security's fundamental value (intrinsic value) can be viewed as the present value of all the cash flows the security will generate in the future. When market prices do not reflect fundamental values, well-informed participants can profit from less-informed participants. To avoid such losses, less-informed participants will withdraw from the market, which is detrimental not only to the financial services industry but also to the economy.

Some exchanges prohibit issuers from creating capital structures that concentrate voting rights in the hands of a few owners who do not own a proportionate share of the equity. These regulations attempt to ensure that companies are run for the benefit of all shareholders and not to promote the interests of controlling shareholders who lack significant economic stakes in the company.

Exchanges derive their regulatory authority from their national or regional governments or through voluntary agreements by their members and their issuers to subject themselves to exchange regulations. In most countries, governmental regulators oversee the exchange rules and the regulatory operations. Most countries also impose financial disclosure standards on public issuers. Examples of governmental regulatory bodies include the Japanese Financial Services Agency, the Securities and Futures Commission of Hong Kong, the U.K. Financial Services Authority, the German

Bundesanstalt für Finanzdienstleistungsaufsicht, the U.S. Securities and Exchange Commission, the Ontario Securities Commission, and the Mexican Comisión Nacional Bancaria y de Valores.

### 3.4 Alternative Trading Systems

Alternative trading systems, also known as electronic communications networks or multilateral trading facilities, are trading venues that function like exchanges but do not exercise regulatory authority over their subscribers. They only control the conduct of those subscribers who use their trading systems. Some alternative trading systems operate electronic trading systems that are otherwise indistinguishable from the trading systems operated by exchanges. Others operate innovative trading systems that suggest trades to their clients based on information that clients share with them or that they obtain through research into their clients' preferences.

Many alternative trading systems are known as **dark pools** because of a lack of transparency; they do not display the orders that their clients send to them. Large investment managers especially like these systems because market prices often move to their disadvantage when other traders know about their large orders. Most alternative trading systems allow institutional traders to trade directly with each other without the intermediation of dealers or brokers, which makes them very low-cost trading venues.

Alternative trading systems may be owned and operated by broker/dealers, exchanges, or banks or by companies organized solely for this purpose, many of which may be owned by a consortium of broker/dealers and banks. Examples of alternative trading systems include Pure Trading (Canada), The Order Machine (the Netherlands), BATS Chi-X Europe (Europe), POSIT (United States), Liquidnet (United States), Baxter-FX (Ireland), and Turquoise (Europe). Many of these alternative trading systems provide services in markets besides the ones in which they are domiciled.

## 4 STRUCTURE OF SECONDARY SECURITY MARKETS AND OF CONTRACT MARKETS

In a **secondary market**, investors trade with each other but not with the original security issuer. In a **contract market**, buyers purchase contracts (typically the derivatives contracts described in Chapter 11: forwards, futures, options, and swaps) from sellers. If the sellers do not hold the contracts, they write (create) new ones. In both the secondary and contract markets, buyers and sellers must find each other.

Trading in these markets is the successful outcome of a bilateral (two-way) search in which buyers look for sellers and sellers look for buyers. Many market structures have been developed to reduce the costs of this search. Markets are liquid when the costs of finding a suitable counterparty to a trade are low.

Trading in securities and contracts takes place in many different market structures. The structures differ by when trades can be arranged, who arranges the trades, how they do so, how traders learn about possible trading opportunities, and how trades

# Structure of Secondary Security Markets and of Contract Markets

are executed (completed). This section introduces the various market structures used to trade securities and contracts, first considering trading sessions, then execution mechanisms, and finally market information systems.

## 4.1 Trading Sessions

Markets are organized either as call markets or as continuous trading markets. In a **call market**, participants can arrange trades only when the market is called at a particular time and place. Call markets usually convene just once a day, but some markets organize calls at more frequent intervals. In contrast, in a **continuous trading market**, participants can arrange and execute trades anytime the market is open.

Buyers can easily find sellers and vice versa in call markets because all traders interested in trading (or orders representing their interests) are present at the same time and place. Call markets thus have the potential to be very liquid when they are called, but they are completely illiquid between calls. In contrast, traders can arrange and execute their trades at any time in continuous trading markets, but doing so can be difficult if the buyers and sellers, or their orders, are not both present at the same time.

Most call markets use single-price auctions to match buyers to sellers. In these auctions, the market operator constructs order books representing all buy orders and all sell orders. The operator then chooses a single trade price that will maximize the total volume of trade. The order books are supply and demand schedules, and the point at which they cross determines the trade price.

Many continuous trading markets start their trading session with a call market auction. During a pre-opening period, traders submit their orders for the market call. At the opening, any possible trades are arranged, and then trading continues in the continuous trading session. Some continuous markets also close their trading with a call.

## 4.2 Execution Mechanisms

The three main types of market structures are

- **quote-driven markets** (also called dealer markets or price-driven markets), in which investors trade with dealers;

- **order-driven markets**, in which a broker, an exchange, or an alternative trading system uses rules to arrange trades based on the orders that traders submit; and

- **brokered markets**, in which brokers arrange trades between their clients.

Note that many trading systems use more than one type of market structure.

### 4.2.1 Quote-Driven Markets

Almost all bonds and currencies, and most commodities for immediate delivery (spot commodities), trade in quote-driven markets. Traders call them quote-driven (or price-driven) markets because investors trade with dealers at the prices quoted by the dealers. Depending on the instrument traded, the dealers work for commercial banks, investment banks, broker/dealers, or proprietary trading houses.

Quote-driven markets also often are called **over-the-counter (OTC) markets** because securities once literally traded over a counter in the dealer's office. Now most trades in over-the-counter markets are conducted over proprietary computer communications networks, by telephone, or sometimes over instant messaging systems.

Dealers in over-the-counter markets often trade with each other. These trades commonly arise when one dealer buys from an investor and another dealer sells the same security to another investor. The first dealer then may sell the security to the second dealer. In some over-the-counter markets, brokers arrange trading among dealers in interdealer markets.

### 4.2.2 Order-Driven Markets

In contrast to most bonds, currencies, and spot commodities that trade in quote-driven markets, many shares, futures contracts, and most standard options contracts trade on exchanges and alternative trading systems that use order-driven trading systems. Order-driven markets arrange trades using rules to match buy orders with sell orders. Orders typically specify the quantity the traders want to buy or sell. The order may also contain price specifications, such as the maximum price that the trader will pay when buying or the minimum price the trader will accept when selling.

Because rules match buyers and sellers, trades are often arranged among complete strangers. Order-driven systems thus must have settlement systems to ensure that buyers and sellers settle their security trades and perform on their contract trades. Otherwise, dishonest traders would not settle their obligations if a change in market conditions made settlement unprofitable.

Two sets of rules characterize order-driven market mechanisms: order-matching rules and trade-pricing rules. The order-matching rules match buy orders with sell orders. The trade-pricing rules determine the prices at which the matched trades take place.

**4.2.2.1 Order-Matching Rules** Order-driven trading systems match buyers and sellers using rules that separately rank buy and sell orders based on price and often other secondary criteria. The order precedence hierarchy determines which orders go first. The first rule is always price priority: The highest-priced buy orders and the lowest-priced sell orders go first. They are the most aggressively priced orders. Secondary precedence rules determine how to rank orders at the same price. Most trading systems use time precedence to rank these orders. The first order to arrive at a given price has precedence over other orders at that price. Some trading systems permit hidden and partially hidden orders—that is, orders exposed only to the brokers or exchanges that receive them. When hidden and partially hidden orders are permitted, displayed quantities at a given price generally have precedence over undisplayed quantities. Thus, the complete precedence hierarchy is given by price priority, display precedence at a given price, and finally, time precedence among all orders with the same display status at a given price. These rules give traders incentives to improve their order prices, display their orders, and arrive early if they want to trade quickly. These incentives are designed to increase market liquidity.

The trading systems match the highest-ranking buy order with the highest-ranking sell order. If the buyer is willing to pay at least as much as the seller is willing to receive, the system will arrange a trade for the minimum of the buy and sell quantities. The remaining size, if any, is then matched with the next order on the other side, and the process continues until the system can arrange no further trades. More information about orders, including an example, is provided in Section 6.

**4.2.2.2 Trade-Pricing Rules** Once the orders are matched, the trading system then uses its trade-pricing rule to determine prices. The three rules that various order-driven markets use to price their trades are the uniform pricing rule, the discriminatory pricing rule, and the derivative pricing rule.

Call markets commonly use the **uniform pricing rule**. Under this rule, all trades execute at the same price. The market chooses the price that maximizes the total quantity traded.

Continuous trading markets use the **discriminatory pricing rule**, which involves limit orders. A limit order instructs the trader to obtain the best price immediately available but in no event to accept more than the specified limit price when buying or less than the specified limit price when selling. Under the discriminatory pricing rule, the limit price of the order or quote that first arrived (standing order) determines the trade price.

If trading systems did not use this pricing rule, large traders would break their orders into pieces to price discriminate on their own. The term "large traders" refers to traders who hold or control positions that are greater than a specified reporting level set up by the regulators. A **position** refers to the quantity of a security that a person or an institution owns or owes. The discriminatory pricing rule allows a large trader who wants to trade to discriminate among standing limit orders by filling the most aggressively priced orders first at their limit prices, then filling less aggressively priced orders at their less favorable (from the arriving trader's point of view) limit prices.

Many trades are organized by crossing networks, which are trading systems that match buyers and sellers who are willing to trade at prices obtained from other markets. Crossing networks use the **derivative pricing rule**. Under this pricing rule, trades execute at the midpoint of the best bid and ask quotes published by the exchange at which the security primarily trades. **Bid prices** are the prices at which dealers are willing to buy, and the best bid is the highest price that a buyer is willing to pay. **Ask prices** (or **offer prices**) are the prices at which dealers are willing to sell, and the best ask is the lowest price at which a seller is willing to sell. This pricing rule is called derivative because the price is derived from another market. In particular, the price does not depend on the orders submitted to the crossing network. Some crossing networks are organized as call markets and others as continuously trading markets.

**Internalizing dealers**, who fill their clients' orders by trading directly with their clients rather than by arranging trades with others on behalf of their clients, use the derivative pricing rule. Usually the dealers will fill buy orders at the best offer exposed in the market and sell orders at the best exposed bid. They also often provide slightly better prices. Because these dealers derive their trade prices from other markets' prices, their pricing rule is a derivative pricing rule.

Internalization is controversial because it takes away orders from exchanges on which they may execute at better prices. For example, if the exchange market is 80 bid (buyer's price) and offered at 82 (seller's price), an internalizing dealer may fill a client buy order at 81.9. But if the order were sent to the exchange, the buy order might fill at 81 (a better price) if a hidden sell limit order was standing at 81.

**4.2.2.3 Electronic vs. Floor-Based Trading Systems** Order-driven trading systems may be organized on trading floors or in electronic trading systems. Although electronic trading systems are rapidly replacing floor-based systems, many trading floors continue to operate.

In an electronic trading system, computers conduct the continuous auction. They organize the order book based on the exchange order precedence rules, and they arrange trades, when possible, pricing them through trade-pricing rules. Traders participating in these markets submit electronic orders to these systems.

In most markets with electronic trading systems, high-frequency traders use automated electronic systems to submit and cancel huge numbers of orders. These electronic traders are primarily dealers who compete with each other to provide liquidity to investors. Electronic traders need to be incredibly fast to beat their competitors, who also have fast systems and who generally act on the same information. Generally, the first trader to recognize and act on an opportunity will profit the most.

Electronic trading systems have greatly decreased the costs of arranging trades. They also have permitted high-frequency traders to reduce investors' liquidity costs. The lower costs of trading have increased trading volumes at exchanges that have adopted electronic trading systems. Investors now use many investment strategies involving frequent rebalancing or dynamic risk management that formerly were infeasible because of high transaction costs.

Trading at floor-based exchanges varies by who organizes the market. At the few stock and options exchanges that still maintain floor-based trading systems, exchange clerks or designated dealers manage the continuous auction. Generally with the assistance of electronic systems, they organize the order books using the order precedence rules, ensure that electronically transmitted orders are fairly represented on the floor, and conduct the continuous auction in which trades are arranged. Investors participating in these markets usually can submit electronic orders directly to the exchange, or they can send orders to floor brokers who will represent them on the exchange floor.

Other floor-based exchanges, such as futures markets, use a pit trading system in which exchange members (brokers and dealers) collectively organize the trading. These markets convene in a pit, which literally may be a pit with steps around the sides upon which the traders stand. The pit also may simply be a ring of chairs around an open space. The Chicago Board of Trade is an example of an exchange with many such pits, although the pits are increasingly falling into disuse as electronic trading grows. Exchanges design pits to ensure that all traders have unobstructed sight lines to all other traders. In the pit, the traders shout out their bids and offers and often also use hand signals in the hopes that someone will want to trade with them. Buyers can purchase either by bidding and waiting for someone to sell at their bid price or by taking an offer made by a seller. Likewise, sellers can sell either by offering and waiting for someone to accept their offer or by taking a bid made by a buyer.

To newcomers, pit-based trading seems very chaotic. In fact, the trading is generally very well organized. In particular, exchange rules prohibit traders from bidding and offering when their bids and offers do not represent the best prices in the market. The rules also require that traders arrange their trades with the first buyer to bid a higher price or the first seller to offer a lower price. Experienced floor traders follow these rules exactly and quickly discipline those who violate them. The trading appears chaotic because these markets often operate very quickly. The traders generally use sign language to communicate their bids and offers, and they shout out only the last digits of the price on the assumption that everyone knows the first digits.

Most floor-based exchanges employ price reporters to collect trade price information for immediate public dissemination.

### 4.2.3 Brokered Markets

The third execution mechanism is the brokered market, in which brokers arrange trades among their clients. Brokers organize markets for assets that are unique and thus of interest as a potential investments to only a limited number of people or institutions. Generally, these assets are infrequently traded and expensive to carry in inventory. Examples of such assets include very large blocks of shares and real estate. Because dealers generally are unable or unwilling to hold these assets in their inventories, they will not make markets in them; that is, they will not stand ready to buy or sell these assets if nobody else does. Organizing order-driven markets for these assets does not make sense because too few traders will submit orders to them.

Successful brokers in these markets try to know everyone who might now or in the future be willing to trade such assets. These brokers spend most of their time on the telephone and in meetings building their client networks.

## 4.3 Market Information Systems

Markets vary in the type and quantity of data that they disseminate to the public. Traders say that a market is pre-trade transparent if the market publishes real-time data about quotes and orders. Markets are post-trade transparent if the market publishes trade prices and sizes soon after trades occur.

Buy-side traders value transparency because it allows them to better manage their trading, understand market values, and estimate their prospective and actual transaction costs. In contrast, dealers prefer to trade in opaque markets because, as frequent traders, they have an informational advantage over those who see less than they do.

Many investors assess a market's liquidity by looking at the difference between bid and ask prices, called bid–ask spreads. Recall that bid prices are the prices at which dealers are willing to buy, and ask prices are the prices at which dealers are willing to sell. Thus, bid–ask spreads represent the compensation dealers expect for taking the risk of buying and selling securities. Bid–ask spreads tend to be wider in opaque markets because finding the best available price is harder for dealers in such markets. Transparency reduces bid–ask spreads, which benefits investors.

# 5 POSITIONS

A position refers to the quantity of an instrument that a person or institution owns or owes. A portfolio consists of a set of positions.

In the context of assets and securities, investors have **long positions** when they own assets or securities. Examples of long positions include ownership of stocks, bonds, currencies, commodities, or real assets. Long positions gain when prices rise. In contrast, short positions gain when prices fall. Investors take **short positions** when they sell assets that they do not own, a process that involves borrowing assets, selling them, and repurchasing them later to return them to their owner. Section 5.1 describes the short-selling process more thoroughly.

## 5.1 Short Positions

Short sellers construct short positions in securities by borrowing securities from investors with long positions who then become **security lenders** when they lend their securities. The short sellers then sell the borrowed securities to other traders. Short sellers close (exit) their positions by repurchasing the securities and returning them to the security lenders. If the securities fall in value, the short sellers profit because they repurchase the securities at lower prices than the prices at which they sold them. If the securities rise in value, they will lose. Short sellers who buy to close their positions are said to cover their positions.

The potential gains in a long position generally are unlimited. For example, the stock prices of highly successful companies may have increased manifold since their shares first traded publicly. But the potential losses on long positions are limited to no more than 100%—a complete loss—for long positions with no associated liabilities (debt).

The potential gains and losses in a short position are mirror images of the potential losses and gains in a long position. Thus, the potential gains on a short position are limited to no more than 100%, but the potential losses are unbounded. The unbounded potential losses make short positions potentially very risky.

Although security lenders generally believe that they still own the securities that they lend, they do not in fact own the securities during the periods of the loans. (For tax purposes, they remain the beneficial owners of their securities.) Instead, security lenders own promises made by the short sellers to return the securities. These promises are recorded in security lending agreements. These agreements specify that the short sellers will pay the long sellers all dividends or interest that they otherwise would have received had they not loaned their securities. These payments are called payments in lieu of dividends (or of interest), and they may have different tax treatment than dividends and interest paid by issuers. The security lending agreements also protect the lenders in the event of a stock split.

To secure their security loans, lenders require that the short seller leave the proceeds of the short sale on deposit with them as collateral for the stock loan. Collateral refers to the assets that a borrower pledges to the lender. Security loans are subject to the risk that one of the parties to the contract will fail to honor the contract. This risk is called **counterparty risk**. The lender risks that the borrower will fail to return the security if it rises in value, and the borrower risks that the lender will fail to return the collateral if the security drops in value. To reduce counterparty risk, the short seller must provide additional collateral to secure the loan if the security rises in value, and the lender must return some of the collateral if the security drops in value. These payments adjust the collateral in response to price changes.

## 5.2 Leveraged Positions

In many markets, investors can buy securities on margin—that is, by borrowing some of the purchase price. When investors borrow to buy securities, they are said to leverage (or lever) their positions; in other words, they use leverage (debt). A highly leveraged (or levered) position is one in which the amount of debt is large relative to the equity that supports it.

Buying securities on margin increases the potential gains or losses for a given amount of equity in a position because the buyer can buy more securities on margin than otherwise. The buyer thus earns greater profits when prices rise. But the buyer suffers greater losses when prices fall. Buying securities on margin is thus risky.

Investors usually borrow the money from their brokers. The borrowed money is called a margin loan, and such investors are said to buy on margin. The loan does not have a set repayment schedule and must be repaid on demand. As with any loan, the borrower must pay interest on the borrowed money.

Traders' equity is that portion of the security price represented by the buyer's capital. Traders who buy securities on margin are subject to minimum margin requirements. The **initial margin requirement** is the minimum fraction of the purchase price that must be trader's equity. This requirement may be set by the government, the exchange, or the exchange clearinghouse. In many markets, brokers require more equity than the government-mandated minimum from their clients when lending to them.

The leverage ratio is the ratio of a position's value to the value of the equity in it. This ratio indicates how many times larger a position is than the equity that supports it. If the trader's equity represents 40% of the value of the position, then the leverage ratio is 2.5.

$$2.5 = 100\% \text{ position} \div 40\% \text{ equity}$$

The leverage ratio also indicates how much more risky a leveraged position is relative to a debt-free position. For example, if a stock bought on 40% margin rises 10%, the buyer will experience a 25% return on the equity investment in her leveraged position.

$$25\% = 2.5 \times 10\%$$

But if the stock falls by 10%, the return on the equity investment will be −25%. These calculations do not count interest on the margin loan and commission payments, both of which lower realized returns.

If prices drop by more than the buyer's original margin, the buyer's equity will become negative. The investor then would owe his broker more than the stock is worth. Brokers lose money in such situations if the buyer does not repay the loan out of other funds. To prevent such losses, brokers require that margin buyers always have a minimum amount of equity in their positions. This minimum is called the maintenance margin requirement. It is usually 25% of the current value of the position, but it may be higher or lower depending on the instrument's volatility and the broker's policies.

If the value of the equity falls below the maintenance margin requirement, the buyer will receive a **margin call**, which is a request for additional equity. If the buyer does not deposit additional equity (money) with the broker in a timely manner, then the broker will sell all or part of the position to prevent further losses and thereby secure repayment of the margin loan.

Traders who sell securities short are also subject to margin requirements because they have borrowed securities. Initially, the trader's equity supporting the short position must be at least equal to the margin requirement multiplied by the initial value of the short position. If prices increase, equity will be lost. At some point, the short seller will have to contribute additional equity to meet the maintenance margin requirement. Otherwise, the broker will buy back the security to cover the short position to prevent further losses and thereby secure repayment of the stock loan.

Many investors, hedge funds, and investment banks get into trouble when they use too much leverage. In an attempt to obtain greater profits by borrowing to increase their positions, they often underestimate the risks to which they are exposed. If prices move against their positions, their losses can put them into financial distress or, in extreme cases, bankruptcy.

## 6  ORDERS

Buyers and sellers communicate with the buy-side traders, brokers, dealers, and exchanges that arrange their trades by issuing orders. All orders specify what instrument to trade, how much to trade, and whether to buy or sell. Most orders also have other instructions attached to them. These additional instructions may include execution, validity, or settlement instructions. Execution instructions indicate how to fill the order. Validity instructions indicate when the order may be filled. Settlement instructions indicate how to arrange the final settlement of the trade.

At most markets, dealers and various other proprietary traders often are willing to buy from or sell to other traders seeking to sell or buy. As defined earlier, the prices at which dealers are willing to buy are called bid prices and those at which they are willing to sell are called ask prices or offer prices. The ask prices are invariably higher than the bid prices.

Traders may also indicate the quantities that they will trade at their bid and ask prices. These quantities are called bid sizes for bids and ask sizes for offers. Depending on the market, these quotation sizes may or may not be exposed to other traders or dealers in that market.

Traders quote a market when they expose their bids and offers. Dealers often quote both bid and ask prices, in which case they quote a two-sided market. The highest bid in the market is the best bid, and the lowest ask in the market is the best ask. The difference between the best bid and the best offer is the **market bid-ask spread**. The market bid–ask spread generally is smaller than every dealer's bid–ask spread (it can never be more) because dealers often quote better prices on one side of the market than the other. Accordingly, the bids and asks that make up the best bid and best ask often come from different traders.

In markets with narrow (small) bid–ask spreads, the costs of trading are low for orders smaller than the quoted bid and ask sizes.

## 6.1 Order Execution Instructions

Execution instructions indicate how exchanges and brokers should arrange trades for their clients. Market and limit orders are the most common execution instructions. A **market order** instructs the broker or exchange to obtain the best price immediately available when filling the order. A **limit order** conveys almost the same instruction: Obtain the best price immediately available, but in no event accept a price higher than the specified limit price when buying or accept a price lower than the specified limit price when selling.

Many people mistakenly believe that limit orders specify the prices at which the orders will trade. Although limit orders often do trade at their limit prices, remember that the first instruction always is to obtain the best price available. If better prices are available than the limit price, brokers and exchanges should, and regularly do, obtain those prices for their clients.

Market orders generally execute immediately if other traders are willing to take the other side of the trade. The main drawback with market orders is that they can be expensive to execute, especially when the order is placed in a market for a thinly traded security, or more generally, when the order is large relative to normal trading activity in the market. In that case, a market buy order may fill at a high price, or a market sell order may fill at a low price, if no traders are willing to trade at better prices. High purchase prices and low sale prices result from price concessions given to other traders to encourage them to take the other side of the trade. Because the sizes of price concessions can be difficult to predict and because prices often change between when a trader submits an order and when the order finally fills, execution prices for market orders, especially large ones, are often uncertain.

Buyers and sellers who are concerned about the possibility of trading at unacceptable prices add limit prices to their orders. The main problem with limit orders is that they may not execute. Limit orders do not execute if the limit price on a buy order is too low or if the limit price on a sell order is too high. For example, if an investment manager submits a limit order to buy at €20 and nobody is willing to sell at or below €20, the order will not trade. If prices never drop to €20, the manager will never buy. If the price subsequently rises, the manager will have lost the opportunity to profit from the price increase.

Whether traders use market orders or limit orders when trying to arrange trades depends on their concerns about price, trading quickly, and failing to trade. On average, limit orders trade at better prices than do market orders when they trade, but they often do not trade.

The probability that a limit order will execute depends on the price at which the order is placed relative to market prices. An aggressively priced order is more likely to trade than a less aggressively priced order. A limit buy order is aggressively priced when the limit price is high relative to the market bid and ask prices. If the limit price is placed above the best ask, the buy order generally will partially or completely fill at the best ask price, depending on the size available at the best ask. Such limit orders are called marketable limit orders because at least part of the order can trade immediately. A limit buy order with a very high price relative to the market is essentially a market order.

If the buy order is placed above the best bid but below the best ask, traders say the order makes a new market because it becomes the new best bid. Such orders generally will not trade immediately, but they may attract sellers who want to trade. A buy order placed at the best bid is said to make market, although it may have to wait until all other buy orders at that price trade first. Finally, a buy order placed below the best bid is behind the market. It will not execute unless prices drop. Traders call limit orders that are waiting to trade standing limit orders.

Sell limit orders are aggressively priced if the limit price is low relative to market prices. The limit price of a marketable sell limit order is below the best bid. A limit sell order placed between the best bid and the best ask makes a new market on the sell side; one placed at the best ask makes market; and one placed above the best ask is behind the market.

Exhibit 2 presents a simplified limit order book in which orders are presented ranked by their limit prices for a hypothetical market. The best bid is €26 and the best ask is €28.

## Exhibit 2  Terms Traders Use to Describe Standing Limit Orders

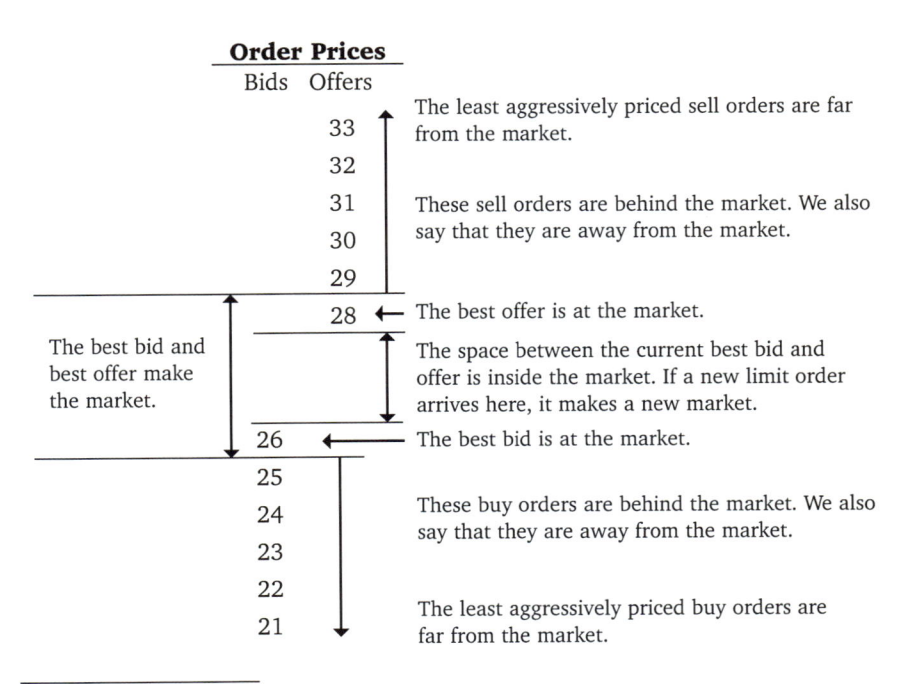

**Order Prices**

| Bids | Offers | |
|------|--------|--|
|      | 33     | The least aggressively priced sell orders are far from the market. |
|      | 32     | |
|      | 31     | These sell orders are behind the market. We also say that they are away from the market. |
|      | 30     | |
|      | 29     | |
|      | 28 ←   | The best offer is at the market. |
|      |        | The space between the current best bid and offer is inside the market. If a new limit order arrives here, it makes a new market. |
| 26 ← |        | The best bid is at the market. |
| 25   |        | |
| 24   |        | These buy orders are behind the market. We also say that they are away from the market. |
| 23   |        | |
| 22   |        | |
| 21   |        | The least aggressively priced buy orders are far from the market. |

The best bid and best offer make the market.

*Source:* Based on a figure in *Trading and Exchanges.*[1]

There is a trade-off between how aggressively priced an order is and the ultimate trade price. Although aggressively priced orders fill faster and with more certainty than less aggressively priced limit orders do, the prices at which they execute are inferior. Buyers seeking to trade quickly must pay higher prices to increase the probability of trading quickly. Likewise, sellers seeking to trade quickly must accept lower prices to increase the probability of trading quickly.

Some order execution instructions specify conditions on size. For example, all-or-nothing orders can trade only if their entire sizes can be traded. Traders can likewise specify minimum fill sizes. This specification is common when settlement costs depend on the number of trades made to fill an order and not on the aggregate size of the order or when a trader who has submitted a large hidden order does not want its existence discovered by another trader using a small order.

### 6.2 Order Exposure Instructions

Exposure instructions indicate whether, how, and sometimes to whom orders should be exposed. Hidden orders are exposed only to the brokers or exchanges that receive them. These agencies cannot disclose hidden orders to other traders until they can fill the orders.

---

[1] Larry Harris, *Trading and Exchanges: Market Microstructure for Practitioners* (New York: Oxford University Press, 2003).

Traders with large orders use hidden orders when they are afraid that other traders might behave strategically if they knew that a large order was in the market. In particular, large buyers fear that they will scare sellers away if they expose their orders. Sellers generally do not want to be the first to trade with large buyers because large buyers often push prices up. Large buyers also fear that other buyers will be able to trade before them (front run) by buying first to profit from any increase in price necessary to fill their large orders. Such front runners increase the costs of filling large orders by taking buying opportunities away from the large traders. Large sellers likewise fear that buyers will shy away from their exposed orders and that other sellers will front run their orders.

Traders can discover the hidden size only by submitting orders that will trade with that size. Thus, other traders can only learn about the hidden size after they have committed to trading with a hidden order if one is present.

Traders also often indicate a specific display size for their orders. Brokers and exchanges then expose only the permitted display size. Any additional size is hidden from the public but can be filled if a suitably large order arrives. Traders sometimes call such orders iceberg orders because most of the order is hidden. Traders specify display sizes when they do not want to display their full sizes but still want other traders to know that someone is willing to trade at the displayed price. Traders on the opposite side who want to trade additional size at that price can discover the hidden size only if they trade the displayed size, at which point the broker or exchange will display any remaining size up to the display size. They also can discover the hidden size by submitting large orders that will trade with that size.

## 6.3 Order Validity Instructions

Validity instructions indicate when an order can be filled. The most common validity instructions, including their potential uses, are listed in Exhibit 3.

# Orders

| Exhibit 3 | Validity Instructions and Potential Uses | |
|---|---|---|
| **Type of Order** | **Explanation** | **Potential use** |
| **Day order** | Orders that are good for the day on which they are submitted. | Traders who review their positions daily may make extensive use of day orders. |
| Good-until-cancelled orders | Orders that are good until they are cancelled. | Most brokers limit how long they will hold an order to ensure that they do not fill orders that their clients have forgotten. |
| Immediate or cancel orders | Orders that are good only on receipt by the broker or exchange. | When searching for hidden liquidity, electronic algorithmic trading systems often submit thousands of immediate or cancel orders for every order that they fill. |
| Good-on-close orders | Orders that are often market orders and that can be filled only at the close of trading. | Traders often use good-on-close orders when they want to trade at the same prices that will be published as the closing prices of the day. This is the case, for example, of mutual funds that value their portfolios at closing prices. |

A **stop order** is an order for which a trader has specified a stop condition. The order may not be filled until the stop condition has been satisfied. For a sell order, the stop condition suspends execution of the order until a trade occurs at or below a trader-specified stop price. After that trade, the stop condition is satisfied and the order becomes valid for execution, subject to all other execution instructions attached to it. If the market price subsequently rises above the sell order's stop price before the order trades, the order remains valid. Likewise, a buy order with a stop condition becomes valid only after price rises above the specified stop price.

Traders often call stop orders stop-loss orders because many traders use them with the hope of stopping losses on positions that they have established. Example 1 provides an example of a stop order.

> **EXAMPLE 1. STOP ORDER**
>
> A trader has bought a stock at €40 and wants to sell the stock if the price falls to less than €30. In this case, the trader might submit a good-until-cancelled, stop €30, market sell order.
>
> If the price of the stock falls to or less than €30, the market order becomes valid, and it should immediately execute at the best price then available in the market. That price may be substantially lower than €30 if the market is falling quickly. The stop order thus does not guarantee to stop losses at the stop price. If potential sellers are worried about trading at too low a price, they can attach

> stop instructions to limit orders instead of to market orders. In this example, if the trader is unwilling to sell below €25, she would submit a good-until-cancelled, stop €30, limit €25 sell order.
>
> If the trader wants to guarantee that she can sell at €30, she can buy a put option with an exercise price of €30. Recall from Chapter 11 that a put option gives its holder the right to sell the underlying at a pre-specified price. In this example, the underlying is the stock, and the pre-specified price, called the exercise price, is €25. The purchase price of the option will include a premium for the insurance that the trader is buying. If the price of the stock falls below €25, then the trader will be able to exercise her put option and receive €25, even if the stock price falls to zero. Thus, options can be viewed as limit orders for which execution is guaranteed at the exercise price. A trader likewise might use a stop buy order or a call option to limit losses on a short position.

Because sell stop orders become valid when prices are falling and buy stop orders become valid when prices are rising, traders using stop orders contribute to market momentum. Market momentum describes the situation in which securities that outperformed in the past continue to outperform, and securities that underperform in the past continue to underperform. Put another way, past winners continue being winners, and past losers continue being losers. Traders who use stop orders contribute to market momentum because their sell orders push prices down further, and their buy orders push prices up further, reinforcing the trend.

### 6.4 Trade Settlement Instructions

Settlement instructions tell brokers how to arrange final settlement of trades. Traders generally do not attach these instructions to each order; instead, they provide them as standing instructions. These instructions indicate which entity is responsible for settling the trade. For retail trades, that entity is the client's broker.

For institutional trades, another broker may settle the trade. When a client employs one broker to arrange trades and another to settle trades, the first broker gives up the trade to the second broker, who is often known as the prime broker. Institutional traders provide these instructions so that they can obtain specialized execution services from different brokers while maintaining a single account for custodial services and other prime brokerage services, such as margin loans.

An important settlement instruction that must appear on security sale orders is an indication of whether the sale is a long sale or a short sale. In long sales, sellers own the security that they are selling. In short sales, traders do not own the securities that they sell. To settle their trades, they must first borrow the securities, as described earlier.

In both cases, the broker handling the sell order must ensure that the seller can deliver securities for settlement. For a long sale, the broker must confirm that the securities held are available for delivery. For a short sale, the broker must either borrow the security on behalf of the client or confirm that the client can borrow the security.

# SETTLEMENT AND CUSTODIAL SERVICES

Financial markets, especially those that arrange trades among strangers, generally need intermediaries to help traders settle their trades and ensure that the resulting positions are not stolen or pledged more than once as collateral.

Clearinghouses arrange for final settlement of trades. The members of a clearinghouse are the only traders for whom the clearinghouse will settle trades. Brokers and dealers who are not members of the clearinghouse must arrange to have a clearing member settle their trades at the clearinghouse.

To ensure that their members settle the trades that they present to the clearinghouse, clearinghouses require that their members have adequate capital and post margins. They also limit the aggregate net quantities (buy minus sell) that their members can settle, and they monitor their members to ensure that these members do not arrange trades that they cannot settle.

This hierarchical system of responsibility generally ensures that traders settle their trades. The brokers and dealers guarantee settlement of the trades they arrange for their retail and institutional clients. The clearing members guarantee settlement of the trades that their clearing clients present to them, and clearinghouses guarantee settlement of all trades presented to them by their clearing members. If a clearing member fails to settle a trade, the clearinghouse settles the trade using its own capital or capital drafted from the other members of the clearinghouse.

The ability to settle trades reliably is very important because it allows strangers to confidently contract with each other without worrying about counterparty risk, which is the risk that their counterparties will not settle their trades. A secure clearing system thus greatly increases liquidity because it vastly expands the number of counterparties with whom a trader can confidently arrange a trade.

In many national markets, clearinghouses clear all securities trades so that traders can trade securities through any broker, dealer, exchange, or alternative trading system. These clearing systems promote competition among these exchange service providers.

In contrast, most futures exchanges have their own clearinghouses. These clearinghouses usually will not accept trades arranged away from their associated exchanges so that a competing exchange cannot trade another exchange's contracts. Competing exchanges may create similar contracts, but moving traders from one established market to a new market is extraordinarily difficult because traders prefer to trade where other traders trade.

## 7.1 Clearing and Settlement Cycles

Trade settlement consists of two processes. **Clearing** refers to all activities that occur from the arrangement of the trade up until settlement. **Settlement** consists of the final exchange of cash for securities.

The most important clearing activity is **confirmation**. Before a trade can be settled, the buyer and seller must confirm that they traded, and they must confirm the exact terms of their trade. Confirmation generally takes place on the day of the trade and is necessary only for manually arranged trades. When electronic trading systems arrange trades, the automated system confirms the trade to both parties.

Following confirmation, settlement may occur in real time (instantaneously) or it may take up to three trading days. The settlement cycle refers to the timing of the procedures used to settle trades. Settlement cycles differ across markets. For example, in most countries, stocks and bonds settle three trading days after negotiating a trade. The seller must deliver the security to the clearing agent and the buyer must deliver cash. The settlement agent then makes the exchange in a process called delivery versus payment, which links the two transfers. If on the day of the trade a trader both bought and sold the same security, then the trader must deliver only the net difference in the securities and cash.

Many markets are reducing the length of their settlement cycles to reduce counterparty risk: the fewer unsettled trades outstanding, the less damage occurs when a trader fails to settle. Also, the shorter the settlement period, the fewer extreme price changes will occur before final settlement that might increase incentives to fail.

Once a corporate security trade is settled, the settlement agent reports the trade to the company's **transfer agent**, which maintains a registry of who owns the company's securities. Most transfer agents are banks or trust companies, but sometimes companies act as their own transfer agents. Companies need to maintain these databases so that they know who is entitled to any interest and dividend payments that they make to their security holders, who can vote in corporate elections, and to whom various corporate communications should be sent. The transfer agents also issue and cancel certificates of ownership if the corporation issues such certificates. Otherwise, the transfer agent maintains book-entry records of ownership. To avoid problems with lost certificates and the costs of handling paper documents, securities increasingly are issued only in electronic form.

Depositories or custodians hold securities on behalf of their clients. Custodial services, which are often offered by banks or trust companies, help prevent the loss of securities through fraud, oversight, or natural disaster. The depositories may hold certificates in their vaults, or they may maintain systems to ensure the validity of book-entry ownership records. Institutional investors who invest globally often must use depositories in different countries.

Broker/dealers generally hold securities on behalf of their retail and small institutional clients. This service allows their clients to avoid holding their securities in certificate form, and it ensures that the clients can easily sell their securities without arranging to deliver securities or confirm book-entry ownership before they trade. Brokers generally deposit their clients' securities in their depositories for safekeeping. Depending on the nature of the account and on the regulatory jurisdiction, the brokers also may lend out these securities. Securities held in a brokerage account are said to be held in street name, and the broker or the broker's depository appears as the registered owner. The client remains the beneficial owner for all purposes.

Many settlement agents also provide systems that allow brokerage clients to transfer securities from one brokerage account to another. These systems make brokers more responsive to their clients' desire for high-quality, low-cost services because dissatisfied clients can easily use them to transfer their accounts to competing brokers.

## 7.2 Dual-Listed Securities

Many corporate issuers list their securities on two or more exchanges. Such securities are dual listed. Dual listing can make the securities available to more potential investors, especially if the listings are in different countries. If the securities trade in liquid secondary markets, more investors may be inclined to purchase them in the primary markets, which will lower the corporate costs of capital.

Dual listing can be costly. In addition to paying listing fees in two or more markets, the company must subject itself to the regulations and disclosure requirements of all markets in which it is listed. Multiple disclosure requirements are particularly burdensome if different accounting standards require that dually listed issuers prepare two or more sets of accounts.

As explained in Chapter 9, securities of foreign issuers often trade as depository receipts. Depository receipts represent ownership of shares that are held by a custodian financial institution. The depository receipts trade in local markets at prices typically denominated in the local currency. Trade settlement also occurs in the local markets. The custodian converts any dividends paid into the local currency and distributes them to those holding receipts. This mechanism permits investors to easily trade and hold securities issued by foreign issuers.

Dual-listed securities often trade less actively in local markets than in their home markets. Accordingly, traders who can easily access an issuer's home market often can obtain better prices than they can find in their own markets.

# TRANSACTION COSTS

8

Trading is expensive. Costs accrue from brokerage commissions, bid–ask spreads, and market impact. Collectively, these costs are called **transaction costs**.

Most market participants employ brokers to trade on their behalf. They pay their brokers **commissions** for arranging their trades. The commissions usually are a fixed percentage of the principal value of the transaction or a fixed price per share, bond, or contract.

The commissions compensate brokers for the resources that they must use to fill orders. They pay fixed costs for order routing systems, market data systems, accounting systems, exchange memberships, office space, and personnel to manage the trading process. Brokers also pay variable costs, such as exchange, regulatory, and clearing fees, on behalf of their clients. Traders who do not trade through brokers pay these fixed and variable costs of trading themselves.

Traders who demand quick trades tend to purchase at higher prices than the prices at which they sell. The difference comes from the price concessions that they give to encourage other traders to trade with them when the impatient traders want to trade. For small orders, the cost of these price concessions is one-half of the bid–ask spread. To understand why, imagine that an impatient trader simultaneously buys and sells the same quantity of the same security in two trades. These two trades will offset each other so that the trader will accomplish nothing but generate transaction costs. The buy will occur at the ask and the sell at the bid, so the trader will lose the bid–ask spread for the two trades or one-half of the spread per trade.

For large trades, impatient buyers generally must raise prices to encourage other traders to sell to them. Likewise, impatient sellers of large trades must lower prices to encourage other traders to purchase from them. These price concessions, called market impact or price impact, often occur over time as large-trade buyers push prices up and large-trade sellers push them down in multiple transactions. For large institutions, the price impact of trading large orders generally is the biggest component of their transaction costs. Because price concessions often limit the scale of their activities, minimizing transaction costs is very important.

Traders who are willing to wait until other traders want to trade with them generally incur lower transaction costs on their trades. In particular, by using standing limit orders instead of marketable orders, they can buy at the bid price or sell at the ask price. But these traders risk that they will not trade when the market is moving away from their orders. They lose the opportunity to profit when their buy orders fail to execute when prices are rising, and they lose the opportunity to avoid losses when the sell orders fail to execute when prices are falling. These costs of not trading are called opportunity costs.

Traders choose their order submission strategies to minimize their transaction costs and their opportunity costs of not trading. Efficient traders ultimately are more successful than those who do not trade well. They buy at lower prices, sell at higher prices, and less often fail to trade when they want to.

Market participants use various techniques to reduce their transaction costs. They employ skillful brokers, use electronic algorithms to manage their trading, and use hidden orders or dark pool trading systems to hide their size.

Most brokers and large institutional traders conduct transaction cost analyses of their trades to measure the costs of their trading and to determine which trading strategies work best for them. In particular, these studies help large institutions better understand how their order submission strategies affect the trade-off between transaction costs and opportunity costs.

## 9 EFFICIENT FINANCIAL MARKETS

Well-functioning financial markets benefit everyone who needs to trade. Most obviously, they allow people to buy and sell financial instruments cheaply. Well-functioning financial markets also increase investor confidence, which ultimately lowers the costs that companies pay to obtain capital.

# Efficient Financial Markets

## 9.1 Operational Efficiency

Markets in which trades are easy to arrange with low transaction costs are operationally efficient. **Operationally efficient markets** have small bid–ask spreads and they can absorb large orders without substantial impact on prices.

The most operationally efficient markets tend to be those in which many people are interested in trading the same instrument on the same exchange. In such markets, buyers can easily find sellers and vice versa. In contrast, markets for instruments that do not interest many people tend to have high transaction costs because buyers and sellers have more trouble finding each other. Instead, they often must trade with dealers who quote large spreads because they face little competition or because they believe that they will not quickly sell their purchases or repurchase their sales.

The benefits of operationally efficient markets are significant. For example, in operationally efficient markets, investors who need to move money to the future can easily connect with entrepreneurs who need money now to develop new products and services. Likewise, producers who would otherwise avoid valuable projects because they are too risky can easily transfer those risks to others who can better bear them. Most importantly, these transactions can take place among strangers so that the benefits from trading can be derived from a large number of potential matches.

In contrast, economies that have poorly functioning financial markets have great difficulties allocating capital among the many companies that could use it. Financial transactions tend to be limited to arrangements within families when people cannot easily find trustworthy counterparties who will honor their contracts. In such economies, capital is allocated inefficiently, risks are not easily shared, and production is inefficient.

## 9.2 Price Efficiency

An important byproduct of operationally efficient markets is the production of informationally efficient prices. **Informationally efficient prices** reflect all available information about fundamental values. They are crucial to an economy's welfare because informationally efficient prices help ensure that the resources available to the economy, such as labor, capital, materials, and ideas, are used wisely.

In a market economy, if people who own a resource value it at less than the market price, they will sell the resource. Likewise, if people without the resource value it at more than the market price, then they will buy the resource. The resulting allocation of the resource will be to those who most value it. However, this allocation occurs only if the market price reflects the resource's value. If the market price is too low, some people who value the resource at more than the market price will be unable to obtain it because the resource holder may not want to sell it at too high of a discount. In this event, the economy would be better off if the market price increased. Likewise, if the market price is too high, then some people who own the resource but value it at less than the market price will not be able to sell it to people who value it more than they do but not as much as the market price. In this event, the economy would be better off if the market price decreased.

**Allocationally efficient economies** are economies that use resources where they are most valuable. Economies that misallocate their resources waste resources and consequently often are quite poor.

Well-informed investors make prices informationally efficient. When they buy assets and contracts that they think are undervalued, they tend to push their prices up toward their estimates of value. Likewise, when investors sell assets and contracts that they think are overvalued, they tend to push their prices down toward their estimates of value. The effect of their trading thus causes prices to reflect their information about values.

How accurately prices reflect fundamental information depends on the costs of obtaining fundamental information and on the liquidity available to well-informed investors. Accounting standards and reporting requirements that produce meaningful and timely financial reporting and disclosures reduce the costs of obtaining fundamental information and thereby allow analysts to form more accurate estimates of fundamental values. Liquid markets allow well-informed investors to fill their orders at low cost. If filling orders is very costly, informed trading might not be profitable. In that case, information-motivated traders will not commit resources to collect and analyze data, and they will not trade. Without their research and their associated trading, prices will be less informative.

## SUMMARY

This chapter provides an overview of financial markets, how they operate, and why they are valuable to the economy. Some important points to remember include the following:

- Issuers first sell their securities in primary markets. The securities then trade in secondary markets.

- Investment banks operate as underwriters for a public offering, advising on pricing the offer and lining up buyers of large blocks of stocks or bonds.

- Other ways to issue securities in the primary markets are through private placement or rights offerings.

- Liquid secondary markets reduce the costs of raising capital because investors value the option to sell their securities at a low cost if their plans change.

- Markets vary by how trades are arranged. In quote-driven markets, dealers arrange all trades. In order-driven markets, exchanges match orders using order precedence rules and price the resulting trades using trade-pricing rules. In brokered markets, brokers introduce buyers to sellers and arrange their trades.

- Dealers provide liquidity in quote-driven markets when they offer to trade at their quoted bid and ask prices. Investors as well as dealers provide liquidity in order-driven markets when they submit limit orders that give other traders options to trade.

## Summary

- The adoption of electronic exchange trading systems and the associated growth of high-frequency trading have greatly reduced trading costs.

- A position is the quantity of an instrument that a person or institution owns or owes. Investors have long positions when they own assets or contracts.

- Short sellers of contracts simply write the contracts that they sell. Security short sellers must borrow securities to deliver them to buyers.

- Margin loans allow investors to buy more securities than their equity otherwise would permit. The larger positions expose investors to more risk so that gains and losses for a given amount of equity will be larger.

- The leverage ratio—the value of a position divided by the value of the equity supporting it—is an important risk measure.

- Orders are instructions to trade. They always specify instrument, side, and quantity. They usually provide several other instructions as well.

- To effectively achieve their goals, investors must understand how to use orders to communicate their intentions to the brokers, dealers, and exchanges that arrange their trades.

- Market orders tend to fill quickly but often at inferior prices. Limit orders generally fill at better prices if they fill, but they may not fill.

- Traders attach stop instructions to their orders to delay efforts to fill them until the stop condition is satisfied. Although traders often use stop orders to stop losses, such orders are not always effective. Investors measure transaction costs to optimize their trading processes.

- Well-functioning financial markets promote economic growth by ensuring that capital allocation decisions are made well. They also promote growth by allowing people to share the risks associated with valuable products in which investment would otherwise not be undertaken.

- Well-functioning financial markets are operationally and informationally efficient. Operationally efficient markets have low transaction costs. Informationally efficient markets have prices that reflect all available information about fundamental values.

# CHAPTER REVIEW QUESTIONS

Test your knowledge of this chapter at **cfainstitute.org/claritasstudy**.

1 A company plans to sell new shares to the public. The sale of the shares will *most likely* occur in the:

   A primary market.

   B contract market.

   C secondary market.

2 Compared with a regular public offering, in a shelf registration, companies are *most likely* to:

   A sell the shares in a single transaction.

   B have lower public disclosure requirements.

   C have more flexibility on the timing of the sale of the shares.

3 A distinction between brokers and dealers is that brokers:

   A are agency traders.

   B are proprietary traders.

   C trade for their organization's own accounts.

4 Which of the following statements about trading service providers is *least likely* correct?

   A Brokers trade directly with their clients.

   B Block brokers provide brokerage service to investors with large orders.

   C Broker/dealers may have a conflict of interest with respect to how they fill their clients' orders.

5 Stock exchanges *most likely* use trading systems that are:

   A price driven.

   B order driven.

   C quote driven.

Copyright © 2012 CFA Institute

**6** Unique assets, such as real estate, are *most likely* traded in a (an):

  **A** dealer market.

  **B** brokered market.

  **C** over-the-counter market.

**7** An investor takes a short position in a share by:

  **A** buying the share.

  **B** lending the share to another trader.

  **C** borrowing the share and then selling it to another trader.

**8** If the price of a security falls, the loss experienced by an investor who bought the security on margin relative to the loss experienced by an investor who did not use leverage will *most likely* be:

  **A** lower.

  **B** higher.

  **C** the same.

**9** Which of the following orders will *most likely* be executed immediately?

  **A** Stop order

  **B** Limit order

  **C** Market order

**10** Which activity is *most likely* a clearing activity?

  **A** Exchanging cash for securities

  **B** Confirming the terms of the trade

  **C** Reporting the trade to the company's transfer agent

**11** Which of the following statements about the settlement cycle is *most likely* correct?

  **A** The settlement cycle is the same across markets.

  **B** A long settlement cycle reduces counterparty risk.

  **C** The settlement cycle refers to the timing of the procedures used to settle trades.

**12** Which of the following costs is *least likely* to be classified as a transaction cost associated with trading a share?

　**A** Listing fee

　**B** Bid–ask spread

　**C** Brokerage commission

**13** Markets in which buyers can easily find sellers are *most likely* to be classified as:

　**A** operationally efficient.

　**B** allocationally efficient.

　**C** informationally efficient.

# ANSWERS

1. A is correct. Primary markets are the markets in which issuers sell their securities to investors. If the company is selling shares in a public market for the first time, it is an initial public offering (IPO). If the company has previously sold shares in a public market, the sale of new shares is a seasoned offering. B is incorrect because in a contract market, buyers purchase contracts (typically derivatives, such as forwards, futures, options, or swaps) from sellers. C is incorrect because a secondary market is the market in which securities trade between investors.

2. C is correct. A shelf registration allows a company to sell the shares directly into the secondary market over time when it needs additional capital. Shelf registrations provide companies with flexibility on the timing of their capital transactions. A is incorrect because unlike in a regular public offering, in a shelf registration, a company that issues shares does not have to sell the shares in a single transaction. The sale of additional shares can occur over time. B is incorrect because in a shelf registration, the company makes the same public disclosures as it does for a regular offering. Companies face lower public disclosure requirements when they issues shares via a private placement. Private placements are restricted to investors who are expected to have sufficient knowledge and experience to recognize the risks they assume and to have sufficient wealth to assume those risks responsibly.

3. A is correct. Brokers are agency traders. Traders are classified as agency traders when they trade on behalf of their clients and as proprietary traders when they trade for their organization's own accounts. Brokers trade on behalf of their clients; thus, they are agency traders. B and C are incorrect because it is dealers, not brokers, who are proprietary traders and trade for their organization's own accounts.

4. A is correct. Brokers do not trade directly with their clients; rather, they search for traders who are willing to take the other side of their clients' orders. B is incorrect because block brokers provide brokerage service to large traders. C is incorrect because broker/dealers may have a conflict of interest with respect to how they fill their clients' orders. When acting as brokers, they must seek the best price for their clients' orders. But when acting as dealers, they profit most when they sell to their clients at high prices or buy from their clients at low prices.

5. B is correct. Many shares trade on exchanges that use order-driven trading systems. Order-driven markets arrange trades using rules to match buy orders to sell orders. A and C are incorrect because price-driven and quote-driven markets are the same thing (they are also called over-the-counter markets). They are markets in which investors trade with dealers at the prices quoted by the dealers. Almost all bonds and currencies, and most commodities for immediate delivery (spot commodities), trade in price-driven/quote-driven markets.

**6** B is correct. Unique assets, such as real estate, are likely to be traded in a brokered market. Brokers organize markets for assets that are unique and thus of interest to only a limited number of buyers and sellers. A and C are incorrect because dealer and over-the-counter markets are the same thing (they are also called price-driven markets). In these markets, investors trade with dealers at the prices quoted by the dealers. Dealers are not likely to make markets in real estate because real estate is infrequently traded and expensive to carry in inventory.

**7** C is correct. Investors take short positions when they sell assets that they do not own, a process that involves borrowing assets, selling them, and repurchasing them later to return them to their owner. If the asset, in this case a share, falls in value, the investor profits because she can repurchase the share at a lower price than the price at which she sold it. If the share rises in value, she loses. A is incorrect because by buying the share, the investor takes a long, not short, position in the share. B is incorrect because by lending the share to another trader, the investor becomes the security lender.

**8** B is correct. Leverage magnifies gains and losses. Thus, if the price of a security falls, the loss experienced by an investor who bought the security on margin (leveraged position) relative to the loss experienced by an investor who did not use leverage (debt-free position) will be higher.

**9** C is correct. A market order instructs the broker or exchange to obtain the best price immediately available when filling an order. B is incorrect because a limit order also instructs the broker or exchange to obtain the best price immediately available, but it sets conditions on price. The price to be paid on the purchase cannot be higher than the specified limit price, or the price to be accepted on a sale cannot be lower than the specified limit price. Thus, the order may not execute. A is incorrect because a stop order is an order to which the trader has specified a stop condition. The order may not be filled until the stop condition has been satisfied.

**10** B is correct. The most important clearing activity is confirmation (confirming the terms of the trade). A and C are incorrect because exchanging cash for securities and reporting the trade to the company's transfer agent are activities that occur after clearing activities.

**11** C is correct. The settlement cycle refers to the timing of the procedures used to settle trades. Settlement may occur in real time (instantaneously), or it may take up to three trading days. A is incorrect because settlement cycles differ across markets. B is incorrect because a short, not long, settlement cycle reduces counterparty risk.

**12** A is correct. Listing fees are costs paid by issuers that list their securities on an exchange. They are not transaction costs associated with trading. B and C are incorrect because bid–ask spreads and brokerage commissions are transaction costs associated with trading. The bid–ask spread is the difference between the price at which a dealer is willing to buy (bid) and the price at which the dealer is willing to sell (ask) securities. Thus, the bid–ask spread represents the

# Answers

compensation the dealer expects for taking the risk of buying and selling securities. Brokerage commissions are the commissions paid to brokers for arranging trades.

**13** A is correct. Markets in which trades are easy to arrange with low transaction costs are operationally efficient. This is the case if buyers can easily find sellers. Operationally efficient markets have small bid–ask spreads, and they can absorb large orders without substantial impact on prices. B is incorrect because allocationally efficient economies are economies that use resources where they are most valuable. C is incorrect because informationally efficient markets are markets in which prices reflect all available information about fundamental values.

# Module 6
# Introduction to Industry Controls

Watch an introductory video at cfainstitute.org/claritasstudy.

This module provides insight into the internal controls that protect organizations and the external controls that safeguard client interests. In the following three chapters, you will learn about the concepts and current practices that relate to or are associated with identifying, quantifying, mitigating, managing, monitoring, and measuring risks and activities within the industry.

Organizations are exposed to a wide range of risks. To leave a risk unmanaged and simply hope for a positive outcome is not an appropriate way to do business. In the context of the investment industry, a robust control framework ensures that risks are identified and categorized. A basic categorization is between acceptable and unacceptable risks. Acceptable risks are closely monitored and managed, and unacceptable risks are eliminated. In the following chapters, you will learn about various ways to control risk—through documentation and risk management as well as through risk measurement and performance evaluation.

Success in risk management hinges on a three-step process: creating a strategy and planning well in advance, managing risks as they arise, and monitoring and evaluating risks. The choice of strategy takes place "before the fact" and usually establishes the rules, guidelines, and methods that an organization intends to use. It also considers any legal and regulatory obligations. Managing the risks takes place "at the fact" and includes operationalizing and complying with the established rules, guidelines, and methods. Monitoring and evaluating the risks takes place "after the fact;" assurance or audit functions identify gaps and ways to improve procedures and processes. This three-step process applies for documentation, risk management, and performance evaluation, although each of these topics has its own specifications.

Documentation, which is covered in Chapter 16, is fundamental to control, whether the documents are external legal documents or internal written guidelines for employees to follow. This chapter focuses on the printed words, although technology has helped automate most processes.

Chapter 17 describes the importance of risk management and how it permeates an organization, making every employee, to some extent, a risk manager. Risk encompasses not only investment risks, but also the risks inherent in a business: its operations, its people, and its systems. There are many examples of risk management failures with severe consequences. Unauthorized trading caused the demise of Barings Bank in 1995, then the oldest merchant bank in London; Enron and WorldCom, once among the largest public companies in the United States, went bankrupt following accounting scandals; and risk management failures contributed to the global financial crisis of 2008.

In Chapter 18, you will learn about controls that surround the investment management process. Performance evaluation does not merely reflect how well or poorly a manager has performed; it provides far greater insights into portfolio management and the associated controls. It allows a client to better understand the source of performance—in other words, whether performance was a result of asset allocation, sector allocation, asset selection, or currency allocation.

Written by Ravi Nevile, CFA, and Robin Solomon.
Copyright © 2012 CFA Institute

No system, activity, or process can be perfectly controlled or completely risk free. Despite advances in technology, people play a large role in the decision-making process, management, and underlying operations of every investment organization. The human element is often the difference between a highly successful investment organization and an average one. Thus, a good understanding of the control mechanisms that are in place to protect organizations and safeguard client interests is important.

# CHAPTER 16

## INVESTMENT INDUSTRY DOCUMENTATION

by Ravi Nevile, CFA, and Robin Solomon

## LEARNING OUTCOMES

After completing this chapter, you should be able to do the following:

**a** Define a document;

**b** Describe objectives of documentation;

**c** Describe document classification systems;

**d** Describe types of internal documentation;

**e** Compare internal and external documentation;

**f** Describe types of external documentation;

**g** Describe document management.

# INTRODUCTION

Documentation touches every aspect of investing, from internal documents to contracts with external parties. It provides evidence of how organisations operate, interact, and deliver their services. Documentation varies across the investment industry and across organisations. But the general rules, structure, and logic of internal, business-to-business, and external client documentation apply to all types of organisations. This chapter explains why documentation is important, provides examples of different types of documents, and describes how documents are managed.

# OBJECTIVES AND CLASSIFICATION OF DOCUMENTATION

A **document** represents an official record. Some documents are for internal use only. They are generally administrative and reflect an organisation's philosophy, approach, and activities. Other documents are for external use. They convey information to and from the public domain and often help limit the risks that this interaction with the public creates.

## 2.1 Objectives of Documentation

In the context of the investment industry, documentation does the following:

- Educates—informs or provides instruction;

- Communicates—conveys ideas, concepts, or information;

- Authorises—provides the basis, and often the authority, for action;

- Formalises—establishes roles, deliverables, and obligations;

- Organises—ensures thoroughness and consistency of action, allowing the organisation to function more efficiently and effectively;

- Measures—provides a benchmark for measurement and audit;

- Records—preserves corporate learning (institutional memory);

- Protects—provides assurance of a system to safeguard interests and manage risks.

Copyright © 2012 CFA Institute

From a legal perspective, documents establish proof: proof of existence, authority, activity, and obligation. When policies and procedures are undocumented, there is room for doubt, and poor-quality documentation may be subject to interpretation or undue influence. Proper documentation removes ambiguity.

## 2.2 Document Classification Systems

When using, developing, or reviewing a document, organisations and individuals should consider three factors: origin, direction, and level of standardisation.

Origin relates to the source of the document. Documents can be classified by their source as

- Original documents,
- Derived documents, or
- Associated documents.

Example 1 describes an activity, traveling for work, and the classification of documents related to this activity.

> **EXAMPLE 1. CLASSIFICATION OF DOCUMENTS**
>
> An employee travels for work and incurs expenses while doing so.
>
> - The receipt for a taxi or a train ticket is the original document.
>
> - The expense claim form the employee has to fill out upon her return is a derived document; this document comes into existence because of other documents—in this case, the taxi receipt or train ticket.
>
> - The organisation's travel policy document is an associated document. When filling out the expense claim form, the employee may have to refer to the travel policy document to determine which expenses will be reimbursed.

Documents flow in different directions. Typically, documents associated with policies and procedures flow "down" through an organisation. Referring back to Example 1, the travel policy document may flow down from the human resources department to all employees via an employee handbook. In contrast, documents associated with reporting flow "up." For example, the monthly reports produced by the sales teams flow up from each team to management.

A distinction can be made between standardised and ad hoc documents:

- **Standardised documents** have the benefit of foresight. They are crafted for a specific purpose and consider various alternative uses. Some standard contracts are tailored by negotiation, but their form, content, and purpose have been pre-established.

- **Ad hoc documents**, such as letters, memos, and e-mails, are typically informal. The free-form nature of these ad hoc documents means they carry additional risk for the organisation, particularly when the records are subpoenaed in a legal dispute. Consequently, organisations may implement policies and procedures to impose a process of peer review for such ad hoc communication. Peer review should be documented and auditable.

In Example 2, the relationship of an organisation's risk management policy with the objective, origin, direction, and level of standardisation of documentation is shown.

**EXAMPLE 2. RISK MANAGEMENT POLICY**

| | |
|---|---|
| Objective | Authorise, formalise, and communicate in order to explain the organisation's attitude toward and tolerance for risk. |
| Origin | Derived from regulation, but original (specific) to the organisation and associated with the investment policy, the risk management plan, and a host of related internal documents. |
| Direction | Internal document that flows from the top down. |
| Level of standardisation | Standardised policy template, formally drafted, approved by the board of directors and adopted by management, and implemented by the corporate risk management group or the compliance group. |

# INTERNAL DOCUMENTATION

**Internal documents**, which formalise all forms of internal documentation—including internal policies, procedures, and processes—are fundamental to conveying an organisation's philosophy, approach, and activities. **Policies** are principles of action adopted by an organisation. **Procedures** identify what the organisation must do to achieve a desired outcome. **Processes** are the individual steps the organisation must take, from start to finish, to achieve that desired outcome. Documentation of policies and procedures helps to communicate the policies and procedures and to ensure compliance with legislation and regulations, as well as with the organisation's policies themselves. To ensure clear communication and compliance, it is critical to understand the context of (or reason for) the documentation. Rather than just outlining what to do or not do in a situation, it is better practice to include a sense of why the policy and required documentation is in place and to whom it applies.

A travel policy that simply states that staff must provide both receipts and boarding cards for air travel is not as effective as one that provides additional context on the reasons for and origin of the policy. For example, the firm's expense management policy should not only clearly state that staff are prohibited from downgrading their class of seat or ticket but should also explain that such a rule prevents staff from booking a higher class of seat, downgrading, and thus benefiting from either a cash credit or free flights. Furthermore, the consequences of violating the policy should be explained.

A policy statement that merely states that the organisation will not engage in insider trading is not as effective as one with additional context to make the statement "real" for the employees. It should be explained that the policy has its origin in law and that violation has penalties for the organisation and the individual. It should also be explained that the policy applies to everyone who has access to sensitive information that could be considered "inside information," which includes not only decision makers but also anyone with access. For example, the boardroom attendant serving refreshments during board meetings may have access to sensitive information and, therefore, would require training.

The importance of understanding the origins of, reasons for, and implications of documentation, for both the company and the individual, should not be underestimated. People create and implement policies and procedures, and they need context in which to learn these policies and procedures, understand them, and attribute the proper degree of importance to them. Without a clear context, employees can become ineffective in the event of a process breakdown or unaware of process failure in more extreme circumstances.

Although context is important, how that context is perceived depends to a large degree on the individual or, more importantly, on the individual's role and training. An investment manager might absorb the investment-related themes or ideas within a document, whereas a legal practitioner might focus on the document's contractually binding obligations and the authority levels it captures. Thus, a single document may have multiple purposes and interpretations, each of which may depend on individual perspectives or situations.

A more standard aspect of document creation relates to the production style—for instance, the use of a standardised template. Documents that are clearly presented in a style that most people are familiar with help individuals read and accept these documents. They are also easier to use, enabling individuals, including board members, to perform their duties more effectively.

A standardised template helps maintain version control. Given the level of legislative and regulatory activity in most organisations, it is rare for policy and procedure documents to remain static. Any changes reflected in a policy document will need to be similarly reflected in all associated procedure and process documents. How a certain issue is treated will be different once the new policy is implemented. Simply stating the document title, the version number, and the date on which the version came into effect will help ensure that, in case of a review, the standards to which an organisation is held reflect the rules it has been operating under for the period of the review.

Policies and procedures are living documents and should be subject to a regular review and confirmation process as a function of good organisational governance. This review and confirmation process should not be merely event driven. Even without a notable event, attitudes and practices will change over time. If policies and procedures are not regularly reviewed, they can become outdated and even obsolete.

A regular review process is often managed with the use of **registers**, which are documents containing obligations, past actions, and future or outstanding requirements. Registers of the previous and next review dates should be maintained by a control function (generally, compliance or an internal audit within an organisation) and scheduled for discussion. A sign-off process is generally also incorporated into the document template and includes amendments identified in the review process to be enacted and formalised by relevant individuals with appropriate authority. In the case of policy documents, reviews are noted formally in the minutes of the board meeting.

## 3.1 Policy Documentation

Policy documents might have their roots in legislation. Policy documents might also describe the organisation's mission, values, and objectives. These documents should be consistent with the firm's constitutional documents and bylaws, which summarise the legal identity, purpose, and activities of the organisation.

One role of the board of directors (or similar governance body) is to translate obligations from laws or regulations to ensure that the organisation works within the defined scope of the law and, in doing so, protects and represents the interests of all stakeholders. This translation process normally results in policy documents that help an organisation develop and implement procedures and processes. Interpreting regulations and then narrowing down what is allowed is a company-specific matter.

Policy documents state an organisation's position on various laws and regulations. In arriving at that position, the board of directors considers a number of factors deemed important to the organisation. The eventual statement thus reflects not only the organisation's position but also its attitude toward and tolerance for the risk associated with that position.

In general, regulation concentrates on outward-facing documentation, such as product disclosures and other client-focused material. Regulators may issue guidelines for internal documents, but those guidelines are usually not prescriptive—that is, organisations generally have flexibility to adopt these guidelines or to develop their own organisational standards and approaches.

Many organisations look externally to identify standards that should be followed. There are numerous standards that can be readily adopted and applied by an organisation, including those issued by professional groups. For example, CFA Institute has established the Global Investment Performance Standards (GIPS®) for the presentation of investment performance information. In some instances, professional standards are considered "best practices".

An organisation's adherence to best practices or achievement of certification (where offered) should only be a means to an end. It may not be economically feasible for many smaller organisations to adhere to best practices. An alternative approach is for such organisations to apply standards that suit their own specific circumstances.

These standards are "fit for purpose", and an organisation using this approach has to critically assess and document its own needs and requirements. The result should strike a balance between practicality and cost on the one hand and control and assurance on the other hand.

Overly prescriptive policy documents (like overly prescriptive legislation) can often cause implementation issues. Policy documents are, therefore, often worded broadly to provide guidance rather than direction. Policy is driven from the top down, with corporate rules cascading down through the various divisions and business units of the organisation.

The keys to good policy documentation are simplicity and transparency. Policy statements do not need to be overly detailed and can be relatively concise. Policy documents should include a statement of intent that explains the purpose and goals of the policy. This statement of intent should cover the circumstances under which the policy is invoked and establish any parameters for its use. Because policies must be implemented, the policy document should clearly designate an individual with the proper delegation of authority.

## 3.2 Procedure and Process Documentation

The role of procedure documentation is often to provide a bridge between the activities that are allowed on a policy level and what needs to happen on a process level. Policy sets the field, procedure interprets the rules, and process divides the activity into manageable parts.

Example 3 shows the policy, procedure, and process for a firm operating in eight different regulatory environments, from developed to emerging markets. To ensure that this policy is embedded in the culture of the firm, various procedures must be adopted across different business and functional areas of the organisation. A single procedure could have hundreds of associated processes that would be followed in specific circumstances.

# Internal Documentation

> **EXAMPLE 3. POLICY, PROCEDURE, AND PROCESS**
>
> **Policy Statement**
> The firm operates in eight different regulatory environments, from developed to emerging markets. To ensure stakeholder confidence, and hence support, it must demonstrate the application of the highest fiduciary standards present within any of those jurisdictions and across all jurisdictions.
>
> **Procedure 1**
> Identify regulatory obligations and changes across eight jurisdictions; identify highest standard of care
>
> **Procedure 2**
> Monitor firm regulatory compliance
>
> **Procedure 3**
> Identify breaches and implement remedial action
>
> **Procedure 4**
> Train staff to mitigate breaches
>
> **Process String 1**
>
> Process 1: Create a register of all obligations across eight jurisdictions
>
> Process 2: Monitor regulatory changes and update register
> ….
> ….
>
> **Process String 2**
>
> Process 1: Check firm compliance with insider trading policies
>
> Process 2: Check that licensed representatives meet compliance requirements
> ….
> ….
>
> **Process String 3**
>
> Process 1: Update quarterly registers from Procedure 2 to identify breaches
>
> Process 2: Remedy each breach
> ….
> ….
>
> **Process String 4**
>
> Process 1: Conduct compliance training for new staff upon hiring
>
> Process 2: Conduct annual compliance training for all staff
> ….
> ….
>
> Starting from a simple and concise statement contained in the policy statement, the firm will implement four procedures. For example, the fourth procedure relates to staff training and includes several processes. The first process is to ensure that each new staff member undergoes compliance training when hired. The second process refers to the compliance training that all staff members must complete every year.

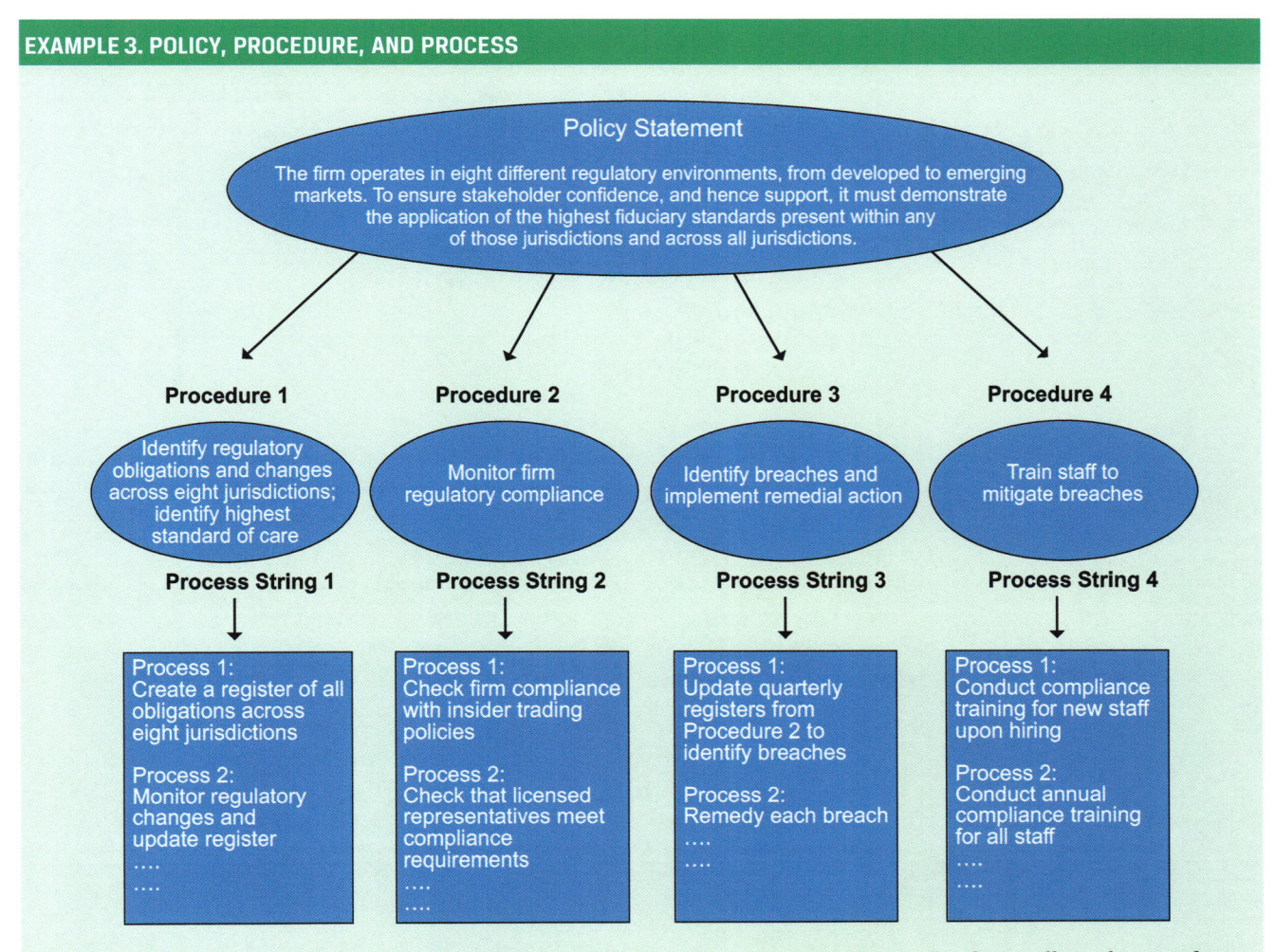

An organisation must continually reassess its procedures and processes and keep them current. It must also make sure that all employees receive adequate training regarding the existing procedures and processes and that they are kept informed when changes are made.

Procedures and processes try to communicate the best possible way to undertake an activity while taking into account external and internal constraints. Finding fault with current practices without understanding the circumstances behind their creation is short-sighted. It is important to understand the history and background of a procedure and the limitations in place at the time of its creation. There may be organisational reasons or system limitations that dictate a specific course of action or, in some cases, a "work-around" that might seem cumbersome but on reflection has merit, given the firm's specific situation. It is not always necessary or effective to duplicate previous efforts or to discount institutional memory at the outset.

Processes should be modular—that is, they should be made up of separate elements that can be reviewed and replaced independently of each other. Modular processes allows organisations to avoid replacing a whole procedure when a single element changes. Similarly, although some processes may be repetitive, in drafting a procedure, each process can be documented once and then referenced as required.

The final consideration when creating or reviewing procedures is risk management. Controls should be embedded in the procedure and drafted with risk management and compliance in mind. This step is important because without a strong control environment, processes are at risk of error. In the worst-case scenario, this risk can lead to economic or reputational losses. Risk management and compliance are covered more completely in Chapter 17.

As with policies and procedures, context is critical for processes. Understanding where inputs come from and where outputs go and what they will be used for provides that context. Process flow diagrams, such as the one shown in Example 4, are a good visual aid for this purpose because they bring multiple processes together by demonstrating the sources of inputs and the uses of outputs. The individual processes take on more significance and can be understood better in the context of the overall procedure. Adherence to the processes can thus be ensured more easily. All procedure documents will, therefore, follow a similar pattern: Each input initiates an activity that results in an output.

- Procedure 1
    - Process 1
        - Input (generally external to the business unit or organisation)
        - Activity
        - Output (used for the next process)
    - Process 2
        - Input (sourced from the previous process output)
        - Activity
        - Output (passed to a different business unit or passed externally)

The process flow diagram creates a chain of linked activities. Checklists are a simple and efficient method when a number of contingent activities are needed. The nature of a checklist lends itself easily to automation.

### EXAMPLE 4. PROCESS FLOW DIAGRAM

Assume that a firm has a policy stipulating that gifts worth more than $100 require compliance approval. An established procedure is provided that employees must follow if they receive such a gift. The policy is intended to prevent conflicts of interest that might arise if the behaviour of the employee were influenced by the gift.

An employee receives a case of wine as a gift from the brokerage firm she regularly uses. Should this employee accept the case of wine? The employee faces an ethical dilemma, similar to those discussed in Chapter 2. She should refer to her firm's gift policy, which includes several procedures and processes. The following process flow diagram should guide the employee.

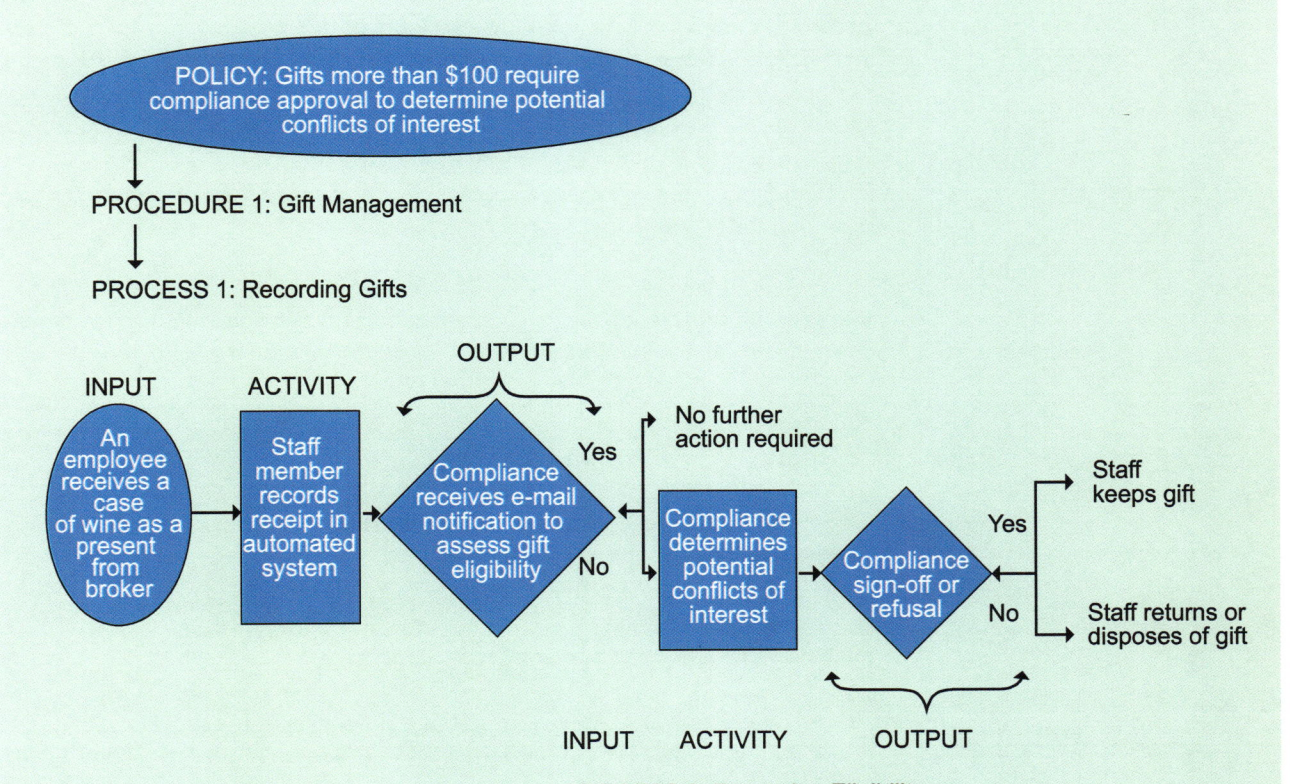

```
                POLICY: Gifts more than $100 require
                compliance approval to determine potential
                          conflicts of interest
                                    ↓
                    PROCEDURE 1: Gift Management
                                    ↓
                    PROCESS 1: Recording Gifts

                                 OUTPUT
    INPUT          ACTIVITY                           No further
                                         Yes         action required                Staff
 An employee      Staff member      Compliance                                   keeps gift
 receives a       records receipt   receives e-mail      Compliance       Yes
 case of wine as  in automated      notification to      determines
 a present from   system            assess gift          potential       Compliance
 broker                             eligibility    No    conflicts of    sign-off or
                                                         interest        refusal    No   Staff returns or
                                                                                         disposes of gift

                                           INPUT      ACTIVITY      OUTPUT
                                         PROCESS 2: Determine Eligibility
```

The first procedure refers to gift management. The first process in that procedure starts when the employee receives the case of wine. Her first activity in the process is to record this gift in the system, which triggers a notification to the compliance department. If the gift is eligible, the employee will receive an automatic notification that she can accept the gift and no further action is required. Alternatively, the compliance department may need to determine whether there is a potential conflict of interest, which would trigger a second activity. If the compliance department then concludes that the gift is eligible, the employee can accept it. If the compliance department decides it is not eligible, the employee has to return it to the brokerage firm or dispose of it.

# EXTERNAL DOCUMENTATION

# 4

External documentation exists between a firm and external parties, including clients, market participants, and service providers. External documents are often legally binding and aim to articulate certain business relationships and obligations undertaken by the parties involved. Examples of external documents within the investment industry are a legal agreement (contract) between a buyer and a seller of an asset, an investment management agreement between a firm and a client, and a "know-your-client" document for a new investment client.

Because contracts are governed by law and are enforceable, involved parties are usually motivated to comply with the agreement. If any of the parties fail to fulfil their obligations, different jurisdictions have distinct governing laws that offer parties varying levels of protection or help. External documents may also be used to inform the public or other external parties about a's activities or changes in its business—for example, a press release announcing the appointment of a new chief executive officer, a marketing presentation for a new investment product, or a statement about the launch of a new website containing company information.

Given the size of the investment industry, the way firms use external documents will vary depending on the parties involved and the capacities in which they are acting. Parties that can be involved in external documents include the following:

- Rule makers and enforcement agencies, such as regulators, governments, and legislators;

- Structural groups that help organise the market, including stock exchanges, clearinghouses, and depositories;

- Market participants that are active in facilitating investments or transactions, such as banks, brokers, and asset managers;

- Professional firms and individuals serving the needs of the industry, including credit rating agencies, auditors, lawyers, consultants, and trustees; and finally,

- Investors, including retail clients and institutional investors.

The relationships between parties dictate how they use documentation to formalise their relationships.

The rest of the discussion focuses on one broad activity—namely, a typical client interaction—and the different types of external documentation that exist at different stages of the client's investment cycle. Differences among products, regulatory agencies, and legislation in different jurisdictions—as well as the client's objectives and constraints—affect the nature of the client interaction and hence the documentation involved.

Exhibit 1 illustrates a client investment cycle. Because it is a cycle, there is no true beginning or end. The typical stages include marketing, client on-boarding, funding, ongoing reporting, investment events, and eventual redemption. At each stage of the cycle, different documentation is required. Samples of documentation at each stage are described in Sections 4.1–4.6.

# External Documentation

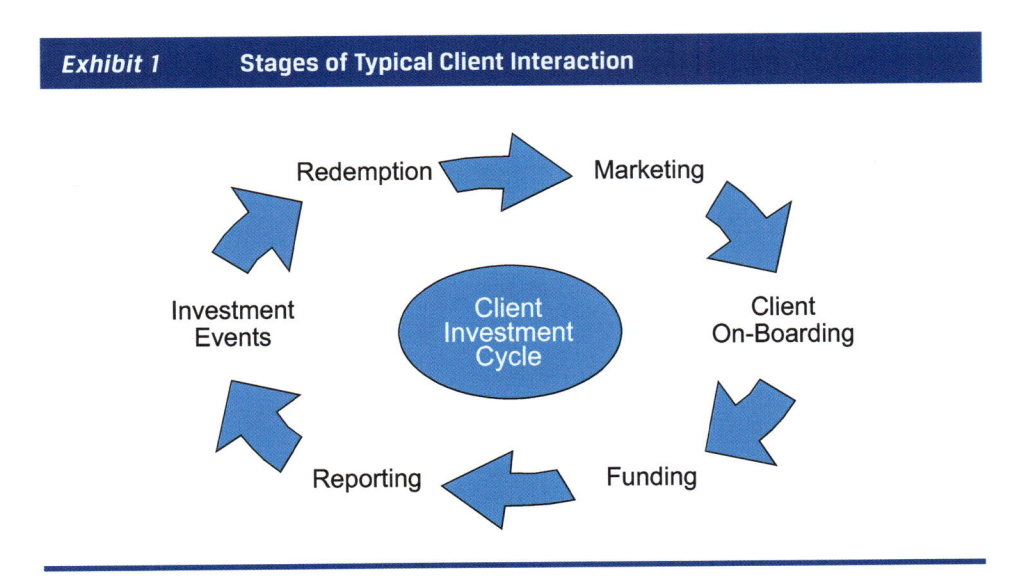

**Exhibit 1  Stages of Typical Client Interaction**

*Client Investment Cycle:* Marketing → Client On-Boarding → Funding → Reporting → Investment Events → Redemption → Marketing

## 4.1 Marketing

Most organisations—whether insurance companies, investment banks, or asset managers—share the same basic objective of winning clients. Thus, most organisations' documentation at the marketing stage of the cycle shares the same purpose: to promote and position the organisation's products and services to persuade the client to invest. The marketing documentation typically includes:

- presentation materials that provide background on the firm and its products.

- offering documentation, such as a prospectus or term sheet. These legal documents contain detailed information about the terms and conditions of the investment opportunity, highlight various risks, and make required disclosures.

- fact sheets about the firm's products that provide short summaries of the investments and typically detail historical performance.

These documents contain information about the people who are to be entrusted with managing the client's capital, including their investment strategy and competitive advantages. Other features include the past performance, risk analytics, and characteristics of the product, such as liquidity, distributed income, and the various fees that will be borne by the client.

Marketing materials are typically regulated to ensure that sellers of financial and investment products provide fair representations of their products, as discussed in Chapter 3. The regulation is normally more onerous as the client's level of investment sophistication decreases. Most developed markets tightly regulate the sale of financial and investment products to retail investors.

## 4.2 Client On-Boarding

**Client on-boarding** is the process by which an organisation accepts a client and inputs client details into its records to enable the organisation to conduct transactions with and on behalf of the client. An organisation has a legal obligation to verify the identity of a potential client by means of a know-your-client (KYC) process before commencing a relationship with the potential client. The typical know-your-client process requires the client to complete a questionnaire, providing personal background information on individuals who have authority to act on the client's behalf, including documentary proof of identity (e.g., passports), addresses, and other personal particulars. The client will also be screened against various global databases to ascertain whether he or she is known or wanted by local or international law enforcement agencies. In addition, the organisation will need to run anti-money-laundering checks at on-boarding and thereafter to identify any potential suspicious transactions that the firm would be obligated to report to a regulator. The firm is responsible for determining the source of the client's funds and verifying that these funds do not originate from an illegal or criminal source. Firms must constantly monitor transactions to ensure that they are not suspicious in nature, and if something suspicious does arise, firms are obligated to report that activity to the authorities. The heavy penalties imposed by most global regulators help combat identity theft and criminal activity and the subsequent flow of funds from these sources into the investment industry.

The know-your-client process also serves to define the client's level of knowledge and sophistication, assign associated and specific risk profiles, and generally assess any possible restrictions. Depending on the type of business, the type of client, and the purpose of the relationship, different and quite detailed information might be required to ensure that the organisation provides the appropriate services for the client's needs.

Moreover, the know-your-client process is important in setting the basis for the relationship. It is important to differentiate between discretionary and non-discretionary relationships. **Discretionary relationships** permit the service provider to act with standing authority on behalf of the client—for example, as a trustee of a trust or as an investment manager with a specific mandate. In such cases, the service provider acts as a fiduciary. In a **non-discretionary relationship**, the service provider undertakes specific tasks that are authorised on a per task basis.

## 4.3 Funding

Once the client on-boarding is complete and the relationship has been initiated and approved by the compliance department, the next stage is the actual cash transfer and investment purchase. The firm will provide wiring instructions to the client, the client will authorise his or her bank to make a payment, and the bank will act on this instruction and provide a confirmation of the transfer. For all of these steps and processes, external documentation exists as a record of the actions taken by each of the parties involved.

After receiving the funds, the organisation will initiate the investment transaction and send a formal confirmation to the client. For example, this documentation could be a share certificate, confirmation of an investment in a mutual fund, or a legal counterparty confirmation of a funded derivatives transaction. Again, numerous steps are involved in this process and each of these steps relies on external documentation to formalise, legalise, and protect the rights and obligations of the buyers and sellers involved.

Moreover, service providers may be involved to provide transaction, safekeeping, or administrative services to the client or the firm, and external documentation would be used to record those activities as well.

## 4.4 Reporting

After funding, regular communication will occur between the firm and the client. For any underlying asset, a valuation (if a market price is available) or an appraisal (an estimation, if no market price is available) will be sent to the client on some predetermined periodic basis. For example, a mutual fund may print the fund's daily net asset value per unit in a national newspaper, a hedge fund manager or administrator may send a monthly statement to clients, or a specialist may value a real estate partnership annually and send an appraisal to the limited partners.

This external documentation takes the form of a statement, often provided by a third-party custodian, administrator, or specialist valuation agent. The statement is a representation of the fair value of the underlying asset at that point in time. The statement will typically contain information on the specific asset, the quantity of units held, and the value per unit. It may also contain performance information, measured by the change in value over various periods of time—a quarter, a year, or perhaps an even longer period. Certain standards, such as the Global Investment Performance Standards standards mentioned earlier, apply to how the valuation is performed or how the performance is presented. Along with valuation statements, clients will receive a range of other reporting, such as investment reports, annual financial statements, and risk management reports.

## 4.5 Investment Events

Over the life of the investment, numerous events may take place that affect the client or require the client to take action; such events lead to further external documentation.

Some events are expected and have a degree of certainty during the lifetime of the investment, such as regular income in the form of interest from a bond, dividends from an equity investment, or rental income from a commercial real estate investment. Typically, income is accompanied by a written confirmation and payment of funds to the client or cash proceeds to be re-invested in some prescribed or previously agreed way. Income will also have to be accounted for in future performance reporting, as well as for income tax purposes.

Other events are uncertain or unexpected, including a host of situations that could affect the client's investment and, therefore, the external documentation between the client and the organisation. Such events include the following:

- Merger and acquisition (M&A) activities. If the firm merges with, spins off from, or acquires another firm, the business and operations may change, affecting the client's investment. Such changes may give certain rights to the client, depending on the underlying investment.

- Bankruptcy. If the firm files for bankruptcy or undergoes a reorganisation, the client may be affected, depending on the nature of the underlying transaction or investment. There will be written communication about the legal process, the rights of the parties involved, and any liquidation.

- Natural disaster. Natural disasters may affect a real asset or even a financial asset. The terms of the investment may give certain rights to the client or the firm.

## 4.6 Redemption

At some stage, a client may want to redeem or sell an investment. Depending on the type of investment, a written request may be required. After verifying the authenticity of the client's instruction, the firm will arrange for the investment to be sold. The timing of redemption depends on the precise details of the investment and its liquidity. Authorised signatories from the organisation allow the bank to release the cash proceeds. A final written confirmation statement is sent to the client.

Although redemption is the end of a transaction, it does not signify the end of the client relationship. The client may want to invest or conduct other transactions with the firm in the future. The documentation relating to the final transaction will be retained, as discussed in Section 5, should there be any future dispute or disagreement between the parties.

It is clear that documents serve an important role in establishing the rules by which a service or product is supplied, formalising the rights and entitlements of ownership, and recording activities pursuant to the purchase and ongoing maintenance of an asset. Clearly, these purposes are not limited to key events but cover the minutiae of daily activity within the industry. Given that typical client interactions occur by the millions each day and given the complexity of all the different parties involved in the industry, the amount of existing external documentation is enormous and constantly growing.

# 5 DOCUMENT MANAGEMENT

This final section closes the loop by describing some of the corporate aspects of managing documentation. This section discusses the role of technology and how firms retain, access, and dispose of documents. The importance of document management cannot be overemphasised because it relates to broad security issues, including confidentiality and companies' protection of client information. Security also encompasses access rights because improper use of or unauthorised access to client information could lead to identity theft and fraud. Additionally, corporations have an ethical obligation to dispose of documents in a safe manner, whether they contain personal information, spending patterns, or levels of wealth or debt. Given the huge amounts of data available on every individual, it is important that organisations take responsibility for the proper retention, security, and ultimate disposal of these documents.

# Document Management

## 5.1 Information Technology

Information technology has greatly enhanced our ability to collect, collate, manage, and distribute documents. It has also greatly advanced the automation of processes, to a large degree eliminating the need for some traditional internal documentation. In the past, rules were physically documented, but rules-based systems now allow enforcement of processes by building controls into operating systems.

Because of the advent of **straight-through processing (STP)**, also referred to as straight-through exception processing (STeP), the need for manual intervention has been removed. It is very often possible to capture inputs—including client interactions—from outside the organisation by directly accessing an organisation's information technology systems, which affects the way external documentation is handled. In some instances, the need for physical documentation has completely disappeared. Examples include the use of internet banking and online share trading, which eliminate the need for deposit/withdrawal slips, trade order tickets, and physical contract notes.

The use of information technology can also reduce risk. For example, the payment of funds from an investment account may be subject to fraud. To limit the risk of fraud, payments typically require a dual sign-off process. If a dual sign-off process is implemented correctly, collusion between two parties can be more easily identified. The manual process involves a physical cheque and two signatories, which is time consuming and prone to errors; a fully automated process involves dual independent (blind) input with automated reconciliation and release, which reduces the risk of errors and time for review.

## 5.2 Retention, Access, Security, and Disposal of Documents

There are logical, legal, and regulatory reasons to retain documents for a period after their initial use. Documents are official records, and therefore, they offer proof and protection. External documents (outgoing and incoming) establish the basis for a given action at a point in time (or for a specified period). It is essential, not only legally but also operationally, that all instructions be retained for a period commensurate with the period of time in which the risk is borne. Issues relating to these documents, however, may also arise years later. Thus, a document does not cease to be important once the action described in that document has been completed. For example, a legal contract that stipulates possible recourse after termination requires that the document be retained for at least the term of that recourse.

There are generally laws or policies in place to prescribe document retention. Each legal jurisdiction will have its own time frames, and some types of documents may have more specific time frames than others. Although most documents today are held electronically, there are still requirements to hold physical, original documents. These documents tend to be asset and jurisdiction dependent and include such items as certificates of title, contracts, and trust deeds. Document retention refers not only to physical documents but also to virtual or system-based documents. Organisations typically store historic information, backups, and physical documents in an off-site location, which is often maintained and managed by a third party.

Documents cannot simply be archived and forgotten. Specific destruction or disposal instructions should be applied to all archived information. Organisations have a responsibility to discard or destroy documentation after the retention period. This responsibility is particularly important with respect to sensitive information, such as personal information about individuals. Most developed markets have strict legislation around data protection and firms' obligations to permanently delete confidential information, whether stored in electronic or paper format.

Finally, documents need to be available and accessible to staff. Although some documents will be restricted, such as staff compensation data or confidential client information, most documents should be easily retrievable. A centralised repository is needed, with appropriate access rights, so that authorised staff can gain access to the documents they require. This repository is normally electronic: a read-only drive, document database, or documentation management system capable of storing internal and external documents relevant to the organisation's business activities.

## SUMMARY

Key points of the chapter include the following:

- Documents provide information or evidence or serve as an official record.

- There are many reasons to document information, including communicating ideas, formalising relationships, authorising actions, recording transactions, and protecting the parties involved.

- Documents can be classified in terms of origin, direction, and standardisation.

- Important features of internal documents include context, version control, and regular review.

- Policy documents, adopted by the board, are high-level documents that state the company's position on various corporate, legal, and regulatory matters.

- Policy documents often reflect a certain standard, such as best practice or market practice, or are "fit for purpose", meaning that they meet the specific needs of the organisation without attempting to benchmark or reference an external standard.

- Policy sets the field, procedure interprets the rules, and process divides the activity into manageable pieces.

- Procedures and processes should be developed so that there are sufficient controls in place to mitigate risk.

- Policies and procedures can be supplemented by useful tools such as checklists, registers, and process flow diagrams to aid users in understanding and completing the appropriate processes.

## Summary

- External documents are often contractual and enforceable by law, providing protection of rights as well as imposing obligations on the parties involved.

- A typical client interaction cycle includes documents related to marketing, on-boarding (including know-your-client and anti-money-laundering processes), funding, reporting, investment events, and redemption.

- Document management includes collection, collation, storage, and retrieval and is generally subject to legislative constraints on retention and disposal.

# CHAPTER REVIEW QUESTIONS

Test your knowledge of this chapter at **cfainstitute.org/claritasstudy**.

1 A stockbroker receives a purchase order by e-mail from a client and a printed memorandum with some policy updates from the human resources (HR) department. Which of the following statements is *most likely* correct?

   A  The client e-mail is considered a document, but not the memorandum.

   B  The memorandum is considered a document, but not the client e-mail.

   C  Both the client e-mail and the memorandum are considered documents.

2 The monthly fund fact sheet of a mutual fund company is available electronically on the company's external website. The fund fact sheet is:

   A  an official record.

   B  not an official record because it is in electronic format.

   C  not an official record because it conveys only information and not evidence.

3 Documentation that protects the organisation is *best* described as providing:

   A  a benchmark for measurement and audit.

   B  the basis and authority to take action when needed.

   C  assurance of a system to safeguard interests and manage risks.

4 A prescribed format for marketing materials used by a company *best* relates to documenting:

   A  origin.

   B  direction.

   C  level of standardisation.

5 A document describing principles of action adopted by a company is *best* described as a:

   A  policy document.

   B  process document.

   C  procedure document.

Copyright © 2012 CFA Institute

## Chapter Review Questions

**6** Version control is *least likely* to:

   **A** be maintained with ad hoc documents.

   **B** indicate when a document was last reviewed.

   **C** assist in establishing when a document became effective.

**7** Compared with external documentation, internal documentation is *more likely* to:

   **A** be legally binding.

   **B** be used to inform the public.

   **C** document policies, procedures, and processes.

**8** Client on-boarding documentation *most likely* refers to:

   **A** wire transfer documentation.

   **B** documentation required to accept a client.

   **C** marketing documentation that should be sent to a client.

**9** When a client wants to sell an investment, the documentation needed from the client *most likely* relates to:

   **A** funding.

   **B** reporting.

   **C** redemption.

**10** The document management process should ensure:

   **A** safekeeping of physical and electronic documentation.

   **B** permanent archiving of all past client information and data.

   **C** that a paper trail exists, even for information technology systems.

**11** Which of the following statements relating to document management is *most* correct?

   **A** Document retention rules tend to apply only to physical documents.

   **B** Organisations should destroy all documentation after the retention period ends.

   **C** For security, documents should be moderately difficult to access by authorized staff.

**12** In the document management process, ease of data retrieval is *best* accomplished by:

**A** maintaining an accessible repository.

**B** retaining information after its initial use.

**C** using sound documentation-safekeeping practices.

# ANSWERS

1. C is correct. Any document is an official record. Some documents, such as the memorandum, are for internal use only. They are generally administrative and reflect an organisation's philosophy, approach, and activities. Other documents, such as the client e-mail, are for external use. They convey information to and from the public domain and often help limit the risks that this interaction with the public creates.

2. A is correct. An official record can be in electronic or printed format. An official record (document) for external use may convey information to and from the public domain. The fund fact sheet is available on the company's external website and is thus an official record.

3. C is correct. Documentation that protects the organisation provides assurance of a system to safeguard interests and manage risks. A is incorrect because documentation that provides a benchmark for measurement and audit better describes the objective of documentation related to measurement. B is incorrect because documentation that provides the basis and authority to take action when needed better describes the objective of documentation related to authorisation.

4. C is correct. A prescribed format for marketing materials describes the level of standardisation, a characteristic used to classify documentation. The level of standardisation determines whether a document is standardised or ad hoc. Standardised documents have pre-established formats, whereas ad hoc documents are free form. A is incorrect because origin refers to the source of the document (i.e., original, derived, or associated documents). B is incorrect because direction refers to the flow of documentation—that is, whether the information flows down (e.g., documents associated with policies and procedures) or up (e.g., documents associated with reporting).

5. A is correct. A policy document describes principles of action adopted by an organisation. C is incorrect because a procedure document identifies what the organisation must do to achieve a desired outcome. B is incorrect because a process document describes the individual steps the organisation must take, from start to finish, to achieve the desired outcome.

6. A is correct. Version control of documentation is difficult to maintain with ad hoc documents, such as letters, memos, and e-mails. The use of standardised documents helps maintain version control. B and C are incorrect because version control indicates when a document was last reviewed and assists in establishing when a document became effective.

7. C is correct. Internal documentation typically documents an organisation's policies, procedures, and processes. A and B are incorrect because external documentation is more likely to be legally binding and is used to inform the public or other external parties.

**8** B is correct. Client on-boarding is the process by which an organisation accepts a client and inputs client details into its records to enable the organisation to conduct transactions with and on behalf of the client. Thus, it refers to documentation required to accept a client. A is incorrect because wire transfer documentation is best described as funding documentation. C is incorrect because marketing documentation sent to a client is best described as marketing documentation.

**9** C is correct. Redemption documentation is required when a client wants to redeem or sell an investment. The firm will arrange for the investment to be sold only after verifying the authenticity of the client's instruction. A is incorrect because funding documentation gives wire instructions to commence a client–firm relationship. B is incorrect because reporting documentation provides regular communication between the client and the firm.

**10** A is correct. Safekeeping of records, whether paper or electronic, is part of the document management process. B is incorrect because past client information and data are not permanently archived. Specific destruction or disposal instructions should be applied to all archived information. This responsibility is particularly important with respect to sensitive information, such as personal information about individuals. Organisations have a responsibility to discard or destroy documentation after the retention period ends. C is incorrect because information technology systems have, in some instances, eliminated the need for physical documentation and often enhance the document management process.

**11** B is correct. Documents cannot simply be archived indefinitely. Specific destruction or disposal instructions should be applied to all archived information. Organisations have a responsibility to discard or destroy documentation after the retention period ends. A is incorrect because document retention rules tend to apply to both physical documents and electronic documentation. C is incorrect because documents need to be available and accessible to authorized staff. Although some documents, such as staff compensation data or confidential client information, will be restricted, most documents should be easily retrievable.

**12** A is correct. Maintaining an accessible repository, with appropriate access rights, helps data retrieval. B and C are incorrect because retaining information after its initial use and using sound documentation-safekeeping practices do not imply that data will be easy to access.

# CHAPTER 17
## RISK MANAGEMENT

by Hannes Valtonen, CFA

## LEARNING OUTCOMES

After completing this chapter, you should be able to do the following:

a   Define risk and identify types of risk;

b   State the importance of risk management;

c   Describe a risk management process;

d   Describe benefits and costs of risk management;

e   Describe limitations of using models and historical information to measure risk;

f   Define operational risks and explain how they are managed;

g   Define compliance risks and explain how they are managed;

h   Define investment risks and explain how they are managed.

# INTRODUCTION

Risk is part of your daily life, and you often act as a risk manager. Before crossing a busy road, you first assess that it is safe for you to do so; if you take a toddler to the swimming pool, you make sure that she is wearing inflatable armbands (floaties) before she gets into the water and that she is never left unattended; you have probably purchased car, home, and/or health insurance to protect you and your family against accidents, disasters, or illnesses. Thus, in the course of your life, you are well acquainted with identifying risks, assessing them, and selecting the appropriate response, which is what risk management is about.

## 1.1 Risk and Investment Decisions

Risk is a critical element of investment decisions. Investors, for instance, buy equity securities, commodities, or real estate properties. Thus, they are exposed to investment risk, the risk associated with investing. These investors may face losses if the company in which they bought common shares goes bankrupt or if commodity or real estate property prices fall. Investment risk is very important for investment professionals, but it is not the focus of this chapter. This chapter puts the emphasis on the types of risks that organizations in the investment industry and people working for these organizations face. Some of these risks are associated with operations. Organizations may be negatively affected by human, system, or process failures and by events that are beyond their control but may disrupt their ability to do business—natural disasters, such as earthquakes or hurricanes, are examples of such events. Organizations also have to comply with laws and regulations, and failure to do so may have a negative effect on their ability to remain in business.

## 1.2 Recognizing Risk

It is important for organizations to develop a structured process that helps them recognize and prepare for a wide range of risks; such a process is called a risk management process. It provides a framework for identifying and prioritizing risks, assessing their potential likelihood and severity, taking preventive or mitigating actions, if necessary, and constantly monitoring and making adjustments. Having a good risk management process in place helps organizations reduce the likelihood and severity of adverse events while enhancing management's ability to realize opportunities.

## 1.3 Risk and the Organization

Although risk management is sometimes viewed as a specialist function, a well-established risk management process will encompass the entire organization and filter down from senior management to all employees, giving them guidance in carrying out their roles. Any action that you take as an employee may affect your organization's risk profile, even if these actions are "only" regular daily activities. If you process

Copyright © 2012 CFA Institute

transactions, recruit people, manage information technology (IT) projects, or interact with clients, you are an integral component of your organization's operations; any failure to follow the appropriate policies, processes, and procedures may have a negative effect on your organization. An unintentional error may cause as much damage as fraud. Thus, it is important that you gain a good understanding of the types of risks an organization faces and that you learn how these risks are managed.

## 2 DEFINITION AND CLASSIFICATION OF RISKS

Risk can take different forms. Although there is no universal classification of risks, this section identifies typical risks to which organizations in the investment industry are exposed.

### 2.1 Definition of Risk

**Risk** arises out of uncertainty. It can be defined as the effect of uncertain future events on an organization or on the outcomes the organization achieves. One of these outcomes is the organization's profitability, which is why the effect of risk on profit or rates of returns is often assessed.

Events that have or could have a negative effect, leading to losses or negative rates of return, tend to be emphasized in discussions of risk. Some of these events are external to the organization. For example, a bank that has a large portfolio of commercial loans may suffer substantial losses if the economy goes into recession and corporate defaults increase. Other events, such as fraud or network failure, are internal to the organization. But not all outcomes from events are negative. Some events can have a positive effect on the organization, creating opportunities for gains. For example, a financial institution that takes the risk of investing in a country with tight capital controls may benefit when the capital controls are partially lifted and it becomes one of the few foreign investors licensed to buy and sell securities in that country.

### 2.2 Classification of Risks

Risks are classified according to the source of uncertainty. There is a long list of sources of uncertainty, so there is a correspondingly long list of risks. Relatively well-defined categories of risk exist, but no standard risk classification system applies to all organizations because risks should be classified in a manner that helps managers make better decisions in the context of their particular organization and its environment.

All organizations face the risk of not being able to operate profitably in a given competitive environment, typically because of a shift in market conditions. This risk is called **business risk** and is associated with the way an organization conducts business and interacts with its environment. For example, a company's ability to grow and remain profitable may be affected by changes in customer preferences, the evolution of the competitive landscape, or product and technology developments. Asset management firms, banks, and insurance companies face business risk, but the response to this risk

# Definition and Classification of Risks

is not specific to the investment industry, which is why business risk is not discussed in the rest of this chapter. This lack of coverage, however, is by no means an indication that this risk is secondary. Business risk management is an important component of any risk management system and involves the basics of good management to create and maintain a competitive advantage. Activities such as strategic business planning, conducting consumer research to understand the market, gathering business intelligence on competitors, and developing products and marketing strategies enable companies to manage business risks and remain profitable.

The two main types of risk covered in this chapter are:

- Operational risk, which refers to the risk of losses from human, system, and process failures and from events that are beyond the control of the organization but that affect its operations. Typical examples include human errors, internal fraud, system malfunctions, technology failure, and contractual disputes.

- Compliance risk, which relates to the risk that an organization fails to follow all applicable laws and regulations and faces sanctions as a result.

Investment risk, which arises from the fluctuation in the value of investments, is an important risk for investment professionals, but less so for individuals involved in support activities. Thus, it receives less coverage in this chapter. The key factors that cause investment risk are changes in market prices (market risks), borrowers' ability and willingness to repay debts (credit risk), and difficulties in buying or selling securities at the required price within a certain period of time (liquidity risk). Depending on the type of investment, a variety of other underlying risks can affect the value of this investment.

Example 1 describes and categorizes some investment risks faced by various organizations in the investment industry.

> **EXAMPLE 1. RISK IN THE INVESTMENT INDUSTRY**
>
> - A retail bank making loans must manage the risk of borrowers not repaying their debts (credit risk). The bank must also consider the risk of business disruption if its IT (information technology) and communication systems fail and its customers are unable to access their accounts or withdraw money (operational risk).
>
> - An investment bank needs to manage the risks of underwriting large issues of common shares, which requires purchasing the issued securities and selling them to other distributors and investors. The bank must bear the risks of investor sentiment changing and/or the difficulty of selling the securities at expected prices and volumes (market and liquidity risk).
>
> - An insurance company must manage the risk of concentrated catastrophic losses at insured properties in casualty insurance business lines and mortality and longevity risks for life insurance (business risks). The company

> must also consider the risks associated with investing insurance premiums and reserves to meet long-term liabilities (a combination of market, credit, and liquidity risks).

# 3 RISK MANAGEMENT

Risk management is an inherent element of the wealth creation process. The evolution of a risk management process may not have been smooth or consistently planned. An organization's risk management process very often evolves in response to financial crises, often incorporating the latest lessons learned and the new regulatory requirements that followed these crises. Well-run organizations will, however, benefit from people and processes that enable forward-looking attention to emerging risks.

## 3.1 Definition of Risk Management

The Committee of Sponsoring Organizations of the Treadway Commission (COSO), which provides guidance about risk management, internal control, and fraud deterrence, defines risk management as "a process, effected by an entity's board of directors, management and other personnel, applied in strategy setting and across the enterprise, designed to identify potential events that may affect the entity, and manage risk to be within its risk appetite, to provide reasonable assurance regarding the achievement of entity objectives."[1] This definition is broad, but it highlights the key concepts associated with a risk management framework.

Risk management is a process—that is, a series of actions to achieve an organization's objectives. These objectives may take different forms, but they are typically driven by the organization's mission and strategy. A common corporate objective is to create value in a business environment that is usually fraught with uncertainty. An important objective of the risk management process is to help managers deal with this uncertainty and identify the risks and opportunities their organization faces. Finding the right balance between risk and reward is one of the main functions of risk management. Shareholders in a company or investors in a fund have invested their money for the promise of a return at some risk level. By limiting the effect of events that may derail the organization's ability to achieve its objectives while benefiting from opportunities to grow the business profitably, risk management plays an important role in delivering value for these shareholders and investors.

The involvement of the board of directors and senior management is critical because they set corporate strategy and strategic business objectives. Although directors and senior managers are in charge of setting the appropriate level of risk to support the corporate strategy, risk management should involve all employees. One individual can

---

[1] COSO, *Enterprise Risk Management: Integrated Framework Executive Summary*, Committee of Sponsoring Organizations of the Treadway Commission (September 2004): www.coso.org/documents/coso_erm_executivesummary.pdf.

damage the reputation of a large institution and even lead to its demise. Reputations take years to build but can be lost in an instant. Markets are increasingly interdependent, and media and the internet can spread the news of a mistake or disaster across the globe in a matter of minutes. Risk management, therefore, is critical to protecting reputations and maintaining confidence among market participants.

## 3.2 Risk Management Process

A structured risk management process generally includes five steps, as illustrated in Exhibit 1.

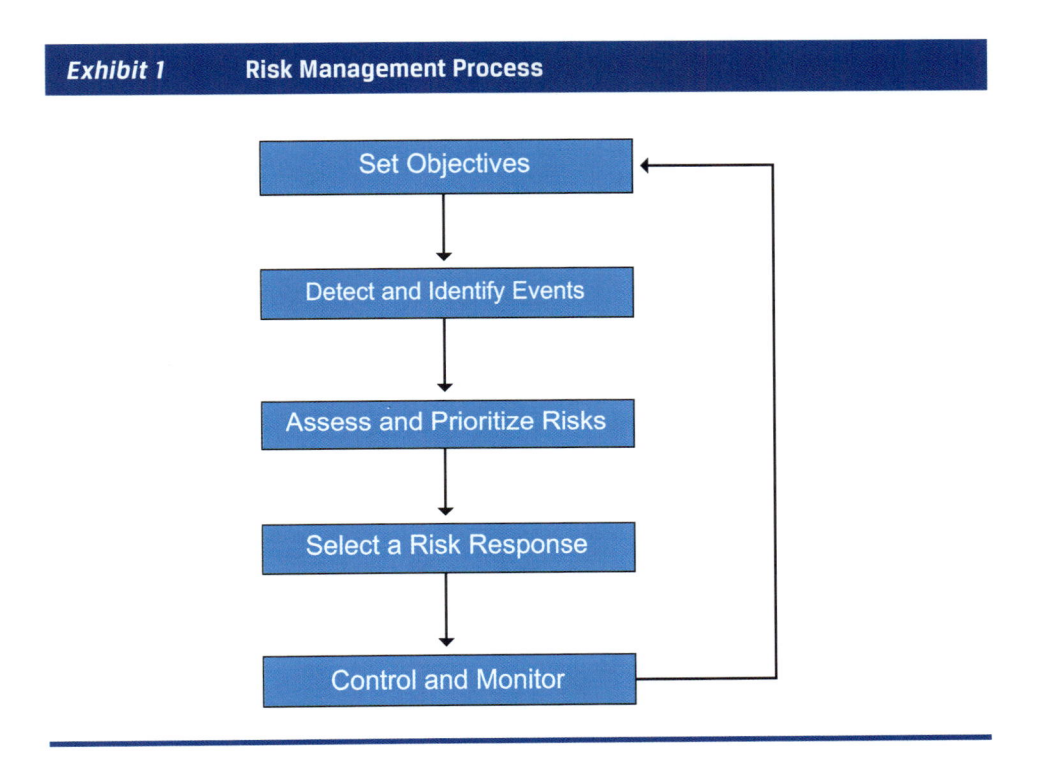

**Exhibit 1   Risk Management Process**

```
          Set Objectives ←──────┐
                │               │
                ▼               │
      Detect and Identify Events │
                │               │
                ▼               │
      Assess and Prioritize Risks│
                │               │
                ▼               │
        Select a Risk Response  │
                │               │
                ▼               │
         Control and Monitor ───┘
```

### 3.2.1 Set Objectives

Setting objectives is an important part of business planning. Risk management enables management to identify potential events that could affect the realization of those objectives. An organization may set strategic objectives, which are typically high-level objectives connected to its mission. It may also define objectives that are related to its operations. Many of these objectives depend on external factors that may be difficult for organizations to influence and control, leading to a high degree of uncertainty. A strong risk management process helps decision makers ensure that the organization is on track to achieve its objectives.

An important element to define at this stage is the organization's risk tolerance. **Risk tolerance** is the level of risk the organization is able and willing to take on. The ability to handle risk is primarily driven by the organization's financial health and depends on its level of earnings, cash flows, and equity capital. Its willingness to take on risk, which is also called its **risk appetite**, depends on its attitude toward risk and on its risk culture.

### 3.2.2 Detect and Identify Events

The next step in the risk management process is to detect and identify events that may affect the organization's objectives. As previously mentioned, the outcome of events can be negative, potentially leading to loss of earnings or assets, or they can be positive. Events may be familiar because they already have happened, either at the organization or at other organizations, or they may be identified as likely to occur based on perceived changes in the business environment.

The aim of risk management is to try to capture the full range of risks, including hidden or undetected ones. Therefore, organizations should involve staff who are in different roles and business areas to detect and identify as many events as possible. But there will always be unforeseen hazards. No matter how hard people try to reduce risk, it can never be completely eliminated. The complexity of the business environment makes it impossible to understand and model the large number of possible outcomes and combinations of outcomes with much hope for accuracy or even comprehensiveness. What risk management provides is a robust framework to help organizations prepare for adverse events, identify their occurrence as early as possible if they do materialize, and thus reduce their impact. The process of identifying potential risks can also at times reveal hidden value-enhancing opportunities.

### 3.2.3 Assess and Prioritize Risks

No matter what form risk takes, two elements are typically considered, in particular for undesirable events: the expected frequency of the event and the expected severity of its consequences. Different expected levels of frequency (highly unlikely, unlikely, possible, likely, or highly likely) and severity of outcomes (negligible, slightly harmful, harmful, extremely harmful, or catastrophic) can be specified. The combination of these two elements (expected frequency of the event and expected severity of its consequences) in a **risk matrix**, as illustrated in Exhibit 2, can be used to prioritize risks and to select the appropriate risk response for each risk identified.

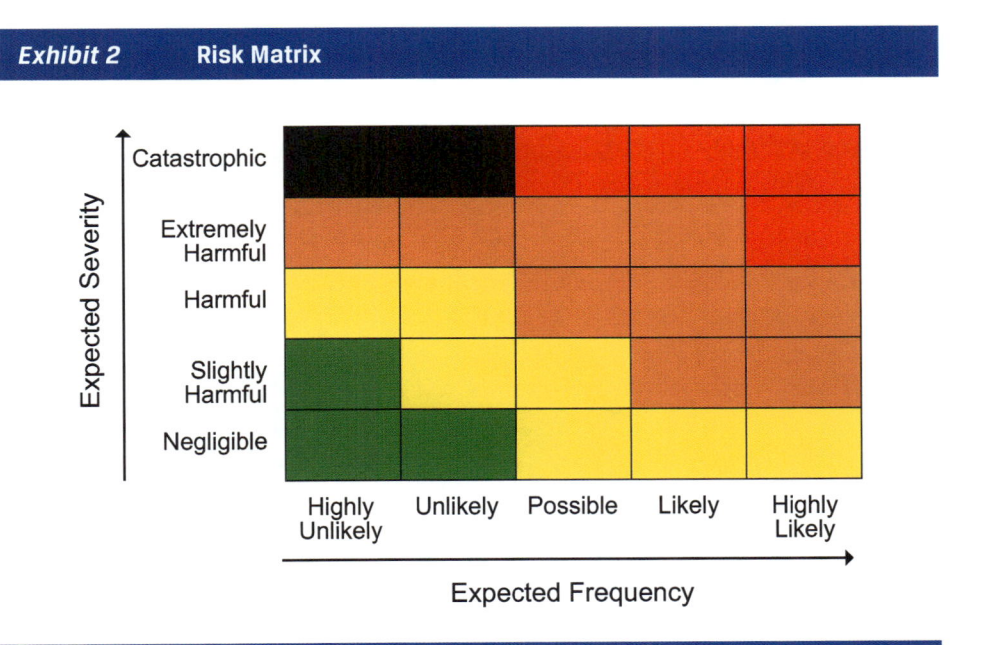

# Risk Management

**Exhibit 2     Risk Matrix**

[Risk matrix chart with Expected Severity (y-axis: Catastrophic, Extremely Harmful, Harmful, Slightly Harmful, Negligible) versus Expected Frequency (x-axis: Highly Unlikely, Unlikely, Possible, Likely, Highly Likely), color-coded from green (low) through yellow and orange to red (high), with a black cell at Catastrophic/Highly Unlikely.]

Depending on their expected level of frequency and severity, risks will receive different levels of attention. Risks in the green area should not receive much attention because they have a low expected frequency and a low expected severity. Risks coded yellow are either more likely but of low severity or more severe but unlikely. Thus, they should receive a little more attention than risks in the green area, but less attention than risks in the orange area. Risks coded orange have a higher expected frequency or higher expected severity, which is the reason why they should be monitored more actively. Risks that are in the red area should receive special attention because their effect on the organization would be very severe. Risks in the black area are highly unlikely but would have a catastrophic effect; these risks are sometimes called black swans, in reference to the presumption in Europe that black swans did not exist until they were discovered in Australia in the 17th century. Frequently, these risks are not identified until after the fact.

In practice, selecting **key risk measures** is very important for the risk management function to be proactive and preventive. Key risk measures should provide a warning when risk levels are rising. They require the collection and compilation of data from various internal and external sources. The set of key risk measures varies among industries and organizations and needs to be reviewed regularly to ensure that the measures are still relevant and sensitive to risk events.

Example 2 shows two key risk measures of many that may be used by a securities brokerage firm. The exhibit identifies the measure, the type of risk that it is concerned with, the source of information, and how to interpret the information.

> **EXAMPLE 2. TWO KEY RISK MEASURES USED BY A SECURITIES BROKERAGE FIRM**
>
> | Key Risk Measure | Type of Risk | Source of Data | Interpretation |
> |---|---|---|---|
> | Client satisfaction index | Operational risk | Client surveys | A decrease in the client satisfaction index may be an indication that the quality of client services is deteriorating, which may have a negative effect on the firm's ability to generate revenue and profit. |
> | Number of fines paid | Compliance risk | Legal or compliance department | An increase in the number of fines paid may be an indication that the firm does not comply with the required laws and regulations, which may result in the firm losing its ability to operate. |

#### 3.2.4 Select a Risk Response

The next critical step in risk management is to formulate responses to deal with the risks identified in the previous step. For each risk, management must select the appropriate response and develop actions to align the company's risk profile with its risk tolerance.

It is important to recognize that all organizations must take risks in the course of their business activities to be able to create value. Restricting activities to those that have no risk would not generate sufficient returns for shareholders or investors. Thus, they would be less willing to provide equity capital to companies or to invest their savings in the range of investments available. Each organization must, therefore, determine the risks that should be exploited, which are very often risks the organization has expertise in dealing with and can benefit from. The organizations must also determine the risks that should be mitigated, which are often risks it has little or no expertise in dealing with. By enabling managers to distinguish between the risks that are most likely to provide opportunities and the risks that are most likely to be harmful, a good risk management process helps to generate superior returns.

In practice, financial firms set **internal risk limits** that incorporate the overall risk tolerance and risk management strategy—for example, by specifying the maximum amount of a risky security that can be held or the maximum aggregate exposure to one asset type or to one specific counterparty. Defining and monitoring limits allows for risk response strategies to be implemented.

# Risk Management

Risk response strategies can be classified into four "T" categories:

- *Tolerate*. This strategy involves accepting the risk and its effect. In some cases, the risk is well understood and taking it provides opportunities to create value. In other cases, the risk must be taken because other risk response strategies are unavailable or too costly.

- *Treat*. This strategy involves taking action to reduce the risk and its effect.

- *Transfer*. This strategy involves moving the risk and its effect to a third party—for example, an insurance company.

- *Terminate*. This strategy involves avoiding the risk and its effect by ceasing activity.

Example 3 illustrates the use of the four risk response strategies by a bank.

> **EXAMPLE 3. RISK RESPONSE STRATEGIES FOR A BANK**
>
> Assume that a bank has expertise making loans to small corporations in its home country. A neighboring country is opening its economy and experiencing strong growth. The bank is looking for value-enhancing opportunities and decides to use its business expertise to make loans to small corporations in the neighboring country. At this stage, the bank is willing to *tolerate* the risks of doing business in a foreign country.
>
> A few years later, the bank has a large portfolio of loans in the neighboring country but the economic situation there is deteriorating. The bank is concerned about the risk of an increasing number of borrowers defaulting on their loans. Thus, it decides to *treat* this credit risk by implementing stricter criteria before granting loans to small corporations and by obtaining additional collateral to back each loan. Recall from Chapter 10 that collateral refers to the assets that secure a loan.
>
> The economic situation in the neighboring country continues to deteriorate, and the bank decides to *transfer* some of the credit risk to another financial institution that is willing to purchase part of the bank's portfolio of loans.
>
> A few months later, the neighboring country faces a recession, leading to social and political unrest. The bank makes the decision that it no longer wants to do business there. It sells the rest of its portfolio of loans to another financial institution and ceases all activities in the neighboring country. In doing so, the bank *terminates* all risks.

### 3.2.5 Control and Monitor

Taking action in response to risk involves a range of controlling and monitoring activities that must be performed in a timely manner. Policies and procedures provide a framework to help ensure that the risk responses are effectively carried out and monitored. Relevant information must be identified, captured, and reported accurately to enable people to carry out their responsibilities.

Risk management, like many processes, should be iterative and subject to regular evaluations and revisions. Results must be used to make appropriate adjustments, leading to a constant improvement in the risk management process.

At some point, risks must be consolidated and managed at the firm level, bringing together different risks into an overall risk exposure. **Enterprise risk management** (ERM) helps a company manage all its risks together in an integrated fashion rather than managing each risk separately. The advantage of this approach is that it aligns risk management with objectives at all levels of the organization, from the corporate level to the business unit level to the project level. ERM also clarifies the ever-changing interactions among risks.

## 3.3 Risk Management Functions

Risk management functions vary by organization, but it is typical for firms in the investment industry to have a stand-alone risk management function with a senior head (often called the chief risk officer) who is capable of independent judgment and action. The chief risk officer often reports directly to the board of directors. Risk and audit committees of the board will often hear presentations from the heads of risk, audit, and compliance. The purpose of establishing a strong independent function is to build checks and balances and to ensure that risks are seriously considered and balanced against other objectives, such as profitability.

Despite the existence of specialist risk managers, risk management remains everyone's responsibility. Risk managers assess, monitor, and report on risks, and in some cases, they may have an approval function or veto authority. But it is the members of the business functions, such as portfolio managers or traders, who "own" the risk of their deals. These employees have the most intimate knowledge of what they trade, and they must monitor their deals on a regular basis. The risk manager must ensure that all relevant risks are identified, but the final judgment on the investment or business decision lies with the business decision makers. Therefore, it is important for risk management to be part of the organization's corporate culture and to be fully integrated with core business activities. Exhibit 3 presents a summary of the risk responsibilities of various roles in an organization.

# Risk Management

**Exhibit 3    Risk Responsibility of Various Roles in an Organization**

| Role | Responsibility |
|---|---|
| Everyone | Risk management is everyone's responsibility. It should be part of the organization's corporate culture and be fully integrated with core business activities. |
| Portfolio managers or traders | They "own" the risk of their deals. They have the most intimate knowledge of what they trade, and they must monitor their deals on a regular basis. |
| Risk managers | They assess, monitor, and report on risks, and in some cases, they may have an approval function or veto authority. They must ensure that all relevant risks are identified. |
| Chief risk officers | They create checks and balances in the system and ensure that risks are seriously considered and balanced against other objectives. |

Organizations will often advocate a three-line-of-defense risk management model. Front-line employees and managers, through their daily responsibilities, form the first line of defense. The risk management and compliance groups operate as a second line of defense, both assisting and advising management while maintaining a certain level of independence. An internal audit function then forms the third line of defense. **Internal audit** is an independent function. Internal auditors follow risk-based internal audit programs, delving into the details of business process controls and ensuring that IT and accounting systems accurately reflect physical transactions. Proactive auditors may also advise business managers on how to improve risk management, controls, and efficiency. Best practice suggests that internal auditors should report directly to the audit committee to ensure their independence.

## 3.4  Benefits and Costs of Risk Management

Risk management provides a wide range of benefits to an organization. It can help by

- Supporting strategic and business planning;

- Incorporating risk considerations in all business decisions to ensure that the organization's risk profile is aligned with its risk tolerance;

- Limiting the amount of risks an organization takes, preventing excessive risk taking and potential related losses, and lowering the likelihood of bankruptcy;

- Bringing greater discipline to the organization's operations, which leads to more effective business processes, better controls, and a more efficient allocation of capital;

- Recognizing responsibility and accountability;

- Improving performance assessment and making sure that the compensation system is consistent with the organization's risk tolerance;

- Enhancing the flow of information within the organization, which results in better communication, increased transparency, and improved awareness and understanding of risk; and

- Assisting with the early detection of unlawful and fraudulent activities, thus complementing compliance procedures and audit testing.

All of these benefits should enhance the company's ability to create value.

The costs of establishing risk management systems range from tangible costs, such as hiring dedicated risk management personnel, putting in place procedures, and investing in systems, to intangible costs, such as slower decision making and lost opportunities. The immediate consequences of inadequate risk management are investment losses and even bankruptcy. Other costly consequences are also possible, such as sanctions for breaching regulations, loss of licenses to carry out financial services, and damage to the organization's and its employees' reputations.

### 3.5 Allocation of Resources

Allocation of resources to risk management should be based on a cost/benefit analysis. It is very difficult to weigh the costs and benefits of risk management precisely because it is impossible to observe, let alone measure, the cost of potential catastrophes that are averted ("near misses" may be recorded in some cases). It is only in hindsight that the cost/benefit trade-offs may be identified. A case in point is Barings Bank's collapse in 1995, which was triggered by huge trading losses hidden in the Singapore branch. At the time, there was no adequate and effective system for reconciling client orders and trades on a global basis, although such a system could have revealed the losses before they wiped out all of the bank's equity capital. It is estimated that implementing this system would have cost about £10 million, a small price to pay compared with the £287 million loss that brought down the bank.

There are limits to the efficacy of risk management because it relies on human judgment. Human failures, such as simple errors, can lead to inadequate risk responses. Controls can also be circumvented, and staff might override risk management decisions. These limitations mean that the board of directors and management can never have absolute assurance that the organization's objectives will be achieved.

## 4 RISK MEASUREMENT

In the context of investments, risk is very often expressed as the potential deviation of actual returns from expected returns. Risk, therefore, captures the variability (also called volatility) of future returns because of uncertainty and is very often measured as the standard deviation of returns, as explained in Chapter 5.

# Risk Measurement

## 4.1 Use and Advantages of Value at Risk

In the late 1980s, a new metric called **value at risk** (VaR) was developed, which is now a widely used technique to measure risk (in particular market risk) in the financial services industry. Value at risk gives an estimate of the minimum loss of value that can be expected for a given period with a given level of probability. For example, an asset management firm may estimate that a portfolio has a value at risk of $1 million for one day with a probability of 5%, which means that there is a 5% chance that the portfolio will fall in value by at least $1 million in a single day (assuming no further trading). Another way of viewing it is that a loss of $1 million or more for this portfolio is expected to occur, on average, every 20 days (1 ÷ 0.05).

Value at risk offers several advantages:

- It is a standard metric that can be applied across different investments, portfolios, business units, companies, and markets.

- It is relatively easy to calculate and well understood by senior managers and directors.

- It is a useful tool for risk budgeting if there is a central process for allocating capital across business units according to risk.

- It is widely used and mandated for use by some regulators.

## 4.2 Weaknesses of Value at Risk

There are weaknesses inherent in the value at risk measure of risk. Value at risk gives an estimate of the minimum but not the maximum loss of value that can be expected. Referring back to the earlier example, the asset management firm can expect a loss of at least $1 million 12 or 13 times a year (5% of the approximately 250 trading days a year). Value at risk does not indicate the maximum loss of value the portfolio manager can expect to bear in one day, and it does not guarantee that a loss in excess of $1 million will not happen more frequently than a dozen times a year.

In practice, value at risk very often underestimates the frequency and magnitude of losses, mainly because of erroneous assumptions and models. First, value at risk primarily relies on historical data to forecast future expected losses. But past returns may not be a good predictor of future returns. In addition, history is not helpful in forecasting events that have far-reaching effects but are unforeseen or considered impossible—that is, black swan events. Second, value at risk makes an assumption regarding the distribution of returns. For example, it is very often assumed that returns are normally distributed and follow the bell-shaped distribution presented in Chapter 5. However, evidence shows that the distribution of returns tends to have "fat tails"—that is, large positive and negative returns are far more frequent in reality than the normal distribution suggests. The use of historical data and the assumption of a normal distribution may work relatively well during times of normal market conditions, but not during periods of market turmoil.

The global financial crisis of 2008 is a case in point. Until 2007, most banks had a very low daily value at risk, which gave them a false sense of security. Once the crisis hit, the number of days when trading losses exceeded the daily value at risk and the amount of those losses were substantially higher than predicted. Some banks reported that the frequency of losses was 10 to 20 times higher than the value at risk predictions, and some banks recorded losses that significantly reduced their equity capital.

### 4.3 Alternatives to Value at Risk

To address these weaknesses, organizations—in particular, financial institutions—often use complementary risk management methodologies in addition to value at risk. These complementary methodologies include scenario analysis and stress testing, which focus on the effect of more extreme situations that would not be fully captured or evaluated with value at risk. For example, an asset management firm may perform a scenario analysis by identifying different scenarios for the economy (strong growth, moderate growth, slow growth, no growth, mild recession, and severe recession) and then determining how each scenario would affect the value of a portfolio and the firm's earnings and equity capital. The firm may also engage in stress testing by examining the effect of extreme market conditions, such as a liquidity crisis, to make sure that it would be resilient and would survive the crisis.

It is worth noting that the value at risk weaknesses apply to all techniques that rely on models. In this context, **model risk** refers to the risk arising from the use of models and ranges from inappropriate underlying assumptions to unavailability and inaccuracy of historical data, data errors, and misapplication of models.

## 5 OPERATIONAL RISKS AND THEIR MANAGEMENT

**Operational risk** has traditionally been less defined, studied, and modeled than market or credit risks, which are more readily quantifiable. But a widely accepted definition is that operational risk is the risk of losses from human, system, and process failures and from events that are beyond the control of the organization but affect its operations.

### 5.1 Managing People

Human failures range from unintentional errors to fraudulent activities. Many organizations are exposed to occupational fraud, which is when an employee abuses his or her position for personal gain by misappropriating the company's assets or resources. In a survey carried out by the Association for Certified Fraud Examiners (ACFE), anti-fraud experts estimated that organizations lose, on average, 5% of their annual revenues to fraud.

One example of operational risk that has a human component and that is more frequent in the financial services industry than in any other industry is rogue trading. **Rogue trading** refers to situations wherein traders bypass management controls and place unauthorized trades, at times causing large losses for the companies they work for. Rogue trading may involve fraudulent trading that is done for personal enrichment or to make up losses. Exhibit 4 lists some of the largest rogue trading incidents.

**Exhibit 4  Examples of Rogue Trading Incidents**

| Year of the Loss | Organization | Rogue Trader | Estimated Loss |
|---|---|---|---|
| 1995 | Barings Bank | Nick Leeson | £827 million |
| 1995 | Daiwa Bank | Toshihide Iguchi | US$1.1 billion |
| 1996 | Sumitomo Corporation | Yasuo Hamanaka | ¥285 billion |
| 2002 | Allied Irish Banks | John Rusnak | US$691 million |
| 2004 | National Australia Bank | Gianni Gray and others | AU$360 million |
| 2004 | China Aviation Oil | Chen Jiulin | US$550 million |
| 2008 | Société Générale | Jérôme Kerviel | €4.9 billion |
| 2008 | Groupe Caisse d'Epargne | Boris Picano-Nacci | €751 million |
| 2011 | UBS | Kweku Adoboli | $2.3 billion |

*Source:* Thomas S. Coleman, *A Practical Guide to Risk Management* (Charlottesville, VA: Research Foundation of CFA Institute, 2011):91–92.

Banks, like most organizations, have tried to learn from past events and plug the holes in their systems and controls to prevent similar events from reoccurring. The failure of Barings Bank in 1995 revealed the danger of not segregating front and back offices properly. In the small bank branch in Singapore, the same individuals managed both sides. An initial trading loss because of a human error was hidden in the accounting system, and subsequent losses accumulated until they exceeded the bank's equity capital. When faced with overwhelming trading losses, it is human nature to be tempted to increase risk taking and double one's bets to recover the losses.

Organizations can mitigate operational risks through education by clearly communicating policies and procedures and by having efficient and effective internal controls. Good human resource (HR) management processes are also critical for business success. Hiring the right people and motivating them with the right incentives are well-known ingredients for success. Risk management from an HR perspective covers such precautions as carrying out background checks (e.g., criminal records and disciplinary records with regulators) for new hires, verifying credentials and previous work experience, performing personality assessment tests, and getting character references to confirm suitability. Although these steps may appear to be standard procedures, studies have shown that discrepancies between presented and actual credentials are very common. Cases in which background checks of senior executives were not appropriately performed are regularly reported. Because of a loss of trust, some of these executives had to resign when the truth was revealed, even if they had performed successfully in their position.

Risk taking should also be considered in the structure of compensation (e.g., bonus payments) for employees—in particular, those exposing the company to significant risks, such as traders and other investment staff. A good compensation system should take into account the level of risk undertaken for a given level of return and should reward those who can achieve returns without taking excessive risks. An example of an incentive that could lead to perverse behavior is rewarding traders for profits regardless of the risks they take. This approach would give them all the upside for trading gains but less downside for trading losses. In practice, traders generating substantial losses typically lose their jobs and reputations, but they do not have to pay back much compared with the vast amounts they typically deal in and the bonus payments they previously received. Some authorities are now imposing new remuneration structures, which include deferred compensation to take into account long-term performance as well as claw-back provisions, whereby staff may have to return their bonuses if reported profitable deals result in losses later.

## 5.3 Managing Systems

Businesses rely heavily on IT systems. Consequently, technology has become an increasingly important source of operational risk. Automated processes can reduce the frequency and severity of operational errors, but they are not infallible. Failures of IT and communication systems very often paralyze business operations or greatly reduce their efficiency, harming the organization's profitability via lower revenues, higher costs, or a combination of both.

IT networks are inherently vulnerable to disruptions and outside interference because of both technical limitations and human factors. One source of risk is the behavior of employees who do not always follow internal company guidelines and download unauthorized applications for personal or business use. The dangers include malicious viruses and unlicensed and perhaps incompatible software getting into company systems. In addition, IT software and security companies are in a constant battle with hackers who exploit weaknesses to penetrate systems. Key controls to protect systems and business information include establishing and communicating policies and standards for users and IT technical staff, creating appropriate security standards and configurations for systems, and in general, allocating adequate personnel and technical resources to maintain a well-controlled IT environment.

Protecting confidential information is also important in the investment industry. Data privacy has received a great deal of prominence recently because of a number of cases in which companies and government agencies lost vast amounts of people's personal information, exposing them to the risk of fraud. An organization should understand how data are produced and flow internally, classify the information by sensitivity, assess the risks of data loss, and adopt appropriate measures. Many countries have strict laws and regulations for protecting customer data, along with severe penalties for violating these laws and regulations.

## 5.4 Managing the Environment

The type of environment in which a company operates can add layers of uncertainty.

### 5.4.1 Political Risk

**Political risk** is inherent in all markets. A change in the ruling political party of a country can lead to changes in policies that can affect taxation, interest rates, investment incentives, public investments, and procurement. Certain industries are heavily influenced by governments that, for example, control natural resources or set prices of raw material inputs or products. In these instances, a change in administration or policies can affect the value of the investment. Even if political risk is perceived to be relatively remote, it must be considered when planning for business continuity.

Because of the immature nature of market institutions and the lack of checks and balances in some emerging markets, political actors can have much greater influence over business decisions in those markets compared with in developed markets. Examples of corruption, politically motivated investigations, lack of independence, and excessive control over government institutions (such as the police, public prosecutors, and judges) regularly emerge and can damage organizations.

Risks in emerging markets are managed in much the same way as in more-developed markets. The difference lies in assessing the level of risk and prioritizing risk management efforts accordingly. Risk response measures should determine whether there is a greater risk that a measure may not be fully implemented as planned and whether additional monitoring and efforts are necessary for a larger margin of security and comfort.

### 5.4.2 Legal Risk

**Legal risk** is the risk that an external party could sue for breach of contract or other violations. Companies and individuals in disputes, for example, may resort to litigation in the form of high-profile class-action lawsuits. An organization should consider how it identifies and conforms to all legal commitments it has undertaken.

The role of an in-house legal expert is crucial in controlling legal risk. Most areas of a company have dealings with external parties, such as deal counterparties, business partners, suppliers, and service providers. An important control in managing the legal risk of these business relationships is to have legal experts review every contract.

Companies should clearly delegate authority and specify who in the organization should review and approve which type of contracts. The most significant deals usually require approval at the board of directors' level. Another control is to use template agreements and standard contract terms and conditions that have been reviewed and approved by legal counsel.

The storage of records, documents, and all forms of communication must also be in line with legal requirements for all relevant jurisdictions, as discussed in Chapter 16.

### 5.4.3 Settlement Risk

**Settlement risk** is the risk that when settling a transaction, a firm performs one side of the deal, such as transferring a security or funds, but the counterparty does not complete its side of the deal as agreed, often because of declaring bankruptcy. This risk is sometimes also called Herstatt risk because of an incident in 1974 when the German Herstatt Bank ceased operations after counterparties had honored their obligation to transfer Deutsche marks to Herstatt but before Herstatt honored its obligation to transfer the equivalent amount in U.S. dollars back to these counterparties.

Although there are usually legal means to compel a counterparty to perform its obligations, such measures are costly and time-consuming. A counterparty is more likely to find it difficult to fulfill its obligations during challenging economic times or when bankruptcy is imminent than during profitable times. In the case of bankruptcy, it may take months or years to receive assets through a bankruptcy resolution procedure and the proceeds may only be a fraction of the original nominal amount of debt.

It is important to distinguish the risks inherent in bilateral arrangements from those in transactions contracted through central counterparties, such as the clearing houses presented in Chapter 13. Clearing houses may step in to assume the risk of a counterparty failing to meet its contractual obligations. Other arrangements to reduce this risk are margin requirements, discussed in Chapter 11, or standardized agreements.

## 5.5 Business Continuity and Disaster Recovery Planning

In today's business environment, it is crucial for businesses to continue essential operations in case of disasters or other unanticipated events. Events can include both risks specific to the firm and market-wide risks, such as natural disasters. **Business continuity planning** refers to the creation of plans to keep business processes running, and **disaster recovery planning** refers specifically to the technical systems side of contingency planning.

The September 11, 2001, attacks in the United States demonstrated an extreme scenario of what businesses should consider when planning for disasters. Despite the massive losses in people and infrastructure, the New York Stock Exchange was able to open six days later, when telecommunications and other essential services had been restored. This experience taught many in the industry a lesson about the importance of having a plan for disaster recovery, including assessing whether back-up facilities are dispersed or concentrated in one area, determining the interdependency of key counterparties and service providers, and evaluating the accessibility of key staff to improve the overall resiliency of the financial systems.

Organizations should perform risk assessments to determine the acceptable parameters for various processes and functions as well as the amount of downtime that is acceptable in the event of disaster. Organizations can thus plan systems and processes accordingly. How much preparation a company must make depends on the nature of the business. For instance, customer-facing services, such as automated teller machines (ATMs) and online banking services, should be very robust, with extra capacity built in to ensure negligible interruptions in services. Electronic trading platforms, which have high volumes of computer-generated transactions, are another example of operations susceptible to disruptions because multiple links to other systems can trigger a chain of disruptions. In contrast, a private equity firm may have limited time-sensitive activities, such as end-of-the-month reporting.

In a world where companies are focusing more and more on their core business competencies and outsourcing non-core activities to specialist service providers, the boundaries of business continuity planning must expand to capture the risk exposure in the activities conducted outside the organization. The decision to outsource a business process in the first place should be informed by the risks associated with loss of management control over the process. Despite due diligence and enquiries to establish the reliability and trustworthiness of service providers, including their business continuity and disaster recovery planning processes, some level of uncertainty will always exist. Many organizations use service level agreements—detailed contracts between service providers and their clients—to specify performance measures, monitoring, and reporting processes. Service level agreements clarify expectations, commitments, and means of recourse for failures in service. It is worth emphasizing that organizations can outsource non-core activities but not all the risks associated with those activities.

# COMPLIANCE RISKS AND THEIR MANAGEMENT

**Compliance risk** is the risk that an organization fails to comply with all applicable rules, laws, and regulations and faces sanctions as a result.

## 6.1 Compliance with Internal Policies and Procedures

The foundation and structure of an organization vary with the size and type of business, but there are common features in all organizations. Power and authority are delegated and responsibilities are assigned within the organization. In smaller entrepreneurial entities, such assignments may be communicated informally, with staff members understanding their individual roles and degrees of authority. In larger and more complex organizations, the roles and levels of authority will be formally defined and the business processes mapped out in more detail, usually even embedded in corporate management systems. Policies and procedures should explicitly set out the delegation of authority and define clear responsibilities and accountability. These definitions form the basis for the monitoring of and control over business processes and provide feedback mechanisms.

The segregation of duties is an important principle that international organizations and authorities in many countries require and recommend. A clear separation needs to exist between the front and back offices. In accounting departments, there should also be a clear separation between those who enter items into the accounts and those who reconcile the bank statements with the cash balances in the accounting system. This separation of roles reduces the risk that staff members who control cash will commit fraud or embezzle funds.

In addition to managing business functions, compliance and internal audit functions are key to ensuring that staff is actually following internal policies and procedures.

## 6.2 Compliance with Laws and Regulations

Ensuring compliance with rules and regulations has often been viewed as a rather mundane chore, but the rapidly changing regulatory environment has recently brought compliance to the forefront of business priorities. Many people believe that the trend toward less regulation contributed to the global financial crisis that began in 2008. The trend has reversed toward the re-imposition of greater regulation and oversight.

### 6.2.1 Framework

Every company has to follow a set of rules, beginning with the statutory laws and other regulations imposed by regulatory bodies. In addition, companies must attend to various forms of guidelines from regulators, stock exchanges, and industry associations that have been given powers to oversee members. There are differences among regulatory environments according to sector because of such factors as systemic significance for the financial system and protection of beneficiaries' pensions. Banking and insurance have historically been subject to very heavy regulation, with detailed rules and scrutiny from regulatory authorities. For example, banks are subject to the Basel Accords. Accords are international agreements, and these international agreements generally take the name of the location where they are signed. The Basel Accords, which define international standards regarding banks' capital, leverage, and liquidity requirements, are discussed on a regular basis in Basel, Switzerland. As of September 2012, the latest version of these accords is Basel III.

Complying with applicable laws and regulations is required of every organization. The consequences of not doing so can be severe and can include financial penalties, loss of business licenses, lawsuits by clients, and in serious cases, even prison terms. Often the greatest consequences are the damage to the firm's reputation and the loss of existing and potential business opportunities.

Companies should have internal reporting procedures to encourage employees to come forward and report instances in which they suspect someone has violated internal policies, procedures, laws, or regulations. Whistle blowing has become an important avenue for authorities to learn about violations, and provisions to protect and reward whistle-blowers have been strengthened in the wake of financial scandals.

The following sections cover typical requirements that companies face and must consider throughout their risk management processes. We start by presenting those that are more general in nature and then highlight those that are more specific.

### 6.2.2 Anti-Corruption Laws

**Corruption,** which is defined as the abuse of power for private gain, has received heightened attention because of tightened laws and regulations on bribery and increased regulatory scrutiny, investigations, prosecutions, and fines. Some national authorities may apply these laws extra-territorially, even to foreign companies. Companies that operate through agents and other third parties should be aware that their responsibility for preventing corruption extends to the actions of these third parties. Ignoring the practices of third parties does not constitute a defense in the event of a regulatory investigation. To safeguard against corruption, companies must start by establishing a tone at the top, with senior management communicating an unambiguous policy of zero tolerance for unethical business practices and bribery. Risk assessments should identify major risk areas and susceptible employees. For instance, employees who deal with government officials for licensing or deal with government or state-owned entities should have enhanced training and be monitored closely. Controls over corporate gifts and hospitality, especially in payment-processing areas, are crucial for preventing illegal or unethical payments.

### 6.2.3 Financial Accounting and Reporting

The integrity of financial reporting is a key element of well-functioning financial markets, and it is crucial for investor confidence. But financial accounting and reporting is not an exact process. Considerable scope exists for recognition of and accounting for items. In addition, company executives have strong incentives to present favorable pictures of their companies' financial strength and performance. Executive compensation packages usually include performance bonuses, such as stock options, which depend on the company's stock price. Higher reported income may lead to a higher stock price, at least in the short run, meaning that managers will receive higher bonuses and can exercise their stock options profitably. The cases of Enron, WorldCom, and Parmalat, in which financial reports were fraudulently manipulated, raised awareness of the vulnerability in financial reporting processes and led to stricter legislation that imposes greater accountability and penalties on company officers.

From a risk management perspective, it is important to have robust accounting systems and processes in place to ensure that financial reporting and accounting standards are met. Controls include reconciling accounts (e.g., between the accounting system and other business systems), internal manager reviews and approvals of account postings, consistency in the application of accounting choices across business units and over time, and internal and external audits to minimize the risk of errors or fraud in financial reporting.

Any organization making investments in financial instruments or in other companies should also understand the accounting and financial reporting associated with these investments. In-house analysis of financial statements and reviews of reports by outside analysts help establish the extent to which financial reports and information should be relied on and whether they present a risk factor to consider in investment decisions. In some types of transactions, such as private equity investments in which a controlling stake is being negotiated, the investor may have greater access to internal financial information of the target company and may perform more detailed due diligence and analysis.

### 6.2.4 Tax Reporting

Compliance with tax regulations is a very complicated issue because the principles and rules vary considerably by jurisdiction. Companies are continuously developing financial and legal structures, often with the intention of minimizing taxes overall. Uncertainty exists in how tax authorities will apply their rules, which is compounded by the fact that rules change regularly. A conservative approach is to conform to tried-and-tested precedents. A more aggressive approach is to seek to exploit loopholes in the tax code, low-tax jurisdictions (so-called off-shore tax havens), and other gray areas.

There is a technical difference between "tax avoidance," which means using tax code provisions to minimize the tax that is owed, and "tax evasion," which means not paying taxes in violation of the tax law. In practice, however, the line between tax avoidance and tax evasion is not always clear and expert tax advice is thus necessary. From a risk management perspective, tax risk should be managed in a consistent manner, incorporating the appropriate expertise at each stage of a transaction or financial reporting cycle.

### 6.2.5 Market Disclosures

Depending on the nature of the business, there can be various types of compulsory regulatory disclosure requirements. Stock exchanges and market regulators typically have a range of disclosures, which may be required as soon as a trigger event occurs or a threshold is reached. For holdings in a particular stock, there can, for example, be significant shareholder disclosures designed to inform the market of potential takeover activity, directors' dealings in shares of the company, or short positions.

Because of the strict timing requirements for these types of notifications, processes must be in place to immediately detect relevant events and to report them promptly according to deadlines. Class-action lawsuits under U.S. securities laws have highlighted the risk companies may face if timely disclosure processes are not followed. A sharp fall in stock price can lead securities lawyers to file class-action lawsuits alleging that shareholders suffered losses because the issuer withheld material financial information. In businesses that operate across a range of markets and exchanges, keeping track of the rules for each market and changes to those rules can entail allocating a great deal of resources.

### 6.2.6 Conflicts of Interest

All organizations should seek to prevent conflicts of interest by requiring clear controls and transparency to ensure adherence to the duties of loyalty and fiduciary responsibilities (managing assets in the best interests of investors and shareholders). If conflicts of interest cannot be avoided, they must be clearly disclosed.

One area that may give rise to conflicts of interest is "front running," which involves placing personal trading orders ahead of the firm's order to benefit from the price change. To prevent individuals from taking advantage of information on company investments and trading plans to place profitable personal trades, employees' personal trading must be disclosed and actively monitored.

Transactions conducted with counterparties that are in some way related to the firm, its employees, or its directors can also create conflicts of interest. Some type of ownership or business interest in the counterparty may bias individuals involved in the decision-making process and lead to sub-optimal decisions for the company and its providers of capital. When organizations are considering third-party transactions, they should implement additional controls, such as independent external valuations and approval by the board of directors. Full disclosure and consent can largely mitigate potential perceptions of conflicts of interest.

### 6.2.7 Insider Trading

There are laws prohibiting firms from trading a security when they are in possession of important confidential information pertaining to the security in question. Most markets have recently tightened laws regulating insider trading, which has not always been considered a serious offense. Another trend is an increase in investigations of insider trading; some such investigations are even relying on techniques similar to those used in investigations of organized crime cases—including tapping telephones, using evidence already collected to make peripheral suspects cooperate, and gradually circling in to catch the central participants of the scheme. Although the use of insider information is clear in cases in which information is obtained directly from an insider of the company in question, many gray areas exist where it is difficult to determine clearly what information is material.

Organizations must implement policies and procedures to ensure that traders understand the laws and that nobody in the organization will be in the position to violate them. For example, a trader must understand how to identify what confidential information meets the definition of material insider information, how to report that the firm is in possession of specific information so that trading by others in the firm can be prevented, and who to ask for advice when needed. Firms that face a high risk of insider trading, such as investment banks, have "control rooms" to monitor information flowing between teams. They also have virtual walls or information barriers to restrict and segregate information and to manage other conflicts of interest. These virtual walls are sometimes called Chinese walls in reference to the screens that were common in China to separate large areas into smaller rooms.

### 6.2.8 Anti-Money Laundering

Anti-money-laundering legislation is a set of rules to prevent proceeds derived from criminal activities from entering the financial system and acquiring the appearance of being from legitimate sources. These rules require financial institutions to obtain sufficient original or certified documentation to perform a formal risk assessment on each client and counterparty; the procedures of such an assessment are called Know Your Customer (KYC) procedures.

International agreements defining basic principles and requirements for anti-money-laundering frameworks have been developed and are implemented with slight variations according to the jurisdiction. A notable feature of most anti-money-laundering regulation is a strict liability approach to compliance; that is, a firm can be subject to severe sanctions as a result of not following required procedures and record-keeping, regardless of whether any suspicious transactions are handled or any actual damage is caused.

### 6.2.9 Product Suitability for Clients

Recent scandals and penalties have highlighted one of the central problems in the investment industry: Financial products are often too complicated for the average consumer to understand, and sellers of these products may have incentives to offer and recommend the wrong products to the consumer. For example, between 2002 and 2008, Hong Kong retail banks and brokerage firms sold a total of HK$14.7 billion of Lehman Brothers' investment products—mainly unlisted notes linked to the credit of various companies—to about 43,700 retail investors. After Lehman's bankruptcy in 2008, investors lost most, if not all, of the principal amount they had invested. Vocal consumer protests ensued, and lengthy investigations by authorities found that many investors were not properly assessed for suitability with regard to the products sold to them nor were the investors clearly advised of the risks associated with these products. The retail banks and brokerage firms were fined, and their reputations suffered.

Today, banks and other institutions in most developed markets have comprehensive systems to ensure that considerations regarding the financial profile and circumstances of each client are incorporated into the advisory/selling process. When a dispute exists, the financial institution may have to demonstrate adequate processes and records of compliance with regulations.

### 6.2.10 *Gatekeepers*

Various service providers act as independent gatekeepers in the financial system. This role applies to custodians (who hold and safeguard investor assets), administrators and registrars (who ensure that shareholdings are recorded and administered accurately and reliably), appraisers and valuers (who independently assess and value investments), and accountants and auditors (who review financial accounting and reporting). Organizations should determine how partnering with independent service providers can mitigate risks internally and how risks related to these relationships should be managed.

## 7 INVESTMENT RISKS AND THEIR MANAGEMENT

**Investment risks** can take different forms depending on the organization's investments and operations. Firms in the investment industry typically experience three broad categories of investment risks: (1) market risk, which arises from price movements in financial markets; (2) credit risk, which arises when borrowers fail to meet repayment obligations; and (3) liquidity risk, which is associated with changes in market demand for securities. A common theme for success in all types of investment risk management is the need to understand the risks and price them accurately.

### 7.1 Market Risk

**Market risk** is the risk caused by changes in market conditions, which affect expected cash flows as well as supply and demand and, therefore, prices. Market risks can be further classified into the risks associated with the underlying market instruments: equity price risk, interest rate risk (for debt securities), foreign exchange rate risk, and commodity price risk.

Market risk can also be divided into systematic risk, which is related to the overall financial market, and non-systematic risk, which is specific to the issuer or to the security. Modern portfolio theory holds that there are benefits to be gained from diversifying investments. As the number of securities in the portfolio increases, the non-systematic risk (also called idiosyncratic risk or specific risk in Chapter 9) decreases, improving the risk–return profile of the portfolio. If securities are not perfectly positively correlated, adding more securities to a portfolio will provide a risk-reduction effect.

The effect of correlation between stocks can be illustrated with the following example. Consider an investor who purchases two stocks, one from a company that manufactures automobiles and the other one from a company that produces oil and gas products. Also assume that the price of oil is the key factor driving the earnings of both companies. When the price of oil rises, it would be expected that the vehicle manufacturer would suffer a loss in sales whereas the oil and gas company would gain an increase in income. In other words, the two stocks are negatively correlated—that is, their stock prices tend to move in opposite directions. When the influence of correlations between stocks is aggregated in a portfolio, it turns out that the greater the diversification, the better the overall risk–return profile. But it is important to note that correlations are not immutable relationships and that they may change, especially during periods of market turmoil.

Many investment firms are in the business of taking investment risks, and they tend to tolerate market risks. But like any other organization, they must align their risk profiles with their risk tolerance. They often implement an approach called **risk budgeting** to determine how risk should be allocated among different business units, portfolios, or individuals. For example, an asset management firm may use the following risk budgeting steps:

- Quantify the amount of risk that can be taken by the organization;

- Set risk budgets and limits for each asset class and/or investment manager;

- Allocate assets in compliance with the risk budgets; and

- Monitor that risk budgets are respected.

Market risks that cannot be tolerated must be mitigated, and organizations have different alternatives available. One of them is to hedge unwanted risks by using derivative instruments, as explained in Chapter 11. For example, a U.K.-based portfolio manager who is concerned that the broad equity market will decrease over the next year may take a short position in a futures contract on the FTSE 100 Index.

## 7.2 Credit Risk

**Credit risk** is the risk for a lender that a borrower will fail to honor a contract and make timely payments of interest and principal. When assessing the creditworthiness of borrowers, it is important to consider both their ability and willingness to repay their debts. For instance, after the fall in real estate prices in 2008, many homeowners in the United States were left with mortgages that had larger balances than the market value of the property. Some of those borrowers still had the ability to keep paying their mortgages but decided to default and let the bank take possession of the property because they were in negative equity. This decision is rational from a purely financial perspective, aside from the side effect of getting a worse credit profile for future borrowing.

The expected loss from credit exposure is a function of three elements: the amount the lender has exposed to a particular borrower, the probability that the borrower defaults, and the loss that would be incurred if the borrower defaults. The amount that is at risk may be reduced if collateral (assets that are pledged to secure the loan) or guarantees from third parties are included. Enforcing contract provisions to take possession of collateral, however, can be a time-consuming legal process. The value of collateral assets for a lender depends on their liquidity and marketability—that is, how easy it is to sell the assets to a third party and at how much of a discount if sold on short notice. Assets for which a steady market demand exists and that can be easily transferred are more valuable than assets that are traded less frequently and are less flexible.

Various sources of independent information exist on borrower creditworthiness, such as credit rating agencies, which should be used in conjunction with internal risk analysis to form a more complete picture of the counterparty. When relying on any analysis, internal or external, a degree of critical judgment and skepticism should always be maintained.

There are various approaches to managing credit risk, including:

- Setting limits on the amount of exposure to a particular counterparty or level of credit rating allowed. For example, a maximum limit of 5% exposure could be set for a particular counterparty.

- Requiring additional collateral and imposing covenants. Covenants, discussed in Chapter 10, are terms for loans that specify both what a borrower must do (positive covenants) and what a borrower is not allowed to do (negative covenants). For example, a bank may restrict borrowers from issuing more debt, paying dividends, or entering into highly risky business ventures. When one of the restrictive conditions is broken, the lender may recall the loan or demand some action, such as the assignment of additional collateral.

- Transferring risk using derivative instruments. Credit default swaps are often used when organizations want to protect themselves against the risk of counterparty default, as discussed in Chapter 11.

Lending to foreign governments or state-owned companies creates another risk. **Sovereign risk** is the risk that a foreign government will not repay its debt because it does not have either the ability or the willingness to do so. A foreign government can also prevent borrowers in its country from repaying their debts—for example, by implementing currency controls to make it difficult or impossible for money to leave the country. The unique aspect of sovereign risk is that lenders have limited legal remedies available to compel the borrower to repay or to be able to recover the assets themselves.

## 7.3 Liquidity Risk

Liquidity refers to the ability to buy and sell quickly without incurring a loss. It is a core concern for companies and is often neglected when sources of finance, such as bank credit, are plentiful. But during the global financial crisis of 2008, an acute shortage of liquidity in the banking systems in many countries led to a general withdrawal of credit lines from borrowers across the board. Business failures increased because some companies were unable to maintain access to sufficient funds to finance their working capital (inventories and receivables from customers net of payables from suppliers) and, therefore, to keep their businesses going.

Firms in the investment industry face a greater level of liquidity risk than, say, manufacturers. **Liquidity risk** comes from the fact that banks, insurance companies, and asset management firms must regularly buy and sell financial instruments. To manage their businesses profitably, they need markets that can accommodate their trades without significant adverse effects on prices. When markets are illiquid—either temporarily, such as during financial crises, or more structurally, such as in some emerging markets—the ability to trade assets is substantially reduced, which has a negative effect on these companies.

## CONCLUSION

This chapter describes how risk management is an integral part of business operations. To some extent, everyone faces and addresses risks at work on a daily basis, whether consciously or not. Although most firms have dedicated risk management functions, it is important to remember that risk is not just the responsibility of the risk management team; everyone is a risk manager. Good risk management frameworks will force responsibilities and objectives to cascade down to all levels of a firm. Therefore, even if you are not a risk management specialist, you should still seek to understand risk management methodology, systems, and tools and participate in risk management activities in your organization.

## SUMMARY

- Risk is defined as the effect of uncertain future events on an organization or on the outcome the organization achieves. Types of risks are often categorized according to the source of risk (e.g., operational risk, market risk, credit risk, or liquidity risk).

- Risk management is an iterative process that helps organizations minimize the chances and effects of adverse events while maximizing the realization of opportunities. This process includes setting objectives, detecting/identifying events, assessing risk, formulating a risk response, and controlling/monitoring activities.

- Risk assessment involves analyzing all risks an organization faces and understanding their likelihood, potential effects, and degree of severity for the organization. Building a risk matrix and selecting key risk indicators are important to prioritize risks and warn appropriate staff members when risk levels are rising.

- Risk response strategies include exploiting risks the organization has expertise dealing with and can benefit from and mitigating risks with which the organization has little or no expertise. Risk mitigation includes treating (reducing) risk, transferring it, or terminating it all together.

- Despite the existence of specialist risk managers, risk management remains everyone's responsibility and must be an integral part of the organization's corporate culture.

- Allocation of resources to risk management should be based on a cost/benefit analysis. Typical costs include tangible costs (e.g., recruiting and training staff) as well as intangible costs (e.g., slower decision-making process and missed opportunities). Risk management should have a positive effect on an organization's ability to achieve its strategic objectives and improve its operations, ultimately leading to value creation.

- Value at risk, which provides an estimate of the minimum loss of value that can be expected for a given period of time with a given probability, is one of the most widely used techniques to measure risk. By relying on historical data and making assumptions about the distribution of returns, value at risk suffers from limitations that are typical to all measures that are based on historical data and models.

- Operational risk is the risk of losses from human, system, and process failures and from external events that affect the organization's operations. Reducing the risk of fraud and rogue trading; investing in robust IT systems; managing political, legal, and settlement risks; and developing business continuity and disaster recovery planning are part of establishing a stronger risk management framework.

- Compliance risks are the risks that an organization faces if it fails to follow all applicable laws and regulations; the organization may face sanctions as a result of non-compliance. Firms in the investment industry must respect market disclosures and anti-money-laundering regulation, prevent front running and insider trading, and ensure product suitability for clients.

- Investment risks take different forms depending on the organization's investments and operations. They include three types of risk: market risk, caused by changes in market conditions affecting prices; credit risk, caused by borrowers' inability and/or unwillingness to make timely payments of interest and principal; and liquidity risk, caused by difficulties in buying or selling securities at the required price.

# CHAPTER REVIEW QUESTIONS

Test your knowledge of this chapter at **cfainstitute.org/claritasstudy**.

1 A type of risk that is **not** directly related to investment risk is:

   A   credit risk.

   B   liquidity risk.

   C   operational risk.

2 Which of the following situations *best* represents a compliance risk?

   A   A counterparty does not fulfill its side of a transaction as agreed.

   B   An organization fails to follow all applicable laws and regulations.

   C   An employee does not complete his or her tasks in a timely manner.

3 Which of the following is **not** an objective of a risk management process?

   A   To eliminate all risks

   B   To identify opportunities

   C   To help managers deal with uncertainty

4 Which of the following is **not** a typical step of a risk management process?

   A   Select a risk response

   B   Assess and prioritize risks

   C   Transfer risk to a third party

5 An organization's risk tolerance level depends primarily on the organization's:

   A   ability to take risk.

   B   willingness to take risk.

   C   both its ability and its willingness to take risk.

Copyright © 2012 CFA Institute

**6** A risk matrix, useful for assessing the level of attention a certain risk should receive, classifies risks according to:

**A** systematic and non-systematic risk exposures.

**B** expected levels of frequency and severity of consequences.

**C** operational, compliance, and investment risk exposures.

**7** An exporter will receive payment in a foreign currency in a month. It decides to hedge the currency risk by using a forward contract to lock in the exchange rate at which it will convert the payment in a month. Which of the following risk response strategies has the exporter *most likely* chosen?

**A** Take the currency risk

**B** Tolerate the currency risk

**C** Terminate the currency risk

**8** A significant benefit of implementing a risk management process is *most likely*:

**A** elimination of risk.

**B** less accountability.

**C** more efficient allocation of capital.

**9** Which of the following is **not** an example of a cost of establishing a risk management system?

**A** Slower decision making

**B** Increased flow of information

**C** Hiring dedicated risk management personnel

**10** Using historical data to forecast future expected losses works relatively well:

**A** all the time.

**B** during times of market turmoil.

**C** during times of normal market conditions.

**11** Rogue trading is *best* described as an example of:

**A** investment risk.

**B** operational risk.

**C** compliance risk.

**12** Which of the following situations *most likely* reduces an organization's operational risk?

  **A** An increase in the number of suppliers of raw materials

  **B** The installation of a backup system for critical information

  **C** A compensation system that focuses on short-term performance

**13** Which of the following situations *most likely* increases an organization's compliance risk?

  **A** Using agents and third parties

  **B** Separating the front and back offices

  **C** Monitoring and controlling business processes

**14** Credit risk is *best* described as the risk of:

  **A** losing money when interest rates rise.

  **B** lacking access to credit lines when needed.

  **C** failing to receive timely payments from borrowers.

# ANSWERS

1. C is correct. Operational risk is not directly related to investment risk. It refers to the risk of losses from human, system, and process failures and from events that are beyond the control of the organization but that affect its operations. A and B are incorrect because credit risk and liquidity risk are risks that are directly related to investment risk. Credit risk refers to a borrower's ability and willingness to repay debts. Liquidity risk relates to the difficulty of buying or selling securities at the required price within a certain period of time.

2. B is correct. Compliance risk is the risk that an organization fails to follow all applicable laws and regulations and faces sanctions as a result. A is incorrect because it describes settlement risk (also called counterparty risk)—the risk of a counterparty's not fulfilling its side of a transaction as agreed. C is incorrect because a situation in which an employee does not complete his or her tasks in a timely manner is an example of operational risk.

3. A is correct. The objective of a risk management process is not to eliminate all risks. It is to find the right balance between risk and reward—that is, to distinguish the risks that should be exploited (they are very often risks the organization has expertise in dealing with and can benefit from) from the risks that should be mitigated (the risks the organization has little or no expertise in dealing with). B and C are incorrect because a risk management process should help managers identify opportunities and deal with uncertainty in making decisions.

4. C is correct. Transferring risk to a third party is not a step in a risk management process but is one of the four risk response strategies. The five steps of a risk management process are (1) set objectives, (2) detect and identify events, (3) assess and prioritize risks, (4) select a risk response, and (5) control and monitor risks. Transferring risk to a third party is not always a suitable risk response strategy. Other strategies that may be more appropriate for some of the risks the organization faces are tolerating, treating, or terminating the risk.

5. C is correct. Risk tolerance is the level of risk an organization is able and willing to take. The ability to take risk is primarily driven by the organization's financial health and depends on its level of earnings, cash flows, and equity capital. Its willingness to take risk, which is also called its risk appetite, depends on its attitude toward risk and on its risk culture.

6. B is correct. A risk matrix is used to assess and prioritize the variety of risks an organization may face. A risk matrix classifies risks according to the expected level of frequency of the event (e.g., highly unlikely, unlikely, possible, likely, or highly likely) and the expected severity of its consequences (e.g., negligible, slightly harmful, harmful, extremely harmful, or catastrophic). A and C are incorrect because although systematic, non-systematic, operational, compliance, and investment risk exposures are risk classifications, they are not identified in a risk matrix.

# Answers

**7** C is correct. By locking in the exchange rate at which it will convert the payment in foreign currency in a month, the exporter has taken action to terminate the currency risk. It has not, however, eliminated all risks because there is settlement risk (also called counterparty risk) associated with the forward contract. A and B are incorrect because the exporter would take or tolerate the currency risk if it had decided not to hedge. In this case, it would have accepted the currency risk and its effects.

**8** C is correct. One of the benefits of implementing a risk management process is greater discipline in operations, leading to more effective business processes, better controls, and a more efficient allocation of capital. A is incorrect because implementing a risk management process can serve to incorporate risk considerations in all business decisions to ensure that the organization's risk profile is aligned with its risk tolerance, but it does not lead to the elimination of risk. Some risks should be eliminated, but others may be exploited—for example, the risks the organization has expertise in dealing with and can benefit from. B is incorrect because implementing a risk management process leads to more rather than less accountability.

**9** B is correct. Establishing a risk management system enhances the flow of information within the organization. It is a benefit, not a cost. A and C are incorrect because slower decision making and hiring dedicated risk management personnel are costs associated with establishing a risk management system.

**10** C is correct. Using historical data to forecast future expected losses works relatively well when past returns are a good predictor of future returns—that is, during times of normal market conditions.

**11** B is correct. Rogue trading, which refers to situations wherein traders bypass management controls and place unauthorized trades that can cause large losses for the companies they work for, is an example of operational risk. Operational risk is the risk of losses from human, system, and process failures and from events that are beyond the control of the organization but affect its operations. A is incorrect because investment risk is the risk associated with investing. C is incorrect because compliance risk is the risk that an organization fails to comply with all applicable laws and regulations and faces sanctions as a result.

**12** B is correct. The installation of a backup system for critical information is likely to reduce operational risk, which is the risk of losses from human, system, and process failures and from events that are beyond the control of the organization but that affect its operations. A and C are incorrect because an increase in the number of suppliers of raw materials and a compensation system that focuses on short-term performance are likely to increase, rather than reduce, operational risk.

**13** A is correct. Using agents and third parties increases compliance risk. It is more difficult to monitor and control these agents and third parties than internal staff, but the organization may still be responsible for the actions of these agents and third parties. B and C are incorrect because separating the front and back offices and monitoring and controlling business processes decrease compliance risk.

**14** C is correct. Credit risk is the lender's risk that a borrower fails to honor contracts and to make timely payments of interest and principal. A and B are incorrect because they are types of investment risk. Losing money when interest rates rise describes market risk. Lacking access to credit lines when needed describes liquidity risk, which is another type of investment risk.

# CHAPTER 18
PERFORMANCE EVALUATION

by Andrew Clare, PhD

## LEARNING OUTCOMES

After completing this chapter, you should be able to do the following:

**a** Describe a performance evaluation process;

**b** Describe measures of return, including holding-period returns and time-weighted rates of return;

**c** Compare arithmetic and geometric means rates of returns;

**d** Describe measures of risk, including standard deviation, downside deviation, and reward-to-risk ratios;

**e** Describe uses of benchmarks and explain the selection of a benchmark;

**f** Explain measures of relative performance, including tracking error and the information ratio;

**g** Explain the concept of alpha;

**h** Explain uses and processes of performance attribution.

# INTRODUCTION

Investors are interested in knowing how their investments have performed. For retail investors, the performance of their investments may determine whether they will enjoy a comfortable retirement, whether they will have enough money to send their children to university, or whether they can afford their dream holiday. The trustees of pension or charitable funds and other institutional investors also want to monitor the performance of their investments to ensure that the assets will be sufficient to cover the needs of the ultimate beneficiaries, such as pensioners. In addition, the performance of a fund and its fund manager is important to a fund management company; after all, if the output of the car industry is cars, then the "output" of the fund management industry is investment returns. For a fund management company, measuring and understanding fund manager performance is vital to managing and improving the investment process in the future.

Knowing the return achieved by an investment or a fund management company is only part of the process of performance evaluation. Investment management is a competitive industry. Both investors and fund management companies will want to know how fund managers have performed relative to familiar and relevant financial market benchmarks (e.g., a stock index, such as the S&P 500 Index in the United States or the Hang Seng Index in Hong Kong) and how their managers have performed against their peers. All interested parties will also want to know how the fund manager achieved the performance—for example, whether the performance was the result of skill or luck or perhaps the result of excessive risk taking.

It is only through the thorough evaluation of investment performance that fund management companies and their investors can make informed decisions about their investments. After reviewing a fund manager's performance, investors can decide whether they want to continue to invest with the manager or to move their funds to another manager. Similarly, the fund management company can decide whether the manager should be asked to manage additional funds, be supported with more resources in an effort to improve the company's performance, or be replaced.

The performance evaluation process includes four discrete but related stages: measuring absolute returns, adjusting returns for risk, measuring relative returns, and attributing performance. These four stages are discussed in turn.

# MEASURING ABSOLUTE RETURNS

The first step of the performance evaluation process is to measure absolute returns. **Absolute returns** are the returns achieved over a certain time period. Absolute returns do not consider the risk of the investment or the returns achieved by similar investments.

Copyright © 2012 CFA Institute

## 2.1 Holding-Period Returns

The performance of a security, such as an equity (stock) or debt (bond) security, over a specific time period, called the holding period, is referred to as the **holding-period return**. The holding-period return measures the total gain or loss that an investor owning a security achieves over the specified period compared with the investment at the beginning of the period. The return over the holding period usually comes from two distinct sources: capital gain or loss and income.

The holding-period return from owning an ordinary or common share of a company typically comes from the change in the price of the share between the beginning and the end of the period, as well as from the dividends received over the period. The change in the price of the shares over the period is the capital gain or loss portion of the return. The dividends received over the period are the income portion of the return. The holding-period returns from owning bonds result from changes in price (capital gain or loss) and receipt of interest (income).

Example 1 illustrates how holding-period returns are calculated. As always, you are *not* responsible for calculations, but the presentation of formulas and calculations may enhance your understanding.

> **EXAMPLE 1. HOLDING-PERIOD RETURNS**
>
> An investor buys one ordinary share in Company A on 1 January at a price of £100. On 31 December, Company A pays a dividend per share of £5, and an ordinary share of Company A is selling for £110.
>
> In this case, the holding period is one year—from 1 January to December 31. The return achieved by the investor from the increase (appreciation) in the share price over this period is calculated as follows:
>
> $$\text{Capital component of the holding-period return} = \frac{110-100}{100} = 0.10 = 10\%$$
>
> But the holding-period return should also include the dividend paid to the investor. The return achieved by the investor from the income received on the share is as follows:
>
> $$\text{Income component of the holding-period return} = \frac{5}{100} = 0.05 = 5\%$$
>
> The total holding-period return is the sum of the capital and income components (i.e., 15%). Mathematically,
>
> $$\text{Total holding-period return} = \frac{110-100+5}{100} = 0.15 = 15\%$$

The change in the value of an investment fund over the course of a given period is typically made up of the capital gains or losses on all of the assets held over that period, plus any income earned on those assets over the same period: dividend income for portfolios of equity securities, interest income for portfolios of debt securities, and rental income for portfolios of commercial real estate properties.

# Measuring Absolute Returns

The effect of the capital and income components of return can be demonstrated by looking at the performance of some representative investment portfolios. Exhibit 1 presents the holding-period returns and the split between the capital gains and losses portion and the income portion for a range of investment portfolios in 2010. Panel A of the exhibit shows the investment performance of four equity portfolios. The global equity portfolio includes equity securities from around the globe; the U.S. and European equity portfolios include equity securities listed in the United States and in Europe; the emerging market equity portfolio includes equity securities listed in emerging markets, such as Brazil, Russia, India, and China (sometimes referred to as BRIC). Panel B of the exhibit presents the investment performance of five bond and commercial property portfolios in 2010. The eurozone government bond portfolio includes bonds issued by eurozone governments, such as France, Germany, Greece, Italy, Ireland, and Spain; the eurozone corporate bond portfolio includes bonds issued by companies headquartered in the eurozone; the European high-yield bond portfolio includes bonds that are rated BB+ or below by Fitch and Standard & Poor's and Ba1 or below by Moody's, the credit rating agencies discussed in Chapter 10; the last two portfolios include U.S. and U.K. commercial property, respectively.

### Exhibit 1  Holding-Period Returns for a Variety of Portfolios, 2010

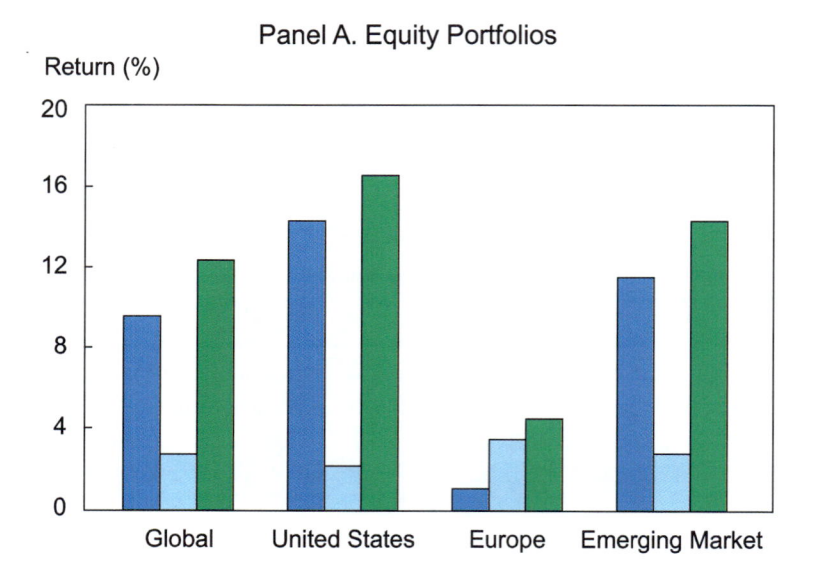

**Panel A. Equity Portfolios**

**Panel B. Bond and Commercial Property Portfolios**

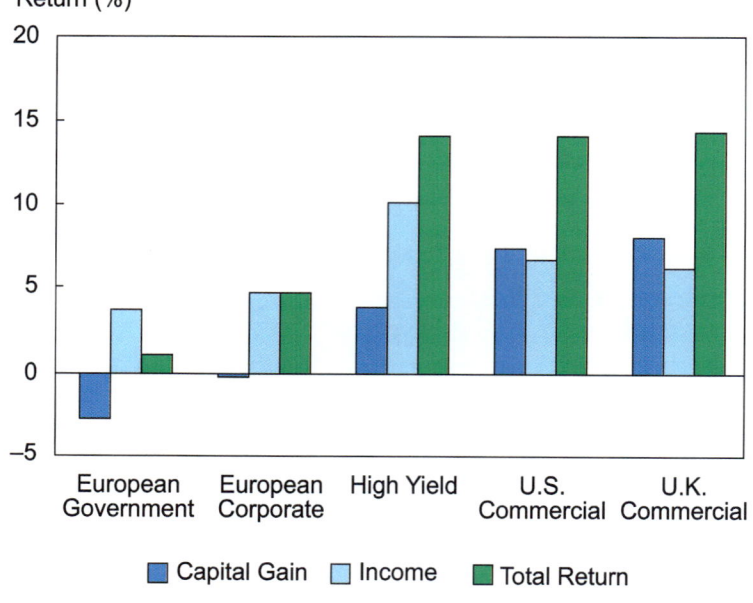

■ Capital Gain   ■ Income   ■ Total Return

*Source*: Based on data from the Centre for Asset Management Research, Cass Business School, London.

Panel A shows that the total holding-period return of all the equity portfolios except the European equity portfolio was more than 12% and that the capital gains portion was much larger than the income portion. The European equity portfolio's total holding-period return was approximately 4% and was made up almost entirely of income return.

Panel B indicates that the total holding-period return of the eurozone government bonds portfolio and the eurozone corporate bonds portfolio were positive. Each of these portfolios experienced a capital loss, which was more than offset by positive

# Measuring Absolute Returns

income returns. Each of the European high-yield bond and two commercial property portfolios had positive total holding-period returns. Each experienced a capital gain and a positive income return.

## 2.2 Cash Flows and Time-Weighted Rates of Return

In the holding-period return calculation in Example 1, the income (the dividend) was received at the end of the holding period. This timing made the calculation of the return relatively easy. In practice, however, calculating a fund's holding-period return is more complex. In particular,

- funds may consist of hundreds of individual investments that pay income at different times throughout the holding period; and

- clients may be making additional investments (cash inflows) in and withdrawals (cash outflows) from a fund throughout the holding period.

In other words, there is a constant flow of cash into and out of most investment funds and portfolios. This flow makes the calculation of holding-period returns considerably more complex than what was described in Example 1. Additional investments and withdrawals from clients will affect the calculated performance of the fund if they are not accounted for properly. Example 2 illustrates this point.

> **EXAMPLE 2. EFFECT OF A DEPOSIT ON A FUND'S INVESTMENT PERFORMANCE**
>
> Suppose that an investment fund has a value of $100 million on 1 January. By 31 December, the fund has grown in value to $110 million. The increase in the value of this fund came from changes in the values of the securities held in the portfolio and from income received and reinvested during the year. The total holding-period return on the fund is 10%, calculated as follows:
>
> $$\text{Fund return} = \left( \frac{\$110 \text{ million} - \$100 \text{ million}}{\$100 \text{ million}} \right) = 0.10 = 10\%$$
>
> However, suppose that one of the fund's clients deposited an additional $5 million into the fund on 30 June. This deposit means that some of the change in the fund's value over the year was not from the performance of the securities or from the income on these securities but was from the receipt of additional client money. A total holding-period return of 10% overstates the fund's investment performance.

The effect of the flow of money into and out of funds over time can be accounted for by dividing the measurement period into shorter holding periods. A new holding period starts each time a cash flow occurs—that is, each time money flows into or out of the fund. If there is only one cash flow during the holding period, the measurement period will be divided into two shorter holding periods; if there are two cash flows, there will be three holding periods; and so on. In practice, client cash inflows and outflows may occur on a daily basis, in which case an annual holding-period return is divided into daily holding-period returns.

Example 3 uses the information in Example 2 to illustrate how the total holding-period return is calculated when a cash flows occurs during the holding period.

> ### EXAMPLE 3. CALCULATION OF A FUND'S RETURN WHEN THERE IS A DEPOSIT
>
> Suppose that the fund introduced in Example 2 received only the one client cash inflow of $5 million at the close of business on 30 June. No other cash inflows or outflows occurred in the period; there was no additional cash from clients, and there was no cash from income on holdings of the fund. The holding period of one year can be divided into two periods of six months. The calculation of the holding-period return is then completed in three steps:
>
> - Calculate the six-month holding-period return for the period from 1 January to 30 June before the additional deposit.
>
> - Calculate the six-month holding-period return for the period from 1 July to 31 December, including the cash inflow of $5 million that increased the value of the fund on 30 June.
>
> - Calculate the annual holding-period return by combining the two six-month holding period returns.
>
> Dividing the holding period in this way ensures that the return calculated in each period is not affected by the inflow. The inflow is not included in the holding-period return calculation for the first six months. The inflow, however, is included in the value of the fund at the start of the next six-month holding-period return calculation. But there is one final piece of information that is needed to calculate the return over each of these two six-month periods: the value of the fund on 30 June immediately before the inflow of $5 million. Assume that the fund's value was as follows (the 30 June value does not include the $5 million deposit):
>
> | Date | Fund's Value |
> | --- | --- |
> | 1 January | $100 million |
> | 30 June | $98 million |
> | 31 December | $110 million |
>
> The holding-period return over the first six months (1 January to 30 June) is as follows:
>
> $$\text{Fund return} = \left(\frac{\$98 \text{ million} - \$100 \text{ million}}{\$100 \text{ million}}\right) = -0.020 = -2.0\%$$
>
> On 30 June, the fund has fallen in value to $98 million. But at this point, the fund experiences the positive cash inflow of $5 million. This event means that at the start of the second holding period on 1 July, the fund has a value of $103 million ($98 million + $5 million). On 31 December, the fund has a value of $110 million. Thus, the holding-period return for the second six months (1 July to 31 December) is as follows:

$$\text{Fund return} = \left(\frac{\$110 \text{ million} - \$103 \text{ million}}{\$103 \text{ million}}\right) = 0.068 = 6.8\%$$

Notice that because there are no cash inflows or outflows during this second six-month period, the holding-period return will be determined only by the choices and actions of the fund manager. Thus, the 6.8% return measures the fund's investment performance from 1 July to 31 December.

The clients of the fund may want to know the return achieved by the fund manager over the full calendar year rather than over each six-month period. As discussed in Chapter 5, there are two approaches used to combine returns. The first approach is to calculate the arithmetic mean by adding the two six-month returns. This approach, however, does not consider compounding; recall from the time value of money discussion that compounding is the process by which interest is reinvested to generate its own interest. The second approach is to calculate the geometric mean, which does consider compounding and is usually the preferred approach. Using our current example, the fund return was −2.0% for the first six months and 6.8% for the last six months. Thus, the geometric mean or fund return for the year is

Fund return = [(1 − 2.0%) × (1 + 6.8%)] − 1 = 0.0466 = 4.66%

So, the fund manager achieved an annual holding-period return of 4.66%, which is the return achieved by the fund manager on the funds under management between 1 January and 31 December. This 4.66% return reflects the fund's investment performance and is less than half the return calculated in Example 2.

Returns calculated in the manner described in Example 3 are known as time-weighted rates of returns. The **time-weighted rate of returns** calculation divides the overall measurement period (e.g., one year) into sub-periods, representing one month, week, or day of that year. The timing of each individual cash flow identifies the sub-periods to use for calculating holding-period returns. Each sub-period has its own separate rate of return. These sub-period returns are then used to calculate the return for the whole period under consideration. By calculating holding-period returns in this manner, client cash inflows and outflows do not distort the measurement and reporting of a fund's investment performance.

To compare the performance of one fund from one year with the next year or to compare the performance of one fund with another fund requires that returns be measured on a consistent basis over time and across fund managers. In 1999, a set of voluntary investment performance standards was proposed for this purpose. Fund management groups around the globe have adopted the Global Investment Performance Standards (GIPS®). Organisations in more than 30 countries sponsor and promote the standards embedded in the principles, which were created by and are administered by CFA Institute. The time-weighted rates of returns method is required in the Global Investment Performance Standards because this measure is not distorted by cash inflows and outflows.

## 3 ADJUSTING RETURNS FOR RISK

The second step of the performance evaluation process involves adjusting the holding-period return for the risk assumed to determine how much return was produced per unit of risk taken. The general principle is that investors want to get as much return as possible for as little risk as possible. Thus, if two investments have a holding-period return of 10% but the first investment has very little risk whereas the second one is very risky, the first investment will be better than the second one on a risk-adjusted basis. The measurement of risk is the topic of this section.

### 3.1 Standard Deviation

As discussed in Chapter 17, risk can take different forms. The risk we refer to in the rest of this chapter is investment risk. Recall from Chapter 5 that this type of risk is referred to as volatility and that the most common measure of volatility is the standard deviation of returns. The standard deviation of returns reflects the variability of returns around the mean (or average) return; the higher the standard deviation of returns, the higher the volatility of returns and the higher the risk.

Exhibit 2 shows the standard deviation of the annual returns for 2006–2010 on the four equity, three bond, and two commercial property portfolios of Exhibit 1.

## Adjusting Returns for Risk

**Exhibit 2** Standard Deviation of Returns for a Variety of Portfolios, 2006–2010

Panel A. Equity Portfolios

Standard Deviation (%)

| Portfolio | Standard Deviation (%) |
|---|---|
| Global | ~28 |
| United States | ~25 |
| Europe | ~34 |
| Emerging Market | ~41 |

Panel B. Bond and Commercial Property Portfolios

Standard Deviation (%)

| Portfolio | Standard Deviation (%) |
|---|---|
| European Government | ~3.6 |
| European Corporate | ~3.7 |
| High Yield | ~7.7 |
| U.S. Commercial | ~9 |
| U.K. Commercial | ~5.2 |

*Source*: Based on data from the Centre for Asset Management Research, Cass Business School, London.

Exhibit 2 supports the common perception that equities are riskier than bonds. As seen in Panel A, the standard deviation of annual returns for the equity portfolios exceeded 20%, reaching 41% for the emerging market equity portfolio. In contrast, Panel B indicates that the standard deviation of annual returns for the bond and commercial property portfolios were much less than for the equity portfolios: less than 5% for the eurozone government and corporate bond portfolios and less than 10% for the high-yield bond and the two commercial property portfolios.

There are at least two reasons why investors care about historical volatility—that is, the standard deviation of past returns. First, past variability of returns might be indicative of how variable returns may be in the future. But it is important to be aware that volatility may change over time and that there is no guarantee that future returns will behave like past returns. Second, the variability of returns may be a concern given an investor's objectives. Pension funds invest their funds to generate the returns necessary to pay their beneficiaries; life insurance companies invest to generate returns for their policyholders; general insurance companies invest to have the funds to meet the insurance claims on their policies; and individuals invest because they usually have a future expenditure in mind. Investing in a fund whose returns vary significantly over time could potentially disrupt investors' plans. If returns are very negative one year, then the fund may not be able to support the investors' commitments, such as pension payments to pensioners. Similarly, retail investors may need to liquidate or draw on funds from their investments because of unforeseen circumstances.

Exhibit 2 shows that the returns generated by the equity portfolios were more volatile during 2006–2010 than those generated by the bond portfolios. In the event that investors needed income or had to sell their holdings for previously unforeseen reasons, there is a greater possibility that there may be fewer cash flows from income and the sale of holdings than anticipated with equity investments than with debt investments. Interest payments represent contractual obligations but dividends do not, which explains why the income portion is less predictable for equity investments.

## 3.2 Downside Deviation

Standard deviation is a convenient measure of the variability of returns around the mean. Sometimes there is a positive deviation—that is, the return is greater than the mean—and sometimes there is a negative deviation—that is, the return is less than the mean. Which of these two types of deviation do you think investors would be more concerned about? Not surprisingly, psychologists and economists have discovered that investors dislike losses more than they like equivalent gains. So, investors might be happy about achieving an investment return of +10% but very, very unhappy about achieving a return of −10%. Because of this asymmetry in the way investors view the dispersion around the average, some investment professionals use a modified version of standard deviation known as downside deviation.

**Downside deviation** is calculated in almost exactly the same way as standard deviation, but instead of using all the deviations from the average, positive and negative, downside deviation is calculated using only those deviations that are negative. In other words, it is a measure of return variability that focuses only on outcomes that are less than the mean. Downside deviation may also be calculated by focusing on outcomes that are less than a specified return target; this target does not have to be the mean.

Exhibit 3 presents the standard and downside deviations of returns associated with investing in a diversified portfolio of U.K. equities and in a diversified portfolio of U.K. government bonds between 2001 and 2010.

# Adjusting Returns for Risk

**Exhibit 3** Standard Deviation vs. Downside Deviation for 2001–2010

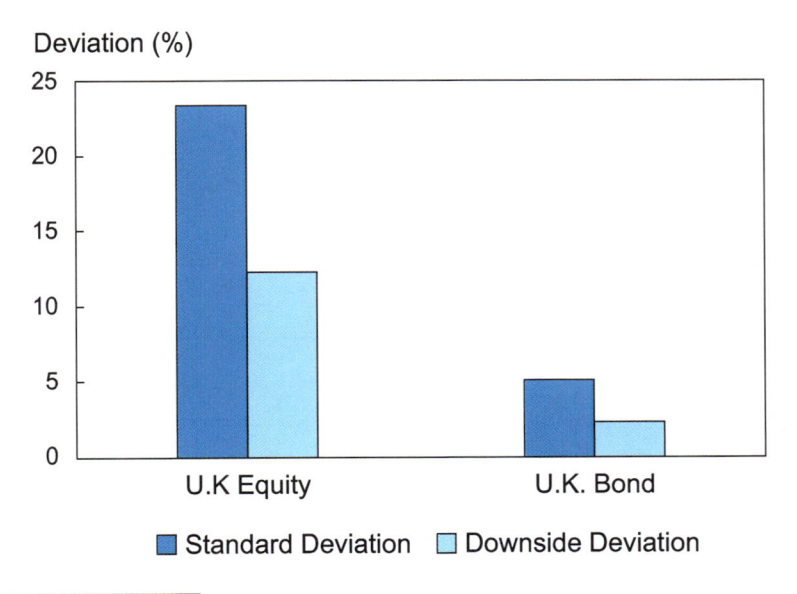

*Source:* Based on data from the Centre for Asset Management Research, Cass Business School, London.

As seen in Exhibit 3, the downside deviations are lower than the standard deviations; this outcome is expected because downside deviations only consider the negative deviations. But both measures convey the same message: The risk of the bond portfolio is lower than that of the equity portfolio.

## 3.3 Reward-to-Risk Ratios

Investors prefer to achieve a high return rather than a low return on their investment portfolios. All other things being equal, they also prefer lower risk (less variability of returns) to higher risk (more variability of returns). Thus, investors are interested in maximising the return on their investments while simultaneously trying to minimise the risks. In other words, they prefer investments that have a high return per unit of risk—that is, investments with a high **reward-to-risk ratio**.

A reward-to-risk ratio is a metric that takes the following basic form:

$$\text{Reward-to-risk ratio} = \frac{\text{Measure of portfolio return}}{\text{Measure of portfolio risk}}$$

The higher the value of the reward-to-risk ratio, the better the risk-adjusted return—that is, the higher the return per unit of risk.

A commonly used reward-to-risk ratio is called the **Sharpe ratio**, first suggested by Nobel Prize–winning economist William Sharpe.[1] The portfolio return is measured as the portfolio's excess return, which is equal to the difference between the portfolio's

---

[1] William F. Sharpe, "Mutual Fund Performance," in Part 2: Supplement on Security Prices, *Journal of Business*, vol. 39, no. 1 (January 1966):119–138.

holding-period return and the return on a "risk-free" investment. The risk-free investment is usually approximated by the return achieved from investing in short-term government bonds because in most countries, government bonds are the investments that carry the lowest level of risk. The portfolio risk is the standard deviation of the portfolio returns. Thus, the Sharpe ratio is calculated as follows:

$$\text{Sharpe ratio} = \frac{\text{Return on portfolio} - \text{Risk-free return}}{\text{Standard deviation of portfolio returns}} = \frac{\text{Excess return on portfolio}}{\text{Standard deviation of portfolio returns}}$$

Example 4 illustrates the calculation of the Sharpe ratio.

### EXAMPLE 4. SHARPE RATIO

Suppose that over a year, the holding-period return on an investment fund was 10%, and the return achieved from investing in government bonds was 4%. Also assume that the standard deviation of the investment fund's returns over this period was 5%. The Sharpe ratio for this fund is:

$$\text{Sharpe ratio} = \frac{10\% - 4\%}{5\%} = 1.2$$

Exhibit 4 presents the Sharpe ratios for the four equity, three bond, and two commodity property portfolios examined in Exhibits 1 and 2.

# Adjusting Returns for Risk

**Exhibit 4** — Sharpe Ratios for a Variety of Portfolios, 2006–2010

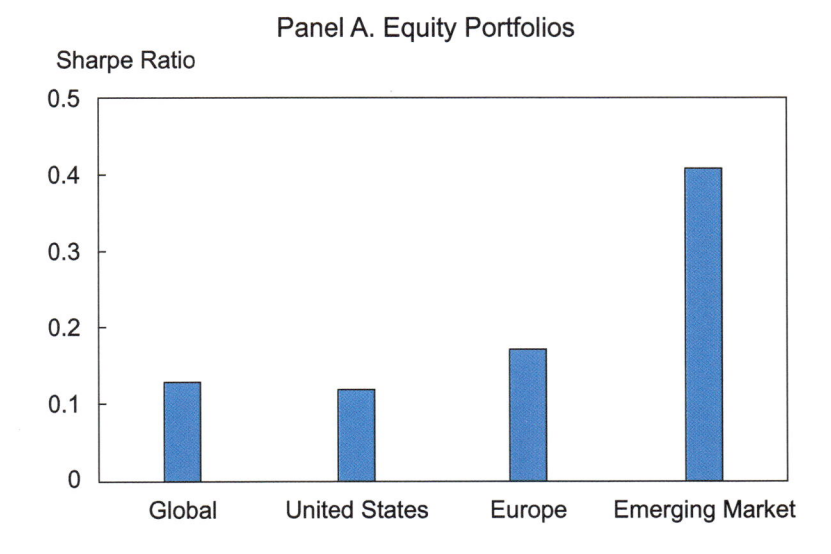

Panel A. Equity Portfolios

[Bar chart showing Sharpe Ratios: Global ≈ 0.13, United States ≈ 0.12, Europe ≈ 0.17, Emerging Market ≈ 0.41]

Panel B. Bond and Commercial Property Portfolios

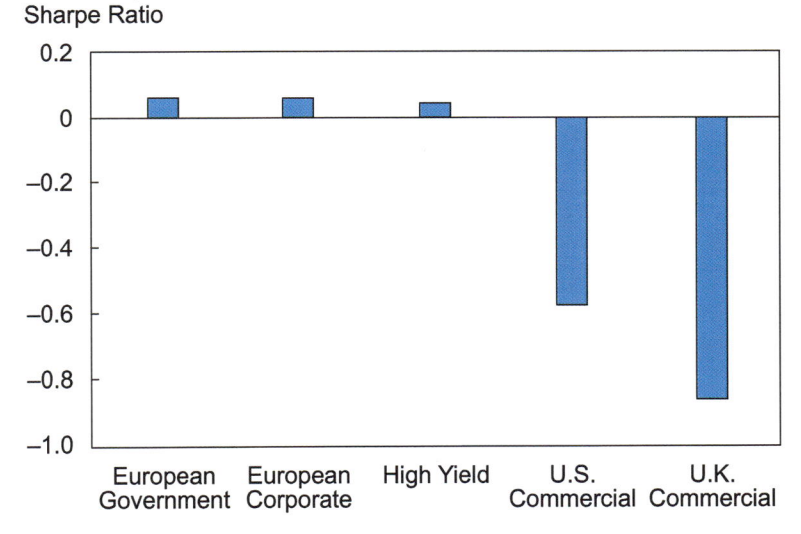

[Bar chart showing Sharpe Ratios: European Government ≈ 0.06, European Corporate ≈ 0.06, High Yield ≈ 0.05, U.S. Commercial ≈ −0.57, U.K. Commercial ≈ −0.86]

*Source:* Based on data from the Centre for Asset Management Research, Cass Business School, London.

Panel A shows that the Sharpe ratios of all the equity portfolios were positive, ranging from 0.10 to 0.40. The emerging market equity portfolio had the highest Sharpe ratio. Thus, this portfolio provided the highest amount of reward for the risk incurred. Panel B indicates that the bond portfolios also had positive Sharpe ratios, although lower than the equity funds. But the commercial property portfolios had negative Sharpe ratios, indicating that these funds generated lower returns than the government bond portfolios during 2006–2010. Thus, they provided a negative reward for the risk taken. You should not conclude, however, that commercial property portfolios are necessarily poor investments. The 2006–2009 period was rather unusual and marked by a global financial crisis that saw a significant drop in property prices.

The Sharpe ratio, along with other reward-to-risk ratios, is an important metric for understanding the quality of the returns produced by a portfolio. A portfolio with high returns but also high return volatility might be said to have produced lower quality returns than a portfolio with similarly high returns but with much lower return volatility. So, in a sense, reward-to-risk ratios, such as the Sharpe ratio, are one of the main "quality control" checks that investors need to make on their investments. Such ratios are also helpful for comparing investment choices.

## 4 MEASURING RELATIVE RETURNS

The third step in the performance evaluation process involves the measurement of **relative returns**—that is, returns relative to a suitable benchmark. By considering relative rather than absolute returns (the holding-period returns measured in the first step), investors can determine whether the money they invested may have done better in other investments. Thus, they can assess their opportunity cost and check that their investments are generating appropriate returns.

### 4.1 Benchmarks and the Calculation of Relative Returns

The calculation of a reward-to-risk ratio, such as the Sharpe ratio, allows investors to compare the performance of one investment fund with another. However, many investors also want to compare the performance of their fund with that of a financial market benchmark, such as a stock index. It is very common practice in all industries, and indeed in many areas of life, to benchmark or compare performance. Benchmarks can be used to assess the quality and/or quantity of a company's performance by comparing its performance with that of its peers and competitors; an application of this principle was provided in Chapter 4 with ratio analysis.

#### 4.1.1 Benchmarks

Fund managers may not only use a benchmark for assessment but may also manage their portfolios to a **benchmark**. This means that the manager must regularly compare the composition and performance of the portfolio with the composition of a financial market index, such as the FTSE 100 Index or the S&P 500. For investors, knowing the financial market index that a fund manager uses as a benchmark will give them some idea of the return and risk that they can expect from investing in that fund.

Before engaging a fund manager, institutional investors will often specify the financial market benchmark that they intend to use to assess the performance of the fund manager. For example, a U.S. equity fund manager may be asked, or mandated, to manage a portfolio of U.S. equities for a client and told that they will be "benchmarked against" the S&P 500. A fund manager could simply match the performance of the S&P 500 by buying all 500 U.S. stocks represented in the index in proportion to their market capitalisations. But the portfolio would underperform by the level of fees charged and transactions costs incurred. Fees would, therefore, need to be very low for the product to attract investors. As discussed in Chapter 13, managers who are expected to manage their clients' money in this way are known as passive fund managers because they simply mimic the holdings of their benchmark.

But the manager might instead have a more specific mandate reflecting specific risk requirements, return targets, or style or sector preferences, such as investing in biotech companies. In this case, simply holding the 500 U.S. stocks that make up the S&P 500 in their appropriate proportions will not produce the performance demanded (and paid for) by clients. To beat this benchmark, the manager will have to use analytical and trading skills and deliver high levels of client service to satisfy the mandate. Managers who manage their portfolios in this manner are known as active fund managers because they actively seek out investments that meet the investment mandate rather than relying on index replication to meet their objectives. Thus, active fund managers' portfolios look different from the benchmark.

Whether defined for retail or institutional clients, to be effective, a financial market benchmark should meet certain criteria—namely,

- Investability. The benchmark should be composed of assets that can be bought and sold by the fund manager. For passive fund managers, it would be difficult to mimic the benchmark if it contained assets that they could not buy. For active fund managers, not being able to invest in some of the benchmark's components could limit the ability to outperform it.

- Compatibility. Investors may not want to invest in assets that carry credit or default risk and may be willing to accept a relatively low return on their assets. In this case, a financial market index of government bonds might be more compatible (based on historical performance) with investor preferences. A benchmark composed of emerging market equities would not be so compatible.

- Clarity. The rules governing the construction of the benchmark (e.g., those rules relating to the weighting of individual index constituents and the method used to calculate index returns) should be clear and unambiguous. This clarity should also extend to the process used for constituent additions to and withdrawals from the index over time.

- Pre-specification. The benchmark should be specified in advance so that the manager is clear about the client's objectives and so that the manager can construct the portfolio that is most appropriate for these objectives.

### 4.1.2 Indices

Many organisations produce financial market indices that allow investors to compare the holding-period return achieved by their fund manager with that generated by the wider market. As discussed in Chapter 14, for most equity exchanges around the world, there is at least one index that represents the majority of its stocks. In addition to these broad indices, stock indices are also available along industrial classification lines, both within a particular country and globally. This arrangement makes it possible, for instance, for investors to compare the performance of a portfolio of global information technology (IT) stocks with the performance of a portfolio of U.K. IT stocks, as long as the indices have been constructed using the same methodology.

Many leading investment banks, such as Barclays Capital and Goldman Sachs, produce bond indices for different types of issuers located in developed or emerging countries. Independent index providers also provide a wide range of bond indices. In addition to aggregate bond indices that are designed to cover the market as a whole, many index providers offer bond indices classified by maturity, credit rating, currency, and industrial category. Many index providers, such as FTSE International, Standard & Poor's, and Morgan Stanley Capital International, produce indices for nearly every asset class, including cash, currencies, commercial property, hedge funds, private equity, and commodities, as well as for bonds and equities.

Despite the widespread availability of independently constructed financial market indices covering nearly every conceivable sector and aspect of the world's financial markets, some investors prefer to compare their fund managers not with broad benchmarks constructed by index providers but instead with the fund manager's peers, for example, comparing the performance of one manager of European equities with that of other managers of European equities. Each manager is then assigned a performance ranking within his or her particular sector of the financial markets. Managers who are in the top 10% of performers among their peers over a specific period are said to be top-decile performers. The performances of individual fund managers are collected and then ranked by independent organisations, such as Morningstar, which then publishes these results, thus allowing investors to see the rankings of their particular fund managers relative to those of other managers that they could have chosen.

#### 4.1.3 Relative Returns

The wide range of financial market indices allows investors to set performance targets (passive or active) for their fund managers and enables them to compare the performance of their fund manager over time against an independent benchmark. In summary, the benchmark allows investors to evaluate relative returns.

### 4.2 Tracking Error and Information Ratio

The **tracking error** of an investment fund reflects how the performance of the investment fund deviates from the performance of its benchmark. The tracking error is measured by taking the standard deviation of the differences between the returns on the fund and the returns on its benchmark. The bigger these differences are, the larger the tracking error is. A passive fund manager may be expected to have a very low tracking error because the manager is seeking to replicate a benchmark. But for an active fund manager, the tracking error will be higher.

Tracking error can also be used to formulate another very popular reward-to-risk ratio, known as the **information ratio**. The "reward" part of the information ratio is the difference between the holding-period return on the portfolio and the return on an appropriate benchmark over the same period, and the "risk" part of the information ratio is based on the tracking error of the fund—that is, its deviations from the performance of the benchmark. It is calculated as follows:

$$\text{Information ratio} = \frac{\text{Difference in average return between portfolio and benchmark}}{\text{Fund tracking error}}$$

# Measuring Relative Returns

Example 5 uses the annual holding-period returns on the U.K. equity portfolio presented in Exhibit 3 to illustrate the calculations of the tracking error and the information ratio.

> **EXAMPLE 5. TRACKING ERROR AND INFORMATION RATIO**
>
> The annual holding-period returns associated with investing in a diversified portfolio of U.K. equities and in the FTSE All-Share Index are reported in the following table. The last column presents the difference in the annual return achieved by the equity portfolio relative to its benchmark.
>
> **Exhibit 5   Tracking Error between an Equity Portfolio and a Benchmark, 2001–2010**
>
> | Year | U.K. Equity Portfolio Total Return | FTSE All-Share Index Total Return | Difference |
> |---|---|---|---|
> | 2001 | 5.00% | 5.05% | −0.05% |
> | 2002 | −15.00 | −15.30 | 0.30 |
> | 2003 | −28.00 | −28.56 | 0.56 |
> | 2004 | 32.00 | 32.96 | −0.96 |
> | 2005 | 15.00 | 15.45 | −0.45 |
> | 2006 | 24.00 | 26.40 | −2.40 |
> | 2007 | 13.00 | 14.30 | −1.30 |
> | 2008 | −3.00 | −3.02 | 0.02 |
> | 2009 | −29.00 | −29.15 | 0.15 |
> | 2010 | 36.00 | 36.36 | −0.36 |
> | Mean | 5.00% | 5.45% | |
> | | | Average Deviation | −0.45% |
> | | | Tracking Error | 0.84% |
>
> *Source:* Based on data from the Centre for Asset Management Research, Cass Business School, London.
>
> The average of the differences in returns is −0.45% per year; in other words, on average, the equity portfolio underperformed the benchmark by 0.45% each year over this 10-year period.
>
> The standard deviation of these differences is 0.84%. The formula used to calculate this standard deviation was presented in Chapter 5, but you are *not* responsible for this calculation. This 0.84% represents the tracking error.
>
> The information ratio is, therefore,
>
> $$\text{Information ratio} = \frac{-0.45\%}{0.84\%} = -0.53$$

> In this case, the information ratio is negative because the fund underperformed its benchmark over the period. If the information ratio had outperformed the benchmark, it would have been positive.

### 4.3 Alpha vs. Beta vs. Luck

The calculation and analysis of reward-to-risk ratios allow an understanding of the price fund investors have to pay in terms of unit of reward for each unit of risk—the total return—generated by the fund's manager. All other things being equal, a manager who produces a consistently high reward-to-risk ratio could be said to be more skilful than one who consistently produces a much lower ratio. Indeed, investors who invest in a fund that is managed on an active rather than on a passive basis are effectively paying for the manager's investment skill and expertise.

Fund manager skill is often referred to as fund manager **alpha**. Perhaps the best way to explain the concept of alpha is to consider the sources of any fund's return, which will be composed of varying amounts of the following three elements:

- market return,
- luck, and
- skill.

**Market return** The manager of a passive investment fund will produce returns for investors. These managers, however, are not looking to add value to the portfolios by picking securities that they believe will outperform other securities. Instead, they typically buy and hold those securities that comprise their benchmark in the appropriate proportions. Although this process is not done without skill, it is not really investment skill. The main skill needed is that of efficient administration. When the passive benchmark rises, the value of the passive fund tracking it should also rise; conversely, when the benchmark falls, the value of the passive fund should also fall. Thus, over time, the fund should produce a return similar to that of the chosen benchmark minus fees.

Given that most active fund managers benchmark their funds against financial market indices, such as the S&P 500, some of the return generated by an actively managed fund will also be caused by broad market movements over which the active fund manager has no control. Arguably, then, the investors in actively managed funds should not pay higher active fees for fund returns that are generated by the market rather than by the investment acumen of their fund manager because they can access market returns at a cheaper price by investing in passively managed funds.

**Luck** Some of the return generated by an investment fund will be the result of luck rather than judgment. The prices of financial assets held in portfolios are very volatile and are affected by many events that could not possibly have been foreseen by a fund manager. Some genuinely good fund managers may be unlucky on occasions, and a genuinely bad fund manager might enjoy some good luck. Because luck will tend to even out over the long term, it is vital that investors be able to identify the element of luck that goes toward the performance of all investment portfolios, although it is difficult to do so.

**Skill**   A skilful fund manager will be able to add value to a portfolio over and above changes to the portfolio's value that are driven by broad market movements and that could have been produced by a passive fund manager. Because luck will tend to even out over time, a skilful manager is one who adds this value consistently over time, year after year. This outperformance over the return of a relevant market benchmark is generally referred to as alpha.

The performance evaluation industry puts a great deal of effort into trying to distinguish between these three sources of fund manager return. To do so, factor models are used to determine the factors that make up returns and the importance of each factor. One such model is the capital asset pricing model (CAPM),[2] from which comes the term alpha. This model also produced a measure of systematic risk: **beta**. Systematic risk was discussed in Chapter 9 and it is also called market risk or non-diversifiable risk. Factor models, such as the CAPM, separate the fund's return into that portion of return that could have been achieved either passively, from market performance (beta); from luck or randomness; or actively, from the investment skills of the fund manager (alpha).

Most active managers benchmark their performance against an independently calculated financial market index. Just as standard deviation is a standardised measure of the deviation of a fund's return relative to its average return, tracking error is a standardised measure of the difference in the performance of the manager's fund relative to the benchmark. And just as the standard deviation of an investment fund's return can be used to produce the Sharpe ratio, a reward-to-risk ratio, the tracking error of an investment fund's return can be used to calculate another reward-to-risk ratio known as the information ratio. Both measures are widely used and referred to in the fund management industry. Finally, alpha is calculated using factor models in an effort to identify the return contributions from a fund manager's skill, whereas beta reflects market performance.

Active and passive investment management are important topics, and we will return to them in Chapter 21.

## ATTRIBUTING PERFORMANCE

**5**

By comparing the performance of a U.K. equity fund manager with the performance of an appropriate U.K. equity index, the fund manager's clients can get an idea of how well the fund manager is performing relative to the market in general, both in terms of average return and in terms of risk, by calculating the fund's tracking error or information ratio. Thus, benchmarks form the basis of **performance measurement**.

---

[2] William F. Sharpe, "Capital Asset Prices: A Theory of Market Equilibrium under Conditions of Risk," *Journal of Finance*, vol. 19, no. 3 (September 1964):425–442.

But benchmarks can also be used to further explore the reasons for the fund manager's performance. By using appropriate financial market indices, the fund manager's performance can be decomposed to reveal where the performance did or did not come from. Depending on the nature of the fund, the performance itself might come from

- asset allocation,
- sector selection,
- stock selection, or
- currency exposure.

Knowing where the fund manager's performance was derived from is useful information both for the clients of the fund and for the investment management company. For example, if a fund manager is good at stock selection but less proficient at sector selection, another fund manager may be asked to give advice on the sector selection aspect of the portfolio, allowing the original fund manager to concentrate on stock selection. Knowing the strengths of fund manager performance can also help investors choose an investment fund.

The process of determining how much of performance is the result of the selection of the best-performing asset classes, sectors, individual securities, and currencies is known as attribution analysis, and it is the last step of the performance evaluation process. Example 6 provides an illustration of performance attribution.

> **EXAMPLE 6. PERFORMANCE ATTRIBUTION**
>
> Consider a fund manager who manages a portfolio that has a value of £100 million on 1 January, the start of an annual evaluation period. The manager's client makes it clear that the benchmark for this fund includes three equity market indices:
>
> - the FTSE 100 (United Kingdom),
> - the S&P 500 (United States), and
> - the Nikkei 225 (Japan).
>
> The mandate also specifies that the performance of the benchmark will equal 60% of the performance of the FTSE 100, 30% of the S&P 500, and 10% of the Nikkei 225. Thus,
>
> Benchmark composition
> = (60% × FTSE 100) + (30% × S&P 500) + (10% × Nikkei 225)
>
> The fund manager is expected to outperform this particular benchmark by 1% per year.
>
> Over the course of the year, assume the three financial indices produce the returns shown in Exhibit 6. For simplicity, the full-year return is equal to the sum of the returns for the two six-month periods; that is, we ignore compounding.

## Exhibit 6   Index and Benchmark Performance over One Year

| Index | Weight | Return 1 January to 30 June | Return 1 July to 31 December | Return 1 January to 31 December |
|---|---|---|---|---|
| FTSE 100 | 60% | 6.0% | 10.0% | 16.0% |
| S&P 500 | 30 | 5.0 | 8.0 | 13.0 |
| Nikkei 225 | 10 | 15.0 | −10.0 | 5.0 |
| Benchmark | 100% | 6.6% | 7.4% | 14.0% |

*Source:* Andrew Clare and Chris Wagstaff, *The Trustee Guide to Investment* (London: Palgrave Macmillan, 2011).

Over the full year, the benchmark generated a return of 14%, composed of a relatively even return of 6.6% in the first half of the year and 7.4% in the second half. But the components of the benchmark produced a more volatile return over these two periods. In particular, the Japanese index was up 15% over the first half of the year but down 10% over the second half.

Assume that over the full year, the fund manager achieved a return of 15%. The manager satisfied the mandate; the return on the fund (15%) is 1% above the benchmark's return (14%). But where did this performance come from? To understand this question, an investor needs more information about the fund manager's decisions throughout the year. In particular, an investor needs to know the proportions of the funds that the manager allocated to U.K., U.S., and Japanese equities over the course of the year.

Exhibit 7 presents the fund manager's broad allocation among the three markets.

## Exhibit 7   Fund Manager Asset Allocation Decisions

| Markets | Fund Allocations 1 January to 30 June | Fund Allocations 1 July to 31 December |
|---|---|---|
| U.K. equities | 60% | 50% |
| U.S. equities | 30 | 20 |
| Japanese equities | 10 | 30 |
| Total | 100% | 100% |

*Source*: Andrew Clare and Chris Wagstaff, *The Trustee Guide to Investment* (London: Palgrave Macmillan, 2011).

Exhibit 7 shows that the fund manager held the equities in benchmark proportions for the first half of the year. But before the start of the second half of the year on July 1, the fund manager reduced the proportion of both U.K. and U.S. equities by 10 percentage points each and increased the holding of Japanese equities by 20 percentage points.

It is possible to calculate the returns that the fund manager would have achieved based on the allocation among the three markets and the returns achieved by the indices. In the first half of the year, the fund would have achieved the following return:

Return from 1 January to 30 June

= (60% × FTSE 100) + (30% × S&P 500) + (10% × Nikkei 225)

= (60% × 6%) + (30% × 5%) + (10% × 15%)

= 6.60%

In the second half of the year, the fund would have achieved the following return:

Return from 1 July to 31 December

= (50% × FTSE 100) + (20% × S&P 500) + (30% × Nikkei 225)

= (50% × 10%) + (20% × 8%) + (30% × −10%)

= 3.60%

This analysis gives a total of approximately 10.2% for the full year, assuming a simple return. However, the fund manager achieved a return of 15%, which means that 4.8% (15.0% − 10.2%) of the return came from a source other than the broad asset allocation decisions that the fund manager made. In fact, had the manager held the equity funds passively but in line with the benchmark proportions, the manager would have achieved a return of 14% over the year—that is, the return for the full year reported in Exhibit 6. This result means that the fund manager's asset allocation decisions cost the fund 3.8% (14% − 10.2%). This conclusion is easy to see from the decision to switch 10% out of U.K. and U.S. equities and into Japanese equities, just after the Japanese market had risen by 15% over the previous six months and just before it fell by 10% over the following six months.

So, the fund manager outperformed the benchmark by 1% even though the asset allocation decision lost 3.8%. This assessment means that the manager added 4.8% to the portfolio from a source other than asset allocation. It is possible that this portion of the return may have been from stock selection or from currency exposure, which is the change in the relative value of the currencies involved (the pound, dollar, and yen). The manager may have added value to the portfolio by buying better-performing stocks or may have earned gains on the changes in the relative values of the currencies.

Using the type of techniques outlined here, it would be possible to further explore the fund manager's performance to understand whether this manager chose good U.S., Japanese, and U.K. stocks or good stocks in all of these markets.

This attribution analysis is summarised in Exhibit 8. Notice that the performance of the benchmark with regard to stock selection is equal to zero by definition because all stocks are included in the index.

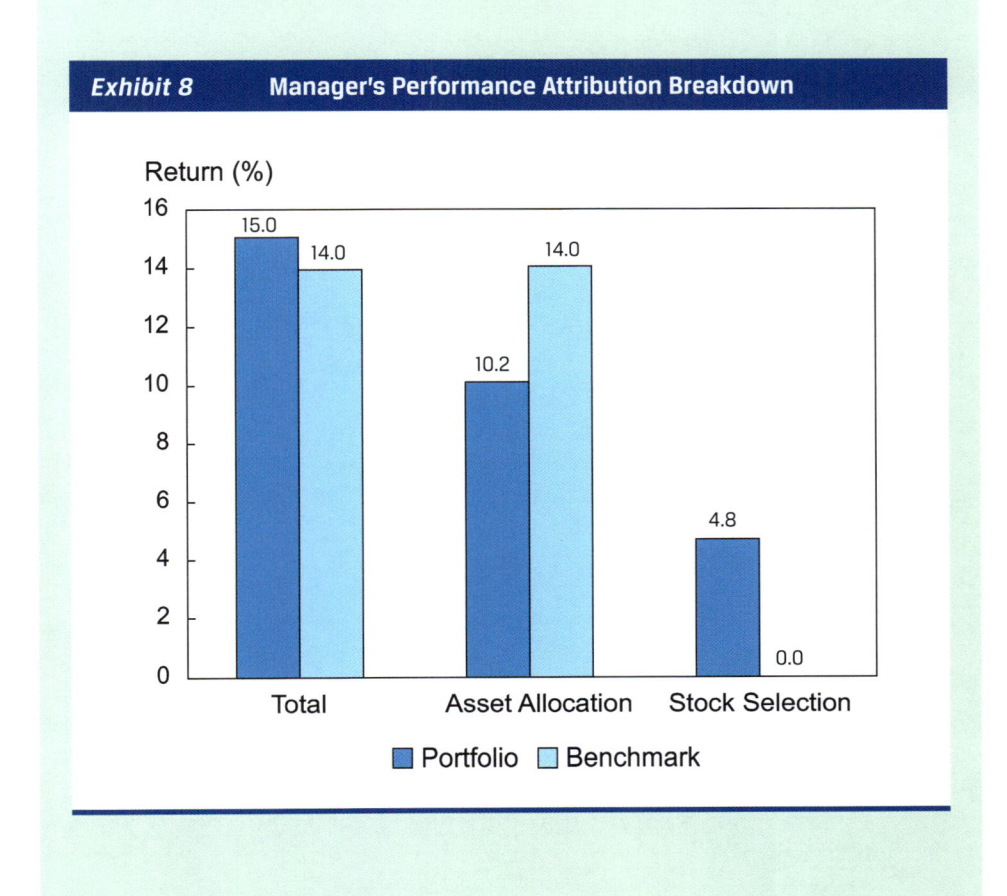

**Exhibit 8    Manager's Performance Attribution Breakdown**

| Category | Portfolio | Benchmark |
|---|---|---|
| Total | 15.0 | 14.0 |
| Asset Allocation | 10.2 | 14.0 |
| Stock Selection | 4.8 | 0.0 |

In Example 6, it was assumed that the return that did not come from the manager's asset allocation decision was instead attributable to stock selection. But because this portfolio is composed of international equities, the additional return may have been from changes in exchange rates over the period. With more detailed attribution analysis, an investor could reveal how much of the performance was from exchange rate movements or how much of the performance on the Japanese fund was from sector selection and so on.

Modern performance attribution software can allow fund management companies to drill down into the detail of a fund to reveal all of this performance information. By doing so, the company may conclude that a particular fund manager is very good at stock selection but weaker in sector selection. Given this information, the company might ask another manager with better sector selection skills to make sector-related decisions, allowing the original manager to continue to pick stocks and thus to continue to add value. In addition, it is important to discuss portfolio strategies and decisions with a manager to try to separate the manager's skill from luck.

## SUMMARY

- Performance evaluation is a crucial process for retail and institutional investors, for fund management companies, and for fund managers. It includes a number of separate but related steps: measuring absolute returns, adjusting returns for risk, measuring relative returns, and attributing performance.

- Absolute returns include two components: a capital gain or loss component and an income component.

- Returns need to be measured properly by taking into account the complex and often daily cash flows into and out of a fund over time.

- Global Investment Performance Standards recommend that investment fund returns be calculated using the time-weighted rate of return method. Time-weighted rates of return are not distorted by cash flows and thus reflect the true performance of the investment fund.

- Standard deviation is the most commonly used measure of investment return risk.

- Downside deviation is similar to standard deviation, except that it only includes "bad" deviations—that is, negative deviations.

- The Sharpe ratio is an important risk–reward ratio that compares a portfolio's excess return with its standard deviation. Thus, it reflects the return achieved per unit of risk taken.

- Relative returns allow comparison of a fund's return with the return of an appropriate benchmark.

- The use of a benchmark allows for the calculation of additional measures of risk, such as tracking error and the information ratio, and also a measure of fund manager skill, known as alpha.

- The use of independently calculated financial market benchmarks allows for the identification of how much of a fund's return was attributable to the fund manager's choice of asset classes, sectors, or individual securities or currencies.

# CHAPTER REVIEW QUESTIONS

Test your knowledge of this chapter at **cfainstitute.org/claritasstudy**.

1. The first step of performance evaluation is:

   A attributing performance.

   B measuring relative returns.

   C measuring absolute returns.

2. The measurement of relative returns involves comparing the fund manager's holding-period return with:

   A a measure of risk.

   B the return on a benchmark.

   C the fund manager's past performance.

3. The measure that *best* reflects a fund's performance when clients make deposits and withdrawals during the holding period is the:

   A time-weighted return.

   B geometric average return.

   C arithmetic average return.

4. The measure that *best* reflects the variability of returns around the mean return is the:

   A standard deviation.

   B reward-to-risk ratio.

   C downside deviation.

5. The measure that is *best* suited for investors who dislike losses more than they like equivalent gains is the:

   A Sharpe ratio.

   B standard deviation.

   C downside deviation.

Copyright © 2012 CFA Institute

**6** The Sharpe ratio is a measure of:

   **A** historical volatility.

   **B** downside deviation.

   **C** risk-adjusted performance.

**7** The criterion that a benchmark should be made up of assets that can be bought or sold by the fund manager is known as:

   **A** investability.

   **B** compatibility.

   **C** pre-specification.

**8** A fund manager who uses analytical and trading skills to beat a benchmark is *best* described as a(n):

   **A** active manager.

   **B** index replicator.

   **C** passive manager.

**9** Relative to an appropriate benchmark, the risk profile of a passive investment fund would *most likely* be:

   **A** lower.

   **B** similar.

   **C** higher.

**10** The tracking error of a passive investment fund would *most likely* be:

   **A** zero.

   **B** low.

   **C** high.

**11** Which of the following information ratios indicates that a fund manager added value to his or her client's portfolio?

   **A** −0.25

   **B** +0.00

   **C** +0.25

## Chapter Review Questions

**12** Alpha measures the portion of the fund manager's return attributable to:

　**A** skill.

　**B** luck.

　**C** market return.

**13** Beta measures the portion of the investment fund's return attributable to:

　**A** randomness.

　**B** broad market movements.

　**C** the fund manager's judgment.

**14** The consistent outperformance of an investment fund compared with its benchmark is *best* described as:

　**A** beta.

　**B** alpha.

　**C** tracking error.

**15** The process of decomposing a fund manager's performance to identify the source(s) of that performance is *best* described as:

　**A** attribution analysis.

　**B** risk-adjusted analysis.

　**C** relative performance analysis.

**16** To determine how much of a fund manager's performance was derived from currency exposure, an investor would *most likely* look at the:

　**A** information ratio.

　**B** attribution analysis.

　**C** capital asset pricing model.

## ANSWERS

1. C is correct. The performance evaluation process begins with the measurement of absolute returns. Absolute returns are the holding-period returns. They measure the total gain or loss that an investor owning a security achieved over the holding period compared with the investment at the beginning of the period. Holding-period returns usually come from the changes in the price of the security between the beginning and the end of the period, as well as the income received over the period (dividend, interest). B and A are incorrect because measuring relative returns and attributing performance are the third and fourth steps of the performance evaluation process, respectively.

2. B is correct. The measurement of relative returns involves comparing the fund manager's holding-period return with the return on an appropriate benchmark. A is incorrect because measures of risk, such as the standard deviation, are used to calculate risk-adjusted returns (the second step of the performance evaluation process) rather than relative returns (the third step of the performance evaluation process). C is incorrect because the fund manager's past performance is not an appropriate benchmark.

3. A is correct. Time-weighted returns take into account the timing of all the cash inflows (deposits) and outflows (withdrawals) made during the holding period. The time-weighted-return calculation divides the overall holding period into sub-periods. The timing of each cash flow identifies the sub-periods to use for calculating holding-period returns. Each sub-period has its own return. These sub-period returns are then used to calculate the return for the overall holding period. B and C are incorrect because the geometric average return and the arithmetic average return do not take into account the timing of cash inflows and outflows during the holding period.

4. A is correct. The standard deviation reflects the variability (or volatility) of returns around the mean (or average) return. B is incorrect because the reward-to-risk ratio is a measure of risk-adjusted performance, which indicates how much return was generated per unit of risk. C is incorrect because the downside deviation is calculated by using only deviations that are negative. In other words, whereas the standard deviation considers all outcomes, both below and above the mean return, the downside deviation focuses only on the outcomes that are less than the mean return.

5. C is correct. The downside deviation focuses only on the negative deviations—that is, the returns that are less than the mean return. Thus, it is an appropriate measure of risk for investors who dislike losses (negative outcomes) more than they like equivalent gains (positive outcomes). A is incorrect because the Sharpe ratio is a measure of risk-adjusted performance that reflects the excess return on a portfolio (the difference between the portfolio's holding-period return and the return on a "risk-free" investment) per unit of risk. B is incorrect because the standard deviation considers all outcomes, both above and below the mean return. It is a better measure for investors who like gains as much as they dislike equivalent losses.

# Answers

**6** C is correct. The Sharpe ratio is a commonly used reward-to-risk ratio, which is a measure of risk-adjusted performance; the higher the value of the Sharpe ratio, the better the risk-adjusted performance. The Sharpe ratio is equal to the excess return on a portfolio (the difference between the portfolio's holding-period return and the return on a "risk-free" investment) divided by the standard deviation of the portfolio's returns. A is incorrect because the measure of historical volatility is the standard deviation. B is incorrect because the downside deviation is a measure of risk that focuses only on the negative deviations—that is, the returns that are less than the mean return.

**7** A is correct. To be effective, a benchmark should be investable (a fund manager should be able to buy and sell the assets that are included in the benchmark). If the benchmark contained assets that could not be bought or sold, it would be difficult for passive fund managers to mimic the benchmark and for active fund managers to outperform the benchmark. B is incorrect because compatibility means that the benchmark's risk profile should be in line with the investor's desired level of risk. C is incorrect because pre-specification means that the benchmark should be specified in advance so that the manager is clear about the client's objectives.

**8** A is correct. Active fund managers use analytical and trading skills to beat a benchmark. They seek out investments that meet the investment mandate, and their portfolios look different from the benchmark. C is incorrect because passive fund managers simply mimic the holdings of the benchmark and do not attempt to outperform the benchmark. B is incorrect because index replication is a passive approach to managing money.

**9** B is correct. A passive investment fund simply mimics the holdings of the benchmark. Thus, the risk profiles of a passive investment fund and its benchmark should be similar.

**10** B is correct. The tracking error reflects how the performance of the investment fund deviates from the performance of its benchmark. Because a passive investment fund is seeking to replicate a benchmark, the tracking error should be very low. The tracking error is unlikely to be zero because the passive investment fund will underperform its benchmark by the level of fees charged and transaction costs incurred.

**11** C is correct. A positive information ratio indicates that a fund manager added value to his or her client's portfolio. An information ratio of +0.25 indicates that the reward (the difference between the holding-period return on the portfolio and the return on an appropriate benchmark) exceeded the risk (measured as the tracking error).

**12** A is correct. Alpha measures the portion of the fund manager's return that reflects the fund manager's skill. B and C are incorrect because luck and market return are sources of return that are beyond the control of the fund manager and that are not a reflection of his or her investment skill.

**13** B is correct. Beta measures the portion of the investment fund's return attributable to broad market movements over which the fund manager has no control. A is incorrect because randomness is the portion of the investment fund's return attributable to luck. C is incorrect because the portion of the investment fund's return attributable to the fund manager's judgment (or skill) is referred to as alpha, not beta.

**14** B is correct. The outperformance of an investment fund compared with its benchmark is generally referred to as alpha. Alpha reflects the investment skill of the fund manager. A is incorrect because beta reflects the market performance, over which the fund manager has no control. C is incorrect because the tracking error reflects how much the performance of the investment fund deviates from the performance of its benchmark.

**15** A is correct. Attribution analysis is used to identify the source(s) of a fund's or fund manager's performance—how much of the return was attributable to the manager's asset allocation, sector selection, security selection, or currency exposure. B is incorrect because risk-adjusted analysis, such as calculating reward-to-risk ratios, is used to determine how much return was generated per unit of risk. C is incorrect because relative performance analysis is the comparison of the fund manager's holding-period return with the return on an appropriate benchmark.

**16** B is correct. Attribution analysis is used to determine the sources of the fund manager's performance. By using an appropriate benchmark, the fund manager's performance can be decomposed into sources of performance. Depending on the type of fund, performance may come from asset allocation, sector selection, security selection, or currency exposure. A is incorrect because the information ratio is a reward-to-risk ratio and would not explain how much of a fund manager's performance was derived from currency exposure. C is incorrect because the capital asset pricing model (CAPM) separates a fund's return into that portion that could have been achieved passively—that is, resulting from market performance (beta)—and the investment skill of the fund manager (alpha). Although the capital asset pricing model identifies a manager's relative performance, it does not explain whether any differences were attributable to asset allocation, sector selection, security selection, or currency exposure.

# Module 7
# Introduction to Serving Client Needs

Watch an introductory video at cfainstitute.org/claritasstudy.

The investment industry provides a range of services—including brokerage, investment advice, and financial asset management—to a wide variety of clients. Because each investor is unique, it is important to understand each investor's needs to provide the best possible service. It is not possible to act in an investor's (client's) best interest if that interest is not recognised and understood. No matter what role you play in the investment industry, being focused on meeting clients' needs and acting in their best interest will serve you and your organisation well.

As discussed in Chapter 19, a crucial part of the investment process is identifying the investor's needs and documenting them in an investment policy statement to guide the construction and management of the investment portfolio. The investment policy statement clarifies what is and is not appropriate for the investor and provides a basis for assessing performance.

Chapter 20 discusses the allocation of resources to assets within a portfolio. Most investors will benefit from holding a portfolio that is diversified among asset classes and among securities or assets within those asset classes. This diversification is meant to keep expected returns consistent with the investor's requirements while potentially reducing risk. There are many asset classes, including shares, bonds, commodities, and real estate, that may be appropriate for an investor's requirements. The investor's portfolio manager or investment adviser will consider the proportions of the portfolio to invest in each asset class to have the best chance of meeting the investor's requirements. The portfolio manager or investment adviser may retain some flexibility to make modest and short-term departures from the agreed-on long-term strategic allocation among asset classes to increase return. These departures may affect the portfolio's risk.

In some cases, a client will use an investment adviser or portfolio manager to structure the portfolio using the broad asset classes. The investment adviser or portfolio manager may then select managers[1] for each of the asset classes. This strategy allows managers to focus on their respective specialties; few managers can be experts in all asset classes. Each asset class manager will still run a diversified portfolio, but the diversification will be in terms of securities within the asset class rather than among asset classes.

Once a decision has been made on the broad mix of assets for the portfolio, the investor must decide on the approach for managing the underlying securities or assets in each asset class. Different approaches to managing a portfolio are discussed in Chapter 21. The investor or manager may attempt to capture the broad return from an asset class or market by investing widely among available securities or assets in the asset class or market. This approach is called passive management, and the costs of such an approach tend to be relatively low. The investor or manager must analyse which securities or assets to hold and in what proportions to capture the asset class return, but extensive analysis of individual assets within the asset class or of asset markets is not necessary. The manager does not try to identify mispriced assets.

---

[1] The managers may represent a mutual fund.

Written by Alistair Byrne, PhD, CFA.

Copyright © 2012 CFA Institute

Alternatively, an investor may believe that higher portfolio returns on a risk-adjusted basis are possible by identifying and holding securities with better prospects and avoiding those that have poor prospects and/or by altering the allocations to different asset classes based on expectations about the markets in those asset classes. This approach is called active management. Successful active management may result in higher returns, but it also has higher costs. The active manager must perform detailed research on individual potential investments or on asset markets to identify the better performers. Research is costly, and these costs are recovered through higher management fees charged to investors. There may also be higher transaction costs from a higher level of turnover in the portfolio.

Investors engaging in active management must be conscious of the challenges presented by the fact that investment markets are highly competitive and contain many skilled participants. Consistently identifying outperforming investments when prices are set by trading among highly informed investors is a daunting task. But there are investment managers with a successful track record of doing just that.

The choice of management approach and asset allocation within a portfolio should be consistent with a client's needs as documented in the investment policy statement. The investment policy statement should be revisited regularly, at least annually, because a client's needs can change over time as his or her circumstances change.

# CHAPTER 19
INVESTOR NEEDS AND INVESTMENT POLICY

by Alistair Byrne, PhD, CFA

## LEARNING OUTCOMES

After completing this chapter, you should be able to do the following:

**a** Describe the importance of identifying investor needs to the investment process;

**b** Describe and contrast types of investors;

**c** Explain how needs differ among investors;

**d** Describe the rationale for and structure of investment policy statements in serving client needs.

# INTRODUCTION

The investment industry provides a range of services—including brokerage, investment advice, and financial asset management—to a wide variety of clients. Individual investor clients range from those of modest means to the very wealthy. The investment industry also provides services to many types of institutional investors, such as pension funds, insurance companies, and endowments.[1] Because every investor is unique, it is important to understand each investor client's circumstances and requirements in order to best meet each client's needs. It is not possible to act in a client's best interests if those interests are not understood and recognised.

Clients differ in terms of their financial resources, personal situations (for individual clients), objectives, attitudes, financial expertise, and so on. These differences affect their investment needs, what services they require, and what investments are appropriate for them. For example, an elderly client with significant resources may be concerned with estate planning, but an elderly client with modest resources may be more concerned about outliving his or her resources. An investment shortfall may have significant consequences for the latter but be a lesser emphasis for the former. Similarly, an endowment client that is restricted from fundraising is likely to have different needs than an endowment that is allowed to raise additional funds. The former has to meet its financial needs from income or the sale of assets, but the latter may also raise funds to meet its financial needs.

Investors may hold such securities as shares and bonds directly, or they may invest in professionally managed funds to get exposure to the assets they want to hold. Investors may choose the securities or funds themselves, or they may engage an investment professional to assist in the selection. The first step in meeting a client's needs for investment services is to get to know the client.

The most basic distinction among investors is that between individual and institutional investors. Individual investors trade (buy or sell) securities or authorise others to trade securities for their personal accounts. Institutional investors are organisations that hold and manage portfolios of assets for themselves or others. The characteristics that define individual investors are usually different from those that define institutional characteristics.

# TYPES AND CHARACTERISTICS OF INVESTORS

Investors are not a homogeneous group; both individual and institutional investors have distinct characteristics.

---

[1] As described in Chapter 13, an endowment is a non-profit organisation that uses its assets to support specified purposes—typically philanthropic.

Copyright © 2012 CFA Institute

## 2.1 Individual Investors

Individual investors are often differentiated based on their resources. Most will have relatively modest amounts to invest. Other, more affluent individuals will have larger amounts. The term "retail investor" can be used to refer to all individual investors, but it is quite common to use the term to refer to individual investors with modest resources to invest. Many investment firms make a distinction between their retail clients, more affluent clients with larger amounts, and high- and ultra-high-net-worth investors with the largest amounts of investable assets.

There is no defined standard in the industry to categorise individual investors; each investment firm designates its own categories and values within those categories. For example, one firm may use four categories (retail, mass affluent, high-net-worth, and ultra-high net worth) and another firm may use six categories (retail, affluent, wealthy, high-net-worth, very-high-net-worth, and ultra-affluent). Firms that use the same categories may have different cut-off points. For example, one firm may classify retail customers as those with investable assets up to €100,000, and another firm may use a cut-off point of €250,000.

The services offered by investment firms and the investments available will typically vary by the amount of money the client has to invest. Some specialist funds may require minimum sizes of investment (e.g., $1 million), and some portfolio management services may have minimum fees, making them uneconomical for smaller account sizes.

An investment firm that focuses on retail investors will have a business that has to service the needs of a large number of relatively small accounts. Often, this means consolidating the retail investors' assets into a smaller number of funds and having automated processes for administration of client fund holdings.

An investment firm or division focusing on high-net-worth investors may have fewer clients than its retail counterpart but higher average account balances. Investor assets may still be invested in funds, but some high-net-worth investors will prefer their own segregated accounts (known as separately managed accounts). Wealthy clients may have higher expectations of client service than retail customers, and usually the service that is provided to them is more personalised.

Individual investors vary in their level of investment knowledge and expertise. Some individual investors have relatively limited investment knowledge and expertise, and others are more knowledgeable, perhaps as a result of their education or work experience. Because individual investors are often thought of as less knowledgeable and experienced than professional investors, regulators in many countries try to protect them by putting restrictions on the investments that can be sold to them. For example, in the United States, the Securities and Exchange Commission (SEC), as of 2011, restricts investments in hedge funds to accredited investors, which in the case of individuals means having a net worth in excess of $1 million and/or an income in excess of $200,000. This restriction is presumably based on the logic that wealthier investors are expected to be more knowledgeable, or at least better able to pay for advice and better able to bear risk.

The personal situations of individual investors—such as their ages and family obligations, which affect cash needs—will also differ and affect their investment needs and decision making. The expected holding period for investments (time or investment horizon), risk and return requirements, and other circumstances also affect investors' needs.

## 2.2 Institutional Investors

There are many different types of institutional investors with varying investment requirements and constraints.

Some institutions manage their investments internally and employ investment professionals whose job it is to select the investments. Other institutions outsource the investment of the portfolio to one or more external investment firms. The choice between internal and external management will often be driven by the size of the institution, with larger institutions better able to afford the resources required for internal management. Some institutions will adopt a mixed model, managing some assets internally that they have expertise to do but also outsourcing assets to external managers—for example, for overseas assets. Those institutions that choose to outsource investment management still have complex decisions to make in terms of which managers to appoint. They may use some internal expertise to make manager selection decisions, or they may employ a consultant.

In many countries, pension funds are significant institutional investors. Money from employer and/or employee contributions is set aside to provide income to plan members when they retire. For example, a company may set up a pension plan to provide benefits to its employees. These assets must be invested until the employee retires and receives the retirement benefits. Pension funds, therefore, typically have relatively long time horizons. Consider a 20-year-old employee joining a plan that will pay a pension from age 65. That individual might be expected to live to age 85, and thus the assets will be accumulating for 45 years and supporting the income being drawn for at least another 20 years. Furthermore, some individuals will live longer than the average expected life span, further extending the investment period.

In a defined benefit pension plan, the sponsoring employer promises its members a certain amount of benefit. For example, it is quite common for the employer to promise a pension that is a set proportion of the employee's final pre-retirement salary for every year worked. For a pension plan with an accrual rate based on 1/60th of the final salary for each year worked, an employee with 40 years' service would be entitled to a pension of 40/60ths of his or her final salary. The employer will make contributions to the pension plan to fulfil the promise. In a defined benefit plan, the employer bears the risk of the investment portfolio. If the investments made by the pension plan fail to perform as expected, the employer will be required to make additional contributions to the plan. Globally, defined benefit plans are becoming less common and are being replaced by defined contribution plans.

In a defined contribution pension plan, the employee and/or employer make pre-specified contributions into the member's (employee's) pension account. The contributions are then invested, normally in funds that the member chooses from a list of eligible funds within the plan. The list is chosen by the plan sponsor (the employer) to provide enough choice to allow members to create a broadly diversified portfolio. The sponsor should also ensure that the fees charged on the funds are reasonable. At retirement, the balance that has accumulated in the account is available for the member. An important distinction with defined contribution plans compared with defined benefit plans is that the risk of the investment portfolio is borne by the employee rather than the employer. The employer has no obligation to make additional contributions if the investments perform poorly. If the retirement fund is less than expected, the employee may have to make do with less retirement income or possibly defer retirement.

Endowments and foundations are also significant institutional investors in many countries. These institutions typically have a charitable or philanthropic purpose for which money has been gifted or raised. For example, the Wellcome Trust is a U.K.-based, global charitable foundation that supports medical research with grants in excess of £600 million per year; its investment portfolio was £14 billion as of September 2010. Many universities have endowments to support their educational activities. For example, Yale University's endowment fund had $19.4 billion as of June 2011. For that year, the fund contributed $992 million of income to the university; this contribution represented 37% of the university's sources of funds (i.e., tuition, government support, and private donations).

Endowments are usually intended to exist in perpetuity and, as such, can be regarded as very long-term investors. But they are also typically required to spend annually on the charitable purpose, so that money needs to be drawn from the fund. Many endowments and foundations establish spending rules; for example, they may establish spending goals within a percentage range of their assets. Often the challenge lies in balancing long-term growth with income or cash-flow requirements. The Wellcome Trust aims to generate a real (inflation-adjusted) return of 6% per year and commits 4.5% of its fund value (averaged over three years) to grants each year. Each endowment or foundation will have its own specific circumstances. Some will be able to raise funds on an ongoing basis, whereas others will be restricted from raising more capital. Some endowments and foundations are required to spend a fixed portion of the portfolio each year, whereas others have more flexibility to vary spending based on their circumstances. These differences have implications for how the institution's assets are invested.

Insurance companies comprise another important category of institutional investor. Insurance companies are paid premiums and need to invest the money raised from premiums until they have to pay out claims. General or property and casualty insurance companies protect their policyholders from the financial loss caused by such incidents as accidents and theft. Life insurance companies make payments to the policyholder's beneficiaries in the event the policyholder dies while the insurance coverage is in force. Property and casualty insurers have short-term horizons and relatively unpredictable payouts; therefore, they prefer low-risk investments. Life insurers have longer-term time horizons and more predictable payouts and, therefore, have more latitude to invest in riskier assets.

Mutual funds can also be considered institutional investors. There are thousands of mutual funds managed by investment management firms. The funds pool the assets of many investors into a single investment vehicle, which is professionally managed and benefits from economies of scale. Mutual funds are set up with particular objectives—for example, to invest in smaller companies (known as small-cap or small-capitalisation companies) globally. The investment management firm receives a fee for managing the fund. As noted in Chapters 13 and 14, although a mutual fund can be regarded as an institutional investor, the term "mutual fund" also refers to the investment vehicle, shares of which an individual or institutional investor can hold in a portfolio.

Hedge funds can similarly be considered as institutional investors that manage private investment pools and as investment vehicles. As noted in Chapter 14, hedge funds are distinguished from other pooled investment products primarily by their availability to a limited number of select investors, by agreements that lock up the investors' capital for fixed periods, and by their managers' performance-based compensation. They can also be distinguished by their use of strategies beyond the scope of traditional mutual funds.

Companies also have investment assets; they may have money that they do not currently need to invest in their operating business. Often, this money will only be available for a short period before being used within the company's business. In this case, the money is more likely to be held in bank deposits or money market funds. If a company has assets that are not needed for current or future business operations, the company may choose to invest the money.

Sovereign wealth funds (SWFs) are an increasingly important type of institutional investor. These funds are set up to invest assets for the future benefit of the sovereign nation or state and its people. A number of funds have been set up to invest revenues from natural resources, such as oil, for the benefit of future generations. Sovereign wealth funds are now some of the largest investment institutions.

Exhibit 1 shows the five largest sovereign wealth funds ranked by assets as of May 2012. In some cases, the asset values were estimated by the Sovereign Wealth Fund Institute, a global organisation that studies sovereign wealth funds and other long-term governmental investors.

### Exhibit 1  Five Largest Sovereign Wealth Funds

| Country | Fund |
| --- | --- |
| United Arab Emirates | Abu Dhabi Investment Authority |
| Norway | Government Pension Fund |
| China | SAFE Investment Company |
| Saudi Arabia | SAMA Foreign Holdings |
| China | China Investment Corporation |

*Source:* Based on data from www.swfinstitute.org/fund-rankings/

Investors—individual and institutional—differ in their financial resources, circumstances, objectives, attitudes, financial expertise, and so on. These differences affect what services the client requires and what types of investments are appropriate for the client. Therefore, it is important to capture the information about the client and the client's needs.

# 3 INVESTORS' NEEDS

Each investor—individual or institutional—has different investment objectives related to varied circumstances, attitudes, and constraints. Key factors to consider that are common to each investor but that will vary by investor include the following:

- Time horizon
- Return requirement
- Risk tolerance

Investors may also have specific needs in relation to liquidity, tax considerations, regulatory requirement, consistency with particular religious or ethical standards, or other unique circumstances. Investors' circumstances and needs change over time, so it is important to re-evaluate their needs at least annually.

## 3.1 Time Horizon

The investor and adviser must be clear on the time horizon for the investments. Some investors will need to access the funds from their portfolio in the short term, whereas others will have a much longer time horizon.

On the institutional side, for example, a general insurance company that expects to have to meet claims in the next few years will have a short horizon, whereas a sovereign wealth fund that is investing oil revenues for the benefit of future generations will have a long horizon, possibly decades.

In the case of individual investors, someone who is planning on buying a new home or paying for college in two or three years will have a short horizon for at least a portion of his or her investments, but an individual in the middle of his or her career who is saving for retirement will typically have a long horizon, probably more than 20 years.

The investment horizon has important implications for how much risk can be taken with the portfolio and the level of liquidity that may be required. Liquidity is the ease with which the investment can be converted into cash. For example, an illiquid private equity investment with a likely payoff in 10 years would be unsuitable for an investor with a 5-year horizon.

Investors with longer time horizons should be able to take more risk because they have more time to adapt to their circumstances. For example, they can save more to compensate for any losses or returns that are less than expected. History shows that over time, markets go up more often than they go down, so an investor with a longer time horizon has more potential to accumulate positive performance. Longer-term investors are also better able to wait for markets to recover from a period of poor performance, although that recovery cannot be guaranteed.

## 3.2 Required Return

Investors differ in how much return they need to meet their goals. The rate of return required—before and after tax—may be calculated using some goal for future wealth or portfolio value. For example, based on a client's age, initial investable assets, expected savings, and tax situation, an adviser may calculate that a 6% rate of return before tax on investments is required for the individual investor to meet her goal of having a €500,000 portfolio value at retirement. If the required rate of return seems unlikely to be achieved, the investor's goals may have to be revised or other factors, such as the level of savings, may have to be adjusted. For an institutional investor, such as a defined benefit pension fund, a particular rate of return may be required to meet the fund's liabilities. If the return is not achieved, contributions to the fund may have to be increased or pension commitments may have to be adjusted. The latter can be very challenging.

An investor may take a total-return perspective, making no distinction between income (for example, dividends and interest) and capital gains (increases in market value); the source of return, changes in value or income, does not matter to a total-return-oriented investor. Alternatively, an investor may distinguish between income and capital gains because the investor links income with current spending and capital gains with long-term needs. This latter perspective reflects the fact that many investors prefer to spend from current income and do not consider capital gains, which can be realised by selling the investment, as available for current spending. Behavioural finance, which attempts to understand and explain observed investor and market behaviours, refers to this segregation of income and capital gains as a mental accounting bias.

The return requirement, particularly for a long-term horizon, should be specified in real terms, which means adjusting for the effect of inflation. This adjustment is important because it maintains the focus on what the accumulated portfolio will be able to purchase rather than just the nominal monetary value. An increase in value that simply matches inflation does not give a client increased spending power.

The investment manager or adviser has to be comfortable that the investor's desired rate of return is achievable within the related constraints. Most clients would like high returns with low risks, but few investments have this expected profile. The adviser or manager has a role in counselling the client. Typically, higher levels of expected return will require higher levels of risk to be taken. Some investors will choose to invest in highly risky assets because they require high levels of return to meet their goals, but the potential consequences (the downside risks) associated with this strategy need to be understood. Other investors will have already accumulated enough assets so that they do not need high returns and can adopt a lower-risk approach with more certainty of meeting their goal. This situation could be the case for a pension plan that has a high funding level, meaning that its assets are sufficient to meet its liabilities. Other investors that have accumulated significant assets may choose to invest in riskier assets because they are capable of bearing the risk and able to withstand losses. Investors, particularly individual investors, may adjust their holdings over time as their circumstances change.

## 3.3 Risk

Investors typically have limits on how much risk they are willing and able to take with their investments. As noted earlier, there is a link between risk and return. Typically, the higher the expected return, the higher the risk associated with that return or the higher the risk taken, the higher the expected return. The investor's risk tolerance is a function of his or her ability and willingness to take risk.

Ability to take risk depends on the situation of the investor, such as the balance between assets and liabilities and the time horizon. If an investor has far more assets than liabilities, any losses that result from risk taking can usually be covered by the assets. If an investor has a long horizon, he has more scope to adjust his circumstances to cope with losses (e.g., to save more or simply to wait for markets to recover, although recovery and its timing cannot be guaranteed).

Willingness to take risk is related to the investor's psychology, which may be assessed using questionnaires completed by the investor. Willingness to take risk is often thought of as more important for individual investors, but even those who oversee institutional investments will have risk guidelines within which they must operate and that help define their ability and willingness to take risk.

Some institutions, such as insurance companies and other financial intermediaries, may also face regulatory restrictions on how much risk they can take with their portfolio.

There may be situations in which an investor's willingness to take risk and his or her ability to take risk differ. In such situations, the investment adviser should counsel the investor on risk and determine the appropriate level of risk to take in the portfolio, taking into account both the investor's ability and willingness to take risk. The lesser of the two risk levels should be the risk level assumed.

## 3.4 Liquidity

Investors vary in the extent to which they may need to withdraw money from their portfolios. They may need to make a withdrawal to fund a specific purchase or to generate a regular income stream. These needs have implications for the types of investments chosen. When liquidity is required, the investments will need to be able to be converted to cash relatively quickly and without too much cost (keeping transaction costs and changes in price low) when the cash is needed.

An individual may also require that a portion of the portfolio be liquid to meet unexpected expenses. In addition, the individual may have known future liquidity requirements, such as a planned future expenditure on children's education or retirement income needs.

For an institution, the liquidity constraint typically reflects the institution's liabilities. For example, a pension fund may expect to begin experiencing net cash outflows at a particular point in the future (i.e., when pension payments exceed new contributions to the plan) and thus will plan on realising the portfolio investments to meet those needs.

# Investors' Needs

## 3.5 Regulatory Issues

Some types of investors have external regulatory requirements that apply to their portfolios. For example, in some countries and for certain types of institutions, there are restrictions on the proportion of the portfolio that can be invested overseas or in such risky assets as equities. Regulations on the holdings of insurance companies are typically quite extensive. Exhibit 2 shows some restrictions that apply to institutional pension funds in selected countries as of September 2012. In all the countries shown, restrictions exist on the amount of the pension fund that can be invested in equity.

**Exhibit 2  Investment Regulations Applying to Pension Funds in Selected Countries**

| Country | Maximum Equity Investment | Maximum Foreign Investment | Other |
|---|---|---|---|
| United States | No limit | No limit | Restrictions on employer-related investments |
| Switzerland | 50% | No limit | 30% limit for real estate |
| Denmark | 70% | No limit | — |
| Austria | 70% | 30% | — |
| Mexico | 30% | 20% | Maximum equity shown is an approximation; it varies by fund category. |
| Korea | 30% | No limit | Real estate investments are not permitted in defined benefit plans. |

*Source:* Based on data from www.oecd.org/dataoecd/9/1/48094890.pdf

## 3.6 Taxes

Tax circumstances vary among investors. Some types of investors are taxed on their investment returns and others are not. For example, in many countries, pension funds are exempt from tax on investment returns. Furthermore, the tax treatment of income and capital gains can vary. It is important to consider an investor's tax situation and the tax consequences of different investments.

Investors should typically care about the returns they earn after taxes and fees because that is what is available to spend. For example, an investor who is subject to higher tax on dividend income than capital gains will typically desire a portfolio of investments seeking capital growth (i.e., from an increase in value of shares) rather than income (i.e., dividends from shares).

Individuals may also face different tax circumstances on different parts of their wealth. For example, income and capital gains on assets held in a pension account (which has restrictions on when it can be accessed) may be tax exempt or tax deferred, whereas income in other accounts may be fully taxable. In this case, the investor may have a preference for holding income-generating assets in a pension account, which is tax exempt or tax deferred. The investor will hold assets expected to generate capital gains (which are taxed at a lower rate than income) in a taxable investment account. Where assets are located (held) can significantly affect an investor's after-tax returns and wealth accumulation.

### 3.7 Unique Circumstances

Many investors have particular requirements or constraints not captured by the standard categories discussed so far.

Some investors have social, religious, or ethical preferences that affect how their assets can be invested. For example, investors may choose not to hold investments in companies whose activities they believe potentially harms the environment. Other investors may require investments that are consistent with certain religious beliefs. For example, Muslims may not invest in conventional debt securities because they do not believe they comply with Islamic law.

Investors may also have specific requirements that stem from the nature of their broader investment portfolio or financial circumstances. For example, an individual who is employed by a company may want to limit investment in that company. This helps the employee reduce single-company exposure and gain broader diversification. Interestingly, many individuals are actually inclined to boost their holdings in their employer's shares on the grounds of loyalty or familiarity, despite the concentration risk that this strategy entails. Such a strategy can have severe consequences if the company fails or its financial position declines. For example, many employees of Enron Corporation, a U.S. energy company, not only lost their jobs, but also suffered significant investment losses when Enron went bankrupt.

Institutional investors may also have unique and specific requirements as a result of their objectives and circumstances. For example, a medical foundation may want to avoid investing in tobacco stocks because it believes encouraging tobacco smoking is counter to its objectives of improving health.

## 4 THE INVESTMENT POLICY STATEMENT

It is good practice to capture information about the client and the client's needs in an **investment policy statement (IPS)**. The investment policy statement—for both individual and institutional investors—serves as a guide for the investor and investment manager or adviser regarding what is required of and acceptable in the investment portfolio. The IPS also forms the basis for determining what constitutes success in managing the portfolio.

The investment policy statement should capture the investor's objectives and any constraints that will apply to the portfolio. The investor and manager/adviser should agree to the investment policy statement and review it on a regular basis, typically once a year. It should also be reviewed when the client experiences a change in circumstances. Creating and reviewing an IPS is a good opportunity for the investment manager and client to discuss the client's goals (and hopes and fears).

A common format for an investment policy statement is to split it into sections covering objectives and constraints. Each section has its own subsections. The investment policy statement identifies the investor's circumstances and goals, following the types of needs and differences discussed in Section 3, as shown in the following common format:

- Objectives
  - Return requirements
  - Risk tolerance
- Constraints
  - Time horizon
  - Liquidity
  - Regulatory constraints
  - Taxes
  - Unique circumstances

Although the standard form of an investment policy statement (IPS) covers objectives and constraints, many investors, especially institutions, will also include procedural and governance issues in the IPS. The IPS may set out the role of any investment committee, its structure, and its authority. It may also set out the roles of investment managers, the basis on which they will be appointed, and the criteria on which they will be reviewed. An important role of the IPS is to provide information that is useful in determining the types and amounts of assets in which to invest and the way the portfolio will be managed over time; the investment policy statement serves as the basis for determining the appropriate portfolio strategies and asset allocations.

# SUMMARY

- The investment industry provides services to individual investors—from those of modest means (retail customers) to the very wealthy with a substantial amount of money to invest. Investment services are also provided to many types of institutional investors, such as pension funds, insurance companies, and endowments.

- Needs vary among different investor types. Clients have their own objectives related to their circumstances and have different constraints that apply to their portfolios. Key dimensions include

  - Time horizon

- Return requirement—before and after tax

- Risk tolerance

■ Investors may also have particular requirements related to liquidity, tax considerations, regulatory requirements, and other unique circumstances, including consistency with particular religious or ethical standards.

■ It is good practice to capture the needs of an investor in an investment policy statement. The IPS serves as a guide for the investment manager or adviser regarding what is required of and acceptable in the investment portfolio

■ The investment policy statement should capture the investor's objectives and any constraints that will apply to the portfolio. An IPS is typically divided into sections that cover objectives and constraints. Each section has its own subsections.

# CHAPTER REVIEW QUESTIONS

Test your knowledge of this chapter at **cfainstitute.org/claritasstudy**.

1 The investment needs of individual investors are *most likely* described as being:

   A the same among investors of similar ages and wealth.

   B similar in many respects to those of institutional investors.

   C unique to each individual's circumstances and requirements.

2 Which of the following types of investors are *least likely* to be identified as institutional investors?

   A Insurance companies

   B Sovereign wealth funds

   C Ultra-high-net-worth investors

3 Which of the following types of institutional investors is *most likely* to have the shortest investment time horizon?

   A Life insurers

   B Endowments

   C Property and casualty insurers

4 An investor with a longer time horizon will *most likely* have a:

   A higher tolerance for risk.

   B reduced investment return expectation.

   C lower ability to invest in illiquid investments.

5 The return requirement for an investor should be:

   A specified in nominal terms.

   B achievable within the relevant constraints.

   C higher for investors with low risk tolerances.

**6** When an investor's willingness and ability to take risk differ, the investment adviser should counsel the investor about risk. The investment adviser is *most likely* to recommend the use of a risk level based on the:

**A** ability to take risk.

**B** willingness to take risk.

**C** lesser of the two risk levels.

**7** An investor's investment policy statement:

**A** ensures that investment plan objectives are met.

**B** should only be reviewed when the client's circumstances change.

**C** outlines what is required of and acceptable in the investment portfolio.

**8** A difference in investment policy statements for institutional investors and individual investors *most likely* relates to the inclusion of:

**A** client constraints.

**B** investment objectives.

**C** procedural and governance issues.

# ANSWERS

1. C is correct. Investment needs are directly affected by personal situations, such as age, wealth level, family obligations, and investment horizon, which are generally unique among individual investors. A is incorrect because the investment needs of individual investors tend to vary among individuals based on factors in addition to wealth and age, such as family obligations, investment horizon, and so on. B is incorrect because the characteristics that define individual investors are usually different from those that define institutional investors. Consequently, investor needs are likely to be different for individual investors compared with institutional investors.

2. C is correct. High-net-worth and ultra-high-net-worth investors are individual investors with the largest amounts of investable assets. A and B are incorrect because insurance companies and sovereign wealth funds are institutional investors.

3. C is correct. Property and casualty insurers have short-term horizons and relatively unpredictable payouts. A is incorrect because life insurers have longer-term time horizons and relatively predictable payouts. B is incorrect because endowments are usually intended to exist in perpetuity and, as such, can be regarded as very long-term investors.

4. A is correct. Investors with longer time horizons can take on more risk because they have more time to adapt to their circumstances. B is incorrect because investors with long time horizons, and consequently a greater ability to take on risk, are likely to have higher return requirements given their higher level of assumed risk. C is incorrect because investors with long time horizons have a greater ability to invest in illiquid investments.

5. B is correct. The investment manager or adviser has to be comfortable that the investor's desired rate of return is achievable within the related constraints. A is incorrect because the return requirement, particularly for a long-term horizon, should be specified in real terms, which means adjusting for the effect of inflation. Adjusting for the effect of inflation is important because it focuses on what the accumulated portfolio will be able to purchase rather than just the nominal monetary value. C is incorrect because for investors with lower risk tolerances, the return requirement will be lower because of the low level of risk in the portfolio.

6. C is correct. There may be situations in which an investor's willingness to take risk and his or her ability to take risk are different. In such situations, the investment adviser should counsel the investor about risk and determine the appropriate level of risk to take in the portfolio, taking into account both the investor's ability and willingness to take risk. The lesser of the two risk levels should be the risk level assumed.

**7** C is correct. The investment policy statement serves as a guide for the investor and investment manager regarding what is required and what is acceptable in the investment portfolio. A is incorrect because the investment policy statement outlines the investment plan objectives and serves as a guide to achieving the objectives but it cannot ensure that investment plan objectives will be met. B is incorrect because the investor and manager/adviser should agree on the investment policy statement and review it on a regular basis, typically once a year or when the client experiences a change in circumstances.

**8** C is correct. Procedural and governance issues are constraints specific to many institutional investors. A and B are incorrect because the investment policy statement for both institutional investors and individual investors will include client constraints and investment objectives.

# CHAPTER 20

## ASSET ALLOCATION

by Alistair Byrne, PhD, CFA

## LEARNING OUTCOMES

After completing this chapter, you should be able to do the following:

**a** Describe how portfolios are constructed to address client investment objectives and constraints;

**b** Compare strategic and tactical asset allocation.

# INTRODUCTION

As discussed in Chapter 19, an investment policy statement (IPS) provides a summary of an investor's circumstances, goals, constraints, return objectives, and risk tolerance. The IPS helps guide asset allocation—which asset classes and how much of each asset class should be included in the investor's portfolio.

Most investors—both individual and institutional—hold a diversified portfolio of investments rather than a concentration in a single investment. A key reason for this diversification is the desire to manage risk, which is consistent with the saying, "Don't put all of your eggs in one basket." Asset allocation has been found to be the most important determinant of portfolio return.

# SYSTEMATIC RISK, SPECIFIC RISK, AND DIVERSIFICATION

Risk occurs when there is uncertainty, meaning that a variety of outcomes are possible from a particular situation or action. In investment terms, risk is the possibility that the actual realised return on an investment will be something other than the return originally expected on the investment. There will be times when the return fails to meet expectations and times when the return exceeds expectations. Fluctuations in the prices and values of investments (capital gains and losses) reflect the risk of investing. Income (e.g., dividends and interest) may also differ from what was expected.

Most investors prefer higher returns and lower risks. That is, they prefer higher outcomes that are more certain, all other things being equal. The trade-off between risk and return is a fundamental issue in investment management. Typically, the higher the risk of an investment, the higher the expected return; the lower the risk, the lower the expected return.

## 2.1 Systematic and Specific Risk

The returns on such investments as shares, bonds, and real estate will be affected by general economic conditions. Returns will also be affected by issues that are specific to the particular investment.

The risk created by general economic conditions is known as systematic or market-related risk because the risk stems from the wider economic system. For example, if the economy enters a recession, many companies will see a downturn in their revenues and profits.

Copyright © 2012 CFA Institute

Risk that is specific to a certain company or security is known as specific, idiosyncratic, non-systematic, or unsystematic risk. Examples include the share price response when a company launches a great new product (e.g., the Apple iPad) or the response to negative news that a promising new drug has failed in trials.

The distinction between systematic and specific risk is important because the two types of risk have different implications for investors. An investor can diversify away specific risk by holding a number of different securities in the portfolio. This is discussed further in Section 2.2. But the investor can do little to avoid systematic risk because all investments will be affected to some extent. Diversifying an equity portfolio by adding investments, such as real estate, will not eliminate systematic risk because rents and real estate values are affected by the same broad economic conditions as the stock market. The extent to which two asset classes move together is captured by the statistical measure of correlation, which is presented in Chapter 5; the higher the correlation between asset classes, the more similar their price movements.

Because systematic risk cannot be avoided and because risk is undesirable, investors have to be compensated for taking on systematic risk; more exposure to systematic risk tends to be associated with higher expected returns. Modern portfolio theory suggests that taking on more specific risk does not necessarily lead to higher returns on average because specific risk can be diversified away. However, some investors may try to identify shares that they expect to outperform (to earn higher returns than expected based on their risk) and invest in them rather than diversifying. In the process, investors take on specific risk; if they turn out to be correct, they may benefit (earn a higher return) from being willing to take on more risk.

## 2.2 Diversification

**Diversification** is one of the most important principles of investing. When assets and/or asset classes with different characteristics are combined in a portfolio, the overall level of risk is typically reduced.

Mathematically, a portfolio that combines two assets has an expected return that is the weighted average of the returns on the individual assets.[1] But provided that the two assets are less than perfectly correlated, the risk of the portfolio (measured by standard deviation of returns) will be less than the weighted average of the risk of the two assets individually.[2] Overall, this means the risk–return trade-off, which is a key concern for investors, is better for the portfolio of assets than for the individual assets.

Most investors hold more than two securities in their portfolios. Adding more securities to a portfolio will reduce risk through diversification, although eventually the additional benefits begin to lessen. Exhibit 1 shows levels of risk for shares chosen at random from the universe of all shares in the U.S. market. Specific risk (non-systematic risk) is reduced by combining additional shares, but as the portfolio moves beyond 30 shares, the incremental risk reduction benefits are lower and the associated trading costs often outweigh any incremental benefit of risk reduction. Exhibit 1 illustrates

---

[1] The expected return on a portfolio of $x$ assets is the weighted average of the returns on the individual assets.
[2] The systematic risk (measured by beta) of a portfolio is the weighted average of the systematic risks of the individual assets. Systematic risk cannot be diversified away.

the concepts of specific risk and diversification. Specific risk is highest at the left side of the exhibit (one share) and lowest at the right side of the exhibit because much of the specific risk is diversified away.

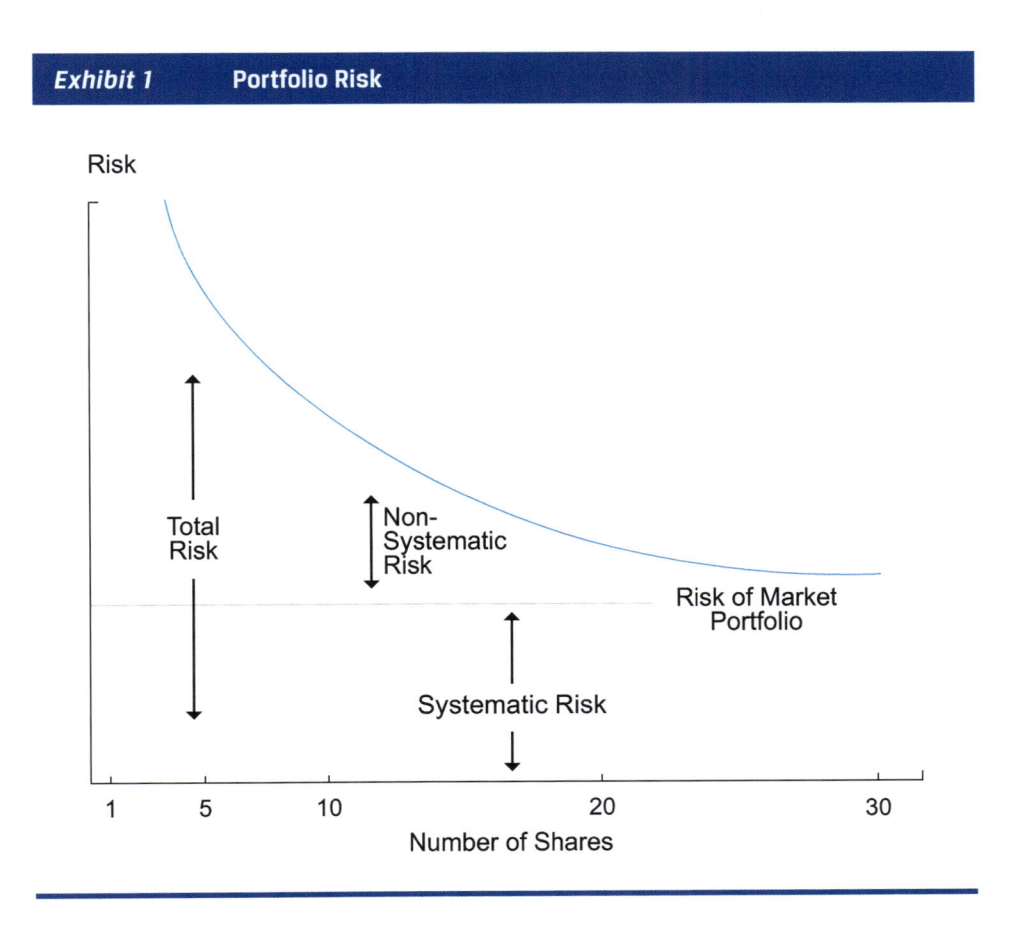

**Exhibit 1    Portfolio Risk**

[Chart showing Risk on the y-axis and Number of Shares (1, 5, 10, 20, 30) on the x-axis. A curve decreases from upper left to lower right, approaching the Risk of Market Portfolio line. Total Risk is indicated on the left, composed of Non-Systematic Risk (above the market portfolio line) and Systematic Risk (below the line).]

The analysis shown in Exhibit 1 assumes randomly chosen shares. The risk reduction benefits have the potential to be greater when the shares are chosen deliberately to have low correlation with each other, perhaps by choosing shares in different industrial sectors (e.g., banks, utilities, pharmaceuticals) or even by choosing shares in different regions and countries.

Diversification also works at the asset class level, so combining different asset types can reduce portfolio risk. For example, the investor might combine investments in various stock and bond markets with investments in real estate and commodities to reduce overall portfolio risk.

# 3 ASSET ALLOCATION AND PORTFOLIO CONSTRUCTION/MANAGEMENT

After the objectives and constraints of the investment policy statement have been established, the next important step is to determine the asset allocation of the portfolio. This step involves decisions regarding which asset classes are eligible for investment (e.g., global equities, domestic government bonds, commodities, or domestic real estate investment trusts) and the proportion of the portfolio to invest in each asset class. In some cases, the asset allocation decision is documented as part of the investment policy statement; in other cases, asset allocation is regarded as part of the subsequent implementation of the IPS.

## 3.1 Strategic Asset Allocation

**Strategic asset allocation** is the long-term mix of assets that is expected to meet the investor's objectives. The desired overall risk and return profile of the portfolio is a factor in determining the strategic asset allocation. A portfolio with a strategic asset allocation dominated by global equities would be expected to have a higher return and be more volatile than a portfolio dominated by domestic bonds because bonds generally have lower returns and lower risk than equities. The strategic asset allocation suitable for one investor may not be suitable for another.

Academic studies have demonstrated that strategic asset allocation significantly affects the average return to a portfolio. Thus, asset allocation warrants considerable attention from investors, investment managers, and investment advisers.

Consider the following example of strategic asset allocation.

> **EXAMPLE 1. STRATEGIC ASSET ALLOCATION**
>
> An institutional investor requires a 6% return on its portfolio. The investment committee wants to invest in global equities and in European government bonds. At the time the investment is made, European government bonds are yielding 4%, and the committee's expectation for the long-term return on the global equity market is 9%.
>
> A portfolio allocation of 60% bonds and 40% equity gives an expected return of 6%:
>
> $(0.60 \times 4\%) + (0.40 \times 9\%) = 6\%$
>
> Of course, the committee has to consider the implied level of risk. If the committee is not comfortable with the risk, the return requirement may need to be reduced. The required portfolio mix may change over the long term as bond yields change and the committee revises its expectations for the return on the stock market.

# Asset Allocation and Portfolio Construction/Management

Strategic asset allocation typically requires the manager to estimate the expected risk and return of each asset class, which can be determined in a number of ways. Historical returns can be used as a guide, but estimates need to be forward looking. The manager also needs to determine the correlation of returns between the asset classes so that he or she can calculate the diversification benefits that may be achieved by combining the various assets in a portfolio.

A common way to build a strategic asset allocation is to use a mean–variance model. In such a model, return and risk are captured by the mean and the variance, respectively; recall from Chapter 5 that variance is the standard deviation squared. To calculate an **efficient portfolio**, the risk, return, and correlation data can be put into a mathematical model. An efficient portfolio is a portfolio that offers the maximum level of return for a given level of risk or, similarly, the minimum level of risk for a given level of return. This idea is based on the fact that investors desire high returns but want to reduce risk. The model used to determine the strategic asset allocation, whether mean–variance or another model, needs to incorporate the investor's objectives and constraints.

The chosen strategic asset allocation is expected to meet the investor's long-term risk and return objectives. An investor may set the strategic asset allocation and simply hold that portfolio for the life of the investment. If the investor does so, the proportions of the portfolio will likely depart from the chosen weights as the different asset classes provide different rates of return and their values increase or decrease by different amounts.

Consider Example 2, which shows the departure from the chosen weights as the asset classes provide different rates of return.

> **EXAMPLE 2. ASSET ALLOCATION OVER TIME**
>
> An investor starts the year with a portfolio worth $200. This portfolio includes $120 of equities and $80 of bonds. Thus, it is 60% invested in equities ($120 ÷ $200) and 40% invested in bonds ($80 ÷ $200).
>
> During the year, equities return +15% and bonds return −2%. Thus, the portfolio's return is 8.2%:
>
> (0.60 × 15%) + (0.40 × −2%) = 8.2%
>
> Because the returns on equities and bonds differ, the weighting of each in the portfolio at the end of the year will be different from the weighting at the beginning of the year. The value of equities at the end of the year is $138.0:
>
> $120 × (1 + 15%) = $138.0
>
> The value of bonds at the end of the year is:
>
> $80 × (1 − 2%) = $78.4
>
> Thus, the value of the portfolio is $216.4 (= $138.0 + $78.4). As summarised in the following table, at the end of the year, the weights of equities and bonds are 64% ($138.0 ÷ $216.4) and 36% ($78.4 ÷ $216.4), respectively.

|  | Equities | Bonds | Portfolio |
|---|---|---|---|
| Value at start of year | $120 | $80 | $200 |
| Weight at start of year | 60% | 40% | 100% |
| Return for year | 15% | −2% | 8.2% |
| Value at end of year | $138.0 | $78.4 | $216.4 |
| Weight at end of year | 64% | 36% | 100% |

The overall portfolio value has increased, and the weighting between equities and bonds has changed. Instead of a 60/40 asset allocation, the investor now has a 64/36 asset allocation. The investor may want to rebalance to return to the initial strategic weights, given his or her risk preferences.

**Rebalancing** involves selling some of the holdings that have increased in proportion and investing the proceeds into the holdings that have decreased as a proportion of the portfolio. In Example 2, equities would be sold and the proceeds invested in bonds. The investor has to decide on a rebalancing policy. For example, the investor may set the frequency of rebalancing or a range of weights beyond which rebalancing occurs. Because there are trading costs associated with rebalancing, most investors will not rebalance on a continual basis but will instead rebalance at specified intervals or weightings.

### 3.2 Tactical Asset Allocation

Although the chosen strategic asset allocation is expected to meet the investor's objectives over the long term, there are times when shorter-term fluctuations in asset class returns may be exploited to potentially increase returns. The short-term adjustment among asset classes is known as **tactical asset allocation**; it is a timing decision among asset classes.

For example, if we continue with the case in which an investor has a strategic asset allocation of 60% global equities and 40% domestic bonds, the manager may think the global equity market is overvalued and likely to face poor returns in the short term. In response, he or she could adjust the asset allocation to 50% equities and 50% bonds. If the manager's expectation is correct, this 50/50 portfolio will perform better than the strategic asset allocation of 60/40. The manager will have added return for the investor versus maintaining the strategic weights on a static basis. That said, forecasting markets is difficult, and tactical deviations do not always work to the benefit of the investor. The difficulty of forecasting explains why investors may choose to maintain the strategic asset allocation within predetermined ranges. For example, the acceptable strategic asset allocation may be determined to be 56–64% global equities and 36–44% domestic bonds rather than 60% global equities and 40% domestic bonds. Such ranges allow for some tactical asset allocation and reduce the frequency of portfolio rebalancing.

The investor or manager typically uses a variety of tools and inputs to make tactical allocation decisions. The decisions may be based on fundamental analyses of economic and political conditions and their likely effects on market returns, on market valuation measures relative to past experience, and/or on trends and momentum in markets. In practice, such decisions are often based on a combination of those factors.

The manager may look at the strength of the economy and likely future trends to gain a perspective on how the central bank might change interest rates and on what might happen to corporate profits. The manager could then look at the level of the price-to-earnings ratio on the stock market and how it compares with recent decades as a measure of valuation or with the level of bond yields relative to historical ranges. The manager could also look at stock and bond market trends as a way of gauging investor sentiment.

Tactical asset allocation is a form of active portfolio management. Active management is discussed in more detail in Chapter 21.

## SUMMARY

- Asset allocation is the largest contributor to portfolio return.

- An investor, in conjunction with the investment manager, must decide on the asset allocation within the investment portfolio.

- The trade-off between risk and return is a fundamental issue in investment management. Typically, the higher the risk of an investment, the higher the expected return; the lower the risk, the lower the expected return.

- The returns on such investments as shares, bonds, and real estate are likely to be affected by general economic conditions. Risk created by general economic conditions is known as systematic risk. Risk specific to a certain security or company is known as specific, idiosyncratic, or unsystematic risk.

- Portfolio theory contends that systematic risk cannot be avoided but that specific risk can be diversified away. Investors should be compensated for systematic risk but not necessarily for specific risk. Thus, taking on more specific risk does not necessarily lead to higher returns.

- Diversification is an important concept in investment theory. When shares or other investments with different characteristics are combined in a portfolio, the overall level of risk is typically reduced. The combination of two or more assets in a portfolio results in an expected return on the portfolio that is the weighted average of the returns on the individual assets. However, provided the assets are less than perfectly correlated, the risk of the portfolio will be less than the weighted average of the risk of the assets.

- Strategic asset allocation is the long-term mix of assets that is expected to meet an investor's objectives. Strategic asset allocation is a decision that has a great impact on the long-term returns on a portfolio.

- Although the strategic asset allocation should meet the investor's objectives over the longer term, the manager or investor can potentially increase returns by exploiting short-term fluctuations in asset class returns. The process of exploiting these short-term fluctuations by adjusting the asset class mix in the portfolio is known as tactical asset allocation.

# CHAPTER REVIEW QUESTIONS

Test your knowledge of this chapter at **cfainstitute.org/claritasstudy**.

1 Systematic risk is the portion of total risk that:

   A is related to a certain company or security.

   B is created by general economic conditions.

   C results from a lack of portfolio diversification.

2 An investor currently owns a portfolio of five securities. If the investor adds another security to the portfolio that is less than perfectly positively correlated with the other five securities, the portfolio's:

   A total risk will likely increase.

   B systematic risk will likely decrease.

   C idiosyncratic risk will likely decrease.

3 The benefits of risk reduction are *most likely* to be greater by combining securities whose expected returns have a:

   A low correlation.

   B perfectly positive correlation.

   C high, but less than perfect, correlation.

4 The long-term mix of assets that is expected to meet an investor's objectives *best* describes:

   A tactical asset allocation.

   B strategic asset allocation.

   C the investor's efficient portfolio.

5 An efficient portfolio can be *best* described as:

   A a common way to build a tactical asset allocation.

   B the portfolio that offers the greatest return for a given level of risk.

   C the portfolio that offers the greatest risk for a given level of return.

**6** The act of an investment manager adjusting her portfolio to take advantage of short-term fluctuations in asset returns *most likely* describes:

**A** rebalancing.

**B** tactical asset allocation.

**C** strategic asset allocation.

# ANSWERS

1. B is correct. Systematic risk (also known as market-related risk) is the risk created by general economic conditions. A is incorrect because the risk that is related to a certain company or security is known as specific, idiosyncratic, non-systematic, or unsystematic risk. C is incorrect because specific risk, not systematic risk, is the result of a lack of diversification.

2. C is correct. Adding securities that are less than perfectly positively correlated with the other securities in the portfolio will likely decrease the idiosyncratic (also known as specific, non-systematic, or unsystematic) risk and, therefore, the total risk. A is incorrect because the total risk of the portfolio will likely decrease, not increase, as a result of the decrease in idiosyncratic risk. B is incorrect because the portfolio's systematic risk is independent of the number of securities in the portfolio. Thus, systematic risk will remain unchanged.

3. A is correct. When securities with different characteristics are combined in a portfolio, the overall level of risk is typically reduced as a result of diversification. The risk reduction benefits resulting from diversification are greatest when the securities have returns that exhibit a low correlation with each other. B is incorrect because there will not be any diversification benefit when the securities in the portfolio have returns that exhibit a perfectly positive correlation. C is incorrect because a less than perfect correlation will reduce risk but not as significantly as a low correlation.

4. B is correct. Strategic asset allocation is the long-term mix of assets that is expected to meet the investor's objectives. The desired overall risk and return profile of the portfolio is a factor in determining the strategic asset allocation. A is incorrect because tactical asset allocation refers to short-term adjustments among asset classes. Although the chosen strategic asset allocation is expected to meet the investor's objectives over the longer term, there may be times when shorter-term fluctuations in asset class returns may be exploited to potentially increase returns. C is incorrect because the efficient portfolio is a portfolio that offers the maximum level of return for a given level of risk (or the minimum level of risk for a given level of return). A common way to build an investor's strategic asset allocation is to create an efficient portfolio using a mean–variance model.

5. B is correct. An efficient portfolio is a portfolio that offers the maximum level of return for a given level of risk. A is incorrect because efficient portfolios are often used to build an investor's strategic, not tactical, asset allocation. C is incorrect because an efficient portfolio is a portfolio that offers the least risk for a given level of return.

6. B is correct. Tactical asset allocation refers to portfolio adjustments to the strategic asset allocation in an effort to take advantage of short-term fluctuations in asset class returns. Although the chosen strategic asset allocation is expected to meet the investor's objectives over the longer term, there may be times when shorter-term fluctuations in asset class returns may be exploited to potentially

increase returns. A is incorrect because rebalancing refers to resetting a portfolio to its initial strategic weights. Rebalancing involves selling some of the holdings that have increased in proportion and investing the proceeds into the holdings that have decreased as a proportion of the portfolio. C is incorrect because strategic asset allocation is the long-term mix of assets that is expected to meet the investor's objectives.

# CHAPTER 21

## ACTIVE AND PASSIVE INVESTMENT MANAGEMENT

by Alistair Byrne, PhD, CFA

# LEARNING OUTCOMES

After completing this chapter, you should be able to do the following:

**a** Compare active and passive investment management;

**b** Explain factors necessary for profitable active management;

**c** Describe how active managers attempt to identify and capture market inefficiencies.

# 1  INTRODUCTION

Beyond deciding which asset classes to invest in and how much to invest in each, an investor must decide whether to use an active or passive management approach. Active managers attempt to add value to a portfolio by selecting investments that are expected, on the basis of analysis, to outperform a specified benchmark. Possible benchmarks include broad market indices, indices for specific market segments, specially constructed benchmarks, and even absolute return targets. Passive managers manage a portfolio designed to track the performance of a specified benchmark. The choice between the two approaches typically hinges on the relative costs of active management and on the investor's expectation of his or her chances of success at active management, which is related to the investor's beliefs about the efficiency of the markets being invested in. Another example of active management is the timing decision among asset classes, as illustrated by tactical asset allocation, which was discussed in Chapter 20.

# 2  MARKET EFFICIENCY

An informationally efficient market is one in which the prices of investments reflect available information about the fundamental values and return prospects of the assets they represent. For example, in a stock market context, a company with good prospects warrants a high stock valuation, which reflects the future profits that will likely accrue to the shareholders. A company with poor prospects will warrant a low valuation to reflect the anticipated low future profitability of the company. If markets are efficient, there is little point to actively managing stock market investments because share prices already reflect the potential of the underlying companies; there is little to uncover via further research. In contrast, in an inefficient market, shares may be over- or undervalued relative to the company's prospects, and an investor may be rewarded with excess returns by successfully identifying such shares. A similar analysis applies for other asset classes.

Some investors argue that stock markets in developed economies are relatively efficient but that markets in emerging economies are less so. They argue that public information flows may not be as extensive or reliable in emerging markets and that it is possible for some investors to access and use information that is not available to others. This situation may exist because there may be less market regulation in emerging markets than in more mature markets or because there may be an absence of skilled analysts investigating emerging markets. Similarly, some investors argue that shares of smaller companies are less efficiently priced than shares of larger companies because fewer investors and analysts take the time to research smaller companies in detail and information is less available. The most efficient markets tend to be those with a reasonably large number of active, informed participants.

Copyright © 2012 CFA Institute

The markets for such investments as real estate or private equity may not be efficient because information on these investments is not publicly available and trading is less active and done privately rather than in a public market in which prices and volumes can be observed. These factors may mean that some investors have access to information and deals that are not available to other investors. An investor may decide to use a passive approach in some markets and an active approach in other markets.

## 3 ACTIVE AND PASSIVE MANAGEMENT

**Passive investment managers** seek to match the return and risk of an appropriate benchmark. Benchmarks include broad market indices, indices for a specific market segment, and specifically constructed benchmarks. Passive investment managers attempt to minimise tracking error. Recall from Chapter 18 that the tracking error is the deviation of the return on the portfolio from the return on the benchmark being tracked. Passive managers may try to fully replicate the benchmark by holding all the benchmark's securities or investments in proportions equivalent to their weighting in the benchmark. But many benchmarks are difficult and costly to fully replicate, sometimes because of the number of securities or because of liquidity and availability issues. Instead of full replication, passive managers may use a tracking approach and hold some subset of the market that is expected to closely track the benchmark's return and risk. The passive manager must consider the difficulties of tracking the return of the benchmark. The tracking approach is typically used if it is impractical to own all the securities or investments in the benchmark. For example, a passive manager in the U.K. equity market might attempt to replicate the FTSE 100 market index directly or attempt to track the index by selecting a subset of shares to represent each industrial sector of the market. Bond index funds typically use the tracking approach because it is almost impossible to own every bond issue in the index. A passive investor must be willing to take on the market exposure and risk of the underlying market.

**Active investment managers** use a variety of approaches. They may attempt to select assets in a benchmark that will outperform the benchmark. These active managers focus on selecting individual securities or assets in an asset class or classes. Active managers may also try to time a market (buying when they believe the market is undervalued and selling when they believe the market is overvalued) and use tactical asset allocation. These active managers focus on identifying asset classes that are expected to perform strongly.

In the case of equity investments, the selection of shares may be based on fundamental analysis of the prospects of companies represented by the securities, on quantitative analysis of the valuation of the share, and/or on technical analysis of trends and momentum in the market. These approaches to analysis are discussed in Section 3.2. Based on their analysis, the active managers will purchase shares that are expected to have superior returns and sell or underweight shares that are expected to underperform. Active managers will periodically update and revise their expectations and adjust their holdings accordingly.

# Active and Passive Management

Passive management is typically cheaper to implement than active management because successfully replicating or tracking a benchmark requires fewer analytical resources than researching and identifying investments with superior return potential does. The passive approach requires knowing which investments are included in the benchmark and their respective values and weights in the benchmark. Although the costs of passive management are lower than the costs of active management, the return earned by the passive investor will typically be less than the index return because of costs.

Active approaches require a much more detailed analysis of each relevant investment or asset class, which is costly. Active management typically also has higher transaction costs because of more frequent trading in the portfolio. If active management does achieve higher-than-benchmark returns, the excess return may compensate for the higher management and transaction costs, and the net returns to the investor may be higher.

Proponents of active management argue that good active managers can more than cover their costs and thus deliver net benefit to investors. Conversely, proponents of passive management argue that the difficulty of identifying superior investments is such that it is not worth paying higher costs for that effort and that passive management will deliver higher net-of-costs returns over the longer term. Although much analysis has been done, the relative merits of active and passive management are still being debated. Some investors hold both active and passive portfolios.

The choice between active and passive management depends in part on the asset class in question. As noted in Section 2, some markets may be regarded as more efficient than others. Active management may be preferred in less efficient markets. Other characteristics can also affect the decision. Passive management of equity portfolios is a well-established discipline and replicating an equity market index is quite straightforward. But for a market such as real estate, where all properties are unique and trading is done in private transactions rather than on a public stock exchange, it is less clear how a passive approach could be put into effect. There may not be a suitable index for passive managers to track. In addition, real estate assets themselves have to be managed (maintained, rented, refurbished, etc.) in a way that equity investments do not. Thus, most investments in real estate are actively managed to some extent. A similar argument applies to private equity and venture capital.

## 3.1 Factors Needed for Active Management to Be Profitable

Active management is a challenging task, but there are managers who have impressive records of success. The prices of shares and other investments are set by the buying and selling activity of many investors in the market. Most developed markets are dominated by well-resourced professional investors from fund management companies and investing institutions. For active managers to be consistently successful, they have to be better at assessing the prospects of investments than other investors. When one active manager buys a share or investment because his or her analysis suggests it has good return prospects, he or she may be buying it from another active manager taking a pessimistic view.

Some of the difficulty in active management is derived from the fact that it is essentially a zero-sum game. For one investor to outperform the market, another investor must underperform by an equivalent amount. Professional investment managers might assume that individual investors trading on their own behalf are likely to make mistakes and to be a source of profits. Non-domestic investors, without good access to local information, might also be a source of mispricing in equity or in other investments that domestic professional investors could exploit. Behavioural finance describes how biases may result in errors of judgment. For example, investors may overreact to new information. Active managers who avoid these biases and errors may add value.

For active managers to identify outperforming shares on a consistent basis, they must either have access to better information than other investors or be able to respond and use the same information faster or with better models to process the information. These requirements are demanding. In many markets, corporate disclosure regulations mean that information on company fundamentals must be made available to all investors at the same time. In fact, laws typically prohibit selective disclosure of material information on company prospects or performance. With hundreds and thousands of profit-motivated investors digesting corporate information, it is a tough requirement to interpret the information faster and better than the aggregate market view.

For active management to be successful, any mispricing of investments has to be substantial enough to cover the costs of exploiting this mispricing. Investing in an undervalued security is only worthwhile to the extent that the excess return covers the cost of the research required to identify the security and the trading costs involved in investing in it. Trading costs will vary by asset type, from relatively low amounts for government bonds and shares of large companies in developed equity markets to much higher amounts for shares of small companies and private market transactions, such as private equity and real estate.

## 3.2 Identifying and Capturing Market Inefficiencies

Active managers often try to identify and capture market inefficiencies through fundamental research. For equity investors, this process means conducting a detailed and thorough analysis of a company's business model, its prospects, and its financial situation. This analysis may involve meeting with company management and interviewing them about their strategy and the prospects of the company. Analysts must take care not to violate laws and regulations when gathering information. Their goal is to identify companies that have better prospects than the stock market is giving them credit for. Typically, an analyst or manager performs some form of fundamental analysis to arrive at an estimated value for a company's shares. If the share price is significantly below the estimated value, the manager will increase the weighting of the shares in the portfolio or add the shares to the portfolio.

Other approaches are also used. Some managers build statistical models that try to identify shares that are likely to outperform. By analysing data, they identify characteristics that have typically been associated with share price outperformance. For example, the analysis might suggest that companies with below-market average valuation levels (for example, the ratio of the share price to earnings per share, known as P/E) and above-average expected earnings growth tend to outperform. This insight can then be used to search for shares currently showing those characteristics. Managers using this approach are often called quants based on the quantitative models they use.

Some managers use a technical approach, seeking to assess price and trading volume trends in the stock market to identify shares that will outperform. For example, a manager who believes in momentum will try to invest in shares that have recently been rising in the market, which is based on the notion that these shares will continue to rise. Other managers might look for signs of imbalance between the potential buyers and sellers of a share to try to predict which direction the share is likely to move.

In practice, many managers use a blend of the techniques discussed here, combining fundamental analysis with quant models and technical analysis to reach a decision regarding which shares to buy.

In other asset classes, similar types of analysis are performed, although the precise variables of interest differ. For example, a real estate manager considers how the value of the property he or she is considering compares with similar properties in the area, how its rental prospects might develop in the future, and whether there is scope to add value to the property through redevelopment.

Once the analysis is complete, managers need to reflect the results in the portfolio. This process involves purchasing or having larger weights in the investments expected to perform well and having smaller or zero weights in the investments regarded as having poor prospects or even short-selling them. For active management to be successful, the portfolio guidelines and restrictions have to be wide enough for managers to be able to implement the results of their analysis in the portfolio—for example, allowing equities to be held $X\%$ over or under the proportion of equities in the index benchmark the fund is being measured against. Portfolio guidelines encourage diversification and prevent excess concentration of the portfolio in any single asset or asset class; diversification is still desirable.

None of the techniques discussed remove the fundamental issue that active management is about forecasting the future in terms of how companies and their associated share prices (or other securities and assets) will perform. Sophisticated techniques cannot remove the inherent uncertainty of the future.

## SUMMARY

- An efficient market is one in which prices reflect the fundamental values and prospects of the assets they represent.

- Active management attempts to add value to the portfolio through the selection of investments that are expected to outperform the benchmark and/or through tactical asset allocations. Passive management is simply managing a portfolio designed to track the performance of a benchmark. The choice between the two approaches typically hinges on the costs of active management and on the investor's expectation of his or her chances of success at active management, which is related to beliefs about the efficiency of the market.

- Passive management is typically cheaper to implement than active management because fewer analytical resources are required to successfully track a market index than to research and identify investments expected to have superior returns. If active management does achieve a higher-than-benchmark return, the excess return may compensate for the higher costs. But it is not certain that the active manager can consistently identify superior investments; consistently successful active management is challenging to achieve.

- At a minimum, the successful active manager needs access to better information or the ability to process information faster and/or better than other investors. These requirements are demanding. Finally, for active management to be successful, any mispricing of investments has to be substantial enough to cover the costs of exploiting it.

- Active managers often attempt to identify and capture market inefficiencies by using fundamental analysis to identify mispriced shares. Other managers (quants) attempt to build statistical models that identify shares that are likely to outperform. Finally, some managers use technical analysis to assess price and volume trends to identify shares that will outperform. In practice, many managers use a blend of the techniques.

# CHAPTER REVIEW QUESTIONS

Test your knowledge of this chapter at **cfainstitute.org/claritasstudy**.

1 Which of the following statements *best* describes passive management? Passive investment managers:

   A  attempt to outperform the benchmark.

   B  tend to earn higher returns than the benchmark.

   C  seek to match the risk and return of the benchmark.

2 Active investment managers are *more likely* than passive investment managers to:

   A  try to time a market.

   B  seek to minimise tracking error.

   C  use strategic asset allocation.

3 Active investment management is *most likely* to be favoured over passive management:

   A  for real estate investments.

   B  when markets are efficient.

   C  for equity investments included in an index.

4 The factor *most likely* to contribute to the success of active management is the:

   A  existence of trading costs.

   B  existence of inefficient markets.

   C  inability for active managers to consistently access better information than other investors.

5 Analysts who review share price and trading volume trends in an effort to identify shares that might outperform are *most likely*:

   A  technical analysts.

   B  fundamental analysts.

   C  quantitative modelers.

# ANSWERS

1. C is correct. Passive investment managers seek to match the risk and return of an appropriate benchmark. A is incorrect because passive investment managers do not try to outperform the benchmark. B is incorrect because although the costs of passive management are lower than the costs of active management, the return earned by the passive investor will typically be less than the benchmark return because of these costs.

2. A is correct. Active managers may try to time a market (buying when they believe a market is undervalued and selling when they believe a market is overvalued). B is incorrect because passive investment managers, rather than active managers, attempt to minimize tracking error. C is incorrect because passive investment managers, rather than active managers, tend to use strategic asset allocation.

3. A is correct. Active management may be preferred in less efficient markets and also for unique assets in which trading occurs in private transactions. Real estate assets are generally unique and are traded in private transactions, thereby increasing the need for and opportunities from active management. B is incorrect because if markets are efficient, there is little point to actively managing investments; asset prices already reflect available information and the potential of the underlying investments. C is incorrect because passive management of equity portfolios is a well-established discipline and replication of an equity market index is quite straightforward.

4. B is correct. The existence of inefficient markets creates an environment in which security mispricing may occur, and active management may prove beneficial in exploiting such mispricing. If markets are efficient, there is little point to actively managing investments because asset prices already reflect the available information and the potential of the underlying investments. A is incorrect because trading costs reduce the expected benefit of active management and may limit the success of active management. For active management to be successful, any mispricing of investments has to be substantial enough to cover the costs of exploiting the mispricing. C is incorrect because the success of active management will be limited if active managers cannot consistently access better information than other investors. Active managers may also be able to use the same information faster than other investors or have better models to process the information.

5. A is correct. Technical analysts use price and trading volume trends within the stock market to identify stocks that will outperform or underperform. For example, managers might look for imbalances between the potential buyers and sellers of a stock as a sign of which direction the share may move. B is incorrect because fundamental analysts conduct a detailed and thorough analysis of a company's business model, its prospects, and its financial situation to identify shares that will outperform or underperform. C is incorrect because quantitative modelers build statistical models to identify shares that are likely to outperform or underperform.

# GLOSSARY

**Absolute advantage**  When a country is more efficient in producing a good or service than other countries—that is, it needs fewer resources to produce the good or service.

**Absolute returns**  The returns achieved over a certain time period. Absolute returns do not consider the risk of the investment or the returns achieved by similar investments.

**Accounting profit**  Net income reported on the income statement.

**Accounts payable**  Money owed by a company to suppliers that have extended the company credit.

**Accounts receivable**  Money owed to a company by customers who purchase on credit.

**Accrual basis**  Accounting method in which revenues and related expenses are recorded when the revenues are earned (expenses recognised) rather than when they are received (paid) in cash.

**Accrued liabilities**  Liabilities related to expenses that have been incurred but not yet paid as of the end of an accounting period.

**Active investment managers**  Managers who actively buy and sell assets and/or alter asset allocations and seek to earn excess risk-adjusted returns.

**Ad hoc documents**  Documents that are typically informal, such as letters, memos, and e-mails.

**Adverse selection**  Tendency for people who are most at risk to buy insurance, causing insurance companies to experience insured losses that are greater than average losses.

**Allocationally efficient economies**  Economies that use resources where they are the most valuable.

**Alpha**  Outperformance relative to a relevant market benchmark.

**Alternative investments**  A diverse set of investment classes, such as private equity, real estate, and commodities, that provide an alternative to traditional investments, such as stocks, bonds, and cash.

**Alternative trading systems**  Venues that match buy and sell orders, but that are not as regulated as exchanges.

**Amortization**  The process of expensing the costs of intangible assets over their useful lives.

**Analysts**  Analysts select, evaluate, and interpret information to arrive at an opinion.

**Annual percentage rate**  The cost of borrowing expressed as a yearly rate without compounding.

**Annuity**  A finite set of level, sequential cash flows; period payments are all the same amount.

**Arbitrage opportunity**  An opportunity to make money by taking advantage of a price difference between two markets.

**Arbitrageurs**  Traders who simultaneously buy and sell identical (or similar) securities, assets, financial contracts, or portfolios of these instruments in two or more markets.

**Arithmetic mean**  The sum of the items in a data set divided by the number of items.

**Ask exchange rate**  See *offer exchange rate*.

**Ask prices**  Prices at which a dealer is willing to sell an asset or a security, typically qualified by a maximum quantity (ask size). Also called *offer price*.

**Asset managers**  See *investment managers*.

**Asset turnover**  A measure that indicates the volume of revenues being generated by the assets used in the business, or how effectively the company uses its assets to generate revenue.

**Asset-backed securities**  Financial securities created by securitization, whose associated payments and value are backed by a pool of underlying assets, such as car loans, credit card receivables, bank loans, or airplane leases.

**Assets**  Resources that a company controls as a result of past events and that are expected to provide future economic benefits.

**Auditors**  An external auditor is an independent accountant that examines financial statements and provides a written opinion on them. An internal auditor is employed by the company and evaluates a company's accounting and internal controls.

**Autocorrelation**  The correlation of a time series with its own past values. For example, a measure of the correlation between successive returns for a single security or portfolio over time.

**Back office**  Administrative and support functions necessary to run the firm, including accounting, human resources, payroll, and operations.

**Balance of payments**  Record that tracks transactions between a country (including individuals, companies, and public authorities) and the rest of the world over some time period (usually a year).

**Balance of trade**  The difference between exports and imports of merchandise; also known as net exports.

**Balance sheet**  A statement of the company's financial position at a specified point in time; essentially, it shows the company's assets, liabilities or debt, and owner-supplied capital.

**Barriers to entry**  Obstacles that prevent competitors from entering the market, such as high required capital investment, licenses and patents, brand loyalty, or control of natural resources.

**Basis point**  Equal to 0.01% or 0.0001.

**Benchmark**  A comparison portfolio (e.g., the S&P 500 Index).

**Beta**  A generic term for market risk, systematic risk, or non-diversifiable risk.

**Bid exchange rate**  The exchange rate at which a bank or currency dealer will buy the foreign currency.

**Bid prices**  Prices at which a dealer is willing to buy an asset or a security, typically qualified by a maximum quantity (bid size).

**Block brokers**  Brokers who provide brokerage services for large-size trades.

**Board of directors**  A group of people whose job is to monitor the company's business activities on behalf of its shareholders.

**Bond**  A formal contract that represents a loan from an investor (bondholder) to an issuer. The contract describes the key terms of the debt obligation such as the interest rate and the maturity.

**Book values**  Balance sheet values of a company's assets, liabilities, and equity.

**Brokerage services**  Services provided to clients who wish to buy and sell securities; they include not only execution services (i.e., processing orders on behalf of clients), but also investment advice or research.

**Brokered markets**  Markets in which brokers arrange trades between their clients.

**Brokers**  Agents who execute orders to buy or sell securities for their clients and provide trading services in exchange for a commission.

**Business continuity planning**  Creating plans to keep business processes running in the event of a disaster or unanticipated event.

**Business cycles**  Economy-wide fluctuations in economic activity.

**Business risk**  The risk of not being able to operate profitably in a given competitive environment because of, for example, changes in customer preferences, evolution of the competitive landscape, products or technology developments, or new laws and regulations.

**Buy-side firms**  Investment managers who purchase transaction services and investment products.

**Buyouts**  Private equity investments in established companies that require capital either to expand (similar to growth equity) or restructure and facilitate a change of ownership.

**Call market**  Market in which trades occur only at a particular time and place (i.e., when the market is called).

**Call option**  The right (but not the obligation) to buy an underlying at the exercise price until the option expires.

**Call risk**  The risk that the issuer will buy back the bond issue prior to maturity through the exercise of a call provision.

**Callable bond**  A bond that provides the issuer with the right to buy back (call) the bond from bondholders prior to the maturity date at a pre-specified price.

**Cap-weighted**  See *capitalization-weighted indices*.

**Capital and financial account**  A component of the balance of payments account that reports capital transfers between domestic entities and foreign entities, investments domestic entities make in foreign entities, and investments foreign entities make in domestic entities.

**Capital markets**  Financial markets for securities that have a maturity longer than a year.

**Capital structure**  The mix of debt and equity that a company uses to finance its business.

**Capitalism**  An economic system that favors private ownership as the means of production and markets as the means of allocating scarce resources.

**Capitalization-weighted indices**  Indices computed by summing up the total market capitalization of all securities on the index list, then dividing by a constant denominator to arrive at the index value. Also called *cap-weighted*, *market-weighted*, or *value-weighted*.

**Capitalized**  Classifying a cost as generating long-term economic benefits and reporting it as an asset rather than charging it as an expense to current operations.

**Carried interest**  A form of incentive fee designed to ensure that a private equity firm's interest is aligned with the limited partners' interest.

**Cartel**  A group of producers that agree to jointly control the production and pricing of goods or services produced by the group.

**Cash flow rights**  The rights of shareholders to distributions, such as dividends, made by the company.

**Clearing**  All activities that occur from the arrangement of the trade up until settlement.

**Clearing and settlement agents**  Investment industry participants that confirm and settle trades after they have been arranged.

**Clearinghouses**  Entities that act as intermediaries between contracting parties and guarantee to each party the performance of the other.

**Client on-boarding**  The process by which an organisation accepts a client and inputs client details into its records to enable the organisation to conduct transactions with and on behalf of the client.

**Closed-end funds** Investment companies that sell shares to the public in initial public offerings (IPOs), then use the proceeds from the initial public offering to purchase investment securities or other assets. Investors who want to buy (sell) closed-end funds must trade with investors willing to sell (buy) these funds.

**Coincident indicators** Measures of economic activity that are intended to measure the current state of the economy rather than the past or to predict the future. Coincident indicators have a tendency to change at the same time as the economy measured as a whole.

**Collateral** Specific assets (generally a tangible asset) that a borrower pledges to a lender to secure a loan.

**Commercial real estate** Commercial property that includes, for example, offices, multi-family residential dwellings, retail and industrial properties, and hotels.

**Commingled account** Pooling together the funds of two or more investors, which are then jointly managed.

**Commissions** Compensation paid by clients to their brokers for arranging their trades, usually a fixed percentage of the principal value of the transaction or a fixed price per share, bond, or contract.

**Commodities** Physical products that are either consumed (e.g., corn, cattle, wheat) or transformed (e.g., copper, gold, oil).

**Common stock** Also known as common shares, ordinary shares, or voting shares, it is the main type of equity security issued by a company. It represents an ownership stake in the company.

**Comparative advantage** A country's ability to produce a good or service relatively more efficiently (i.e., at a lower relative cost) than other countries.

**Complementary products** Products whose consumption is related to another product in a positive way, such as printers and ink cartridges.

**Complements** See *complementary products*.

**Compliance risk** The risk that an organization fails to follow all applicable laws and regulations and faces sanctions as a result.

**Compound interest** Interest that is calculated on principal and interest; it assumes reinvestment of interest received. Compound interest is often referred to as interest on interest.

**Confirmation** Clearing activity that takes place before settlement in which the buyer and seller must confirm that they traded and must confirm the exact terms of their trade.

**Conflict of interest** When either the employee's personal interests or the employer's interests conflict with the interests of the client (conflicts of interest can also arise when employee's and employer's interests conflict).

**Consumer price index** Constructed by determining the weight (or relative importance) of each good and service in a typical household's spending in a particular base year and then measuring the overall price change from year to year.

**Continuous data** Data that can take on an infinite number of values between whole numbers.

**Continuous trading market** Market in which trades can be arranged and executed any time the market is open.

**Contract market** Market in which buyers purchase contracts (typically options, swaps, futures, or forwards) from sellers. If the sellers do not hold the contracts, they write new ones.

**Convertible bond** A bond that offers the bondholder the right to convert the bond into a pre-specified number of shares of common stock of the issuing company.

**Core inflation** The inflation rate calculated based on a price index of goods and services, excluding food and energy.

**Correlation** A measure of the strength of a relationship between two variables; essentially, two variables are correlated when a change in one variable is always accompanied by a change in the other variable. Variables can be positively or negatively correlated.

**Correlation coefficient** A number between −1 and +1 that measures the consistency or tendency for two variables to move in tandem with each other.

**Corruption** The abuse of power for private gain.

**Counterparty risk** Risk that one of the parties to a contract will fail to honor the terms of the contract.

**Coupon rate** The interest rate for a bond. The bond's coupon rate multiplied by its par value equals the annual interest owed to the bondholders.

**Covenants** Actions that the issuer must perform (positive covenants) or is prohibited from performing (negative covenants).

**Credit default swap** A contract that protects the buyer against loss of value of a fixed-income security or index of fixed-income securities. The contract will specify under what conditions the other party has to make payment to the buyer of the CDS.

**Credit rating** Assessment of the credit quality of a bond based on the creditworthiness of the issuer.

**Credit rating agencies** Investment research providers that specialize in providing opinions about the credit qualities of bonds and of their issuers.

**Credit risk** For a lender, the risk of loss caused by a borrower's failure to honor the contract and make a promised payment in a timely manner.

**Credit spread** The difference between a risky bond's yield and the yield on a government bond with the same maturity.

**Cross-price elasticity** The proportional change in quantity demanded for one good in response to a proportional change in the price of another good.

**Crossing networks** Trading systems that match buyers and sellers who are willing to trade at prices obtained from other markets, but who are unwilling to expose their orders for fear of information leaks.

**Currency risk** The risk associated with the fluctuation of foreign exchange rates; also called foreign exchange risk.

**Currency swap** The exchange of debt service obligations denominated in different currencies.

**Current account** A component of the balance of payments that reflects all the inflows and outflows of goods and services, as well as earnings on public and private investments.

**Current account balance** The summation of all flows from trade in goods and services as well as from investment income and current transfers.

**Current account deficit** A negative current account balance.

**Current account surplus** A positive current account balance.

**Current assets** Short-term assets; assets that are expected to be converted into cash, used up, or sold within the current operating period (usually one year).

**Current liabilities** Short-term liabilities that must be repaid within the next year.

**Current ratio** A liquidity ratio calculated as current assets divided by current liabilities.

**Current yield** The annual coupon payment divided by the current market price.

**Custodians** Entities that hold money and securities on behalf of their customers, help arrange trade settlements, and collect interest and dividends for their customers.

**Dark pools** Alternative trading systems that do not display the orders that their clients send to them.

**Data vendors** Vendors that provide historical and current market data and news feeds.

**Day order** Order that is good for the day on which it is submitted. If it has not been filled by the close of the trading session, the order expires unfulfilled.

**Dealers** Financial intermediaries that allow their clients to trade when they want to trade by standing ready to buy (sell) when their clients want to sell (buy) by acting as principals in trades.

**Default** A situation in which the bond issuer fails to make the promised payments.

**Defined benefit pension plan** Pension plans that promise a certain amount to their beneficiaries during their retirement.

**Defined contribution pension plan** Pension plans in which participants contribute to their own retirement plan accounts, usually through employee payroll deductions. In some cases, the pension sponsor also contributes an agreed-on amount to the participants' accounts.

**Deflation** A persistent and pronounced decrease in prices across most goods and services in an economy.

**Demand** The desire for a good or service coupled with the ability and willingness to pay for the desired product.

**Deposit-taking institutions** Institutions that obtain funds primarily from depositors and lend them to borrowers, such as commercial banks, savings and loan banks, mutual banks, and credit unions.

**Depository** Organization that holds securities on behalf of customers whose ownership is recorded as a book entry.

**Depository institutions** See *deposit-taking institutions*.

**Depreciation** The process of allocating the cost of an asset over the asset's estimated useful life.

**Depreciation expense** The amount of depreciation allocated each year and reported in the income statement as an expense.

**Derivative pricing rule** Pricing rule used by crossing networks in which a price is taken (derived) from another market, rather than from the orders submitted to the crossing network.

**Derivatives** Contracts (agreements to do something in the future) that derive their value from the performance of an underlying asset, event, or outcome.

**Devaluation** The decision made by a country's central bank to decrease the value of the domestic currency relative to other currencies.

**Direct investments** Purchase of securities issued by corporations, governments, and individuals of real assets, such as real estate, art, or timber.

**Disaster recovery planning** The technical systems side of contingency planning that includes, for example, plans for back-up facilities to be dispersed geographically or that key staff and service providers are not overly interdependent.

**Disclosure-based** Regulatory system in which regulators emphasize disclosure of material information.

**Discount rate** The rate used to calculate the present value of some future amount.

**Discrete data** Data that show observations only as distinct values.

**Discretionary relationships** Relationships that permit the service provider to act with standing authority on behalf of the client.

**Discriminatory pricing rule** Pricing rule used in continuous markets in which the limit price of the order or quote that first arrived determines the trade price.

**Distribution**  The set of values that a variable can take, showing their observed or theoretical frequency of occurrence.

**Diversification**  The practice of combining assets and types of assets with different characteristics in a portfolio for the purpose of reducing risk.

**Dividend per share**  The amount of cash dividends the company pays for each share outstanding.

**Document**  A piece of written, printed, or electronic matter that provides information or evidence or that serves as an official record.

**Downside deviation**  A measure of return dispersion similar to the standard deviation but that focuses only on negative deviations.

**Duty of care**  The legal and professional obligations that investment professionals have when acting for or on behalf of their clients.

**Earnings per share**  The amount of income earned during a period per share of common stock; net income divided by the number of shares outstanding.

**Economic growth**  The percentage change in real output (real GDP) for an economy.

**Economic profit**  Equal to accounting profit minus the implicit opportunity costs not included in total accounting costs; the difference between total revenue and total cost.

**Economics**  The study of choices in the presence of scarce resources.

**Economies of scale**  Reduction in cost per unit resulting from increased production.

**Effective annual rate**  The amount by which a unit of currency will grow in a year, with interest on interest included.

**Efficient portfolio**  A portfolio offering the highest expected return for a given level of risk as measured by variance or standard deviation of return.

**Elasticity**  In economics, the responsiveness of one variable, such as the quantity demanded (or supplied), to changes in a related variable, such as price, income, and the price of a substitute or complementary product.

**Endowment funds**  Long-term funds owned by non-profit institutions.

**Enterprise risk management**  A framework that helps organizations consolidate and manage all its risks together in an integrated fashion.

**Equal-weighted**  An index weighting method in which an equal weight is assigned to each constituent security at the inception of the index.

**Equity**  Assets minus liabilities; the shareholders' (owners') investment in the company.

**Equity-indexed annuity**  See *equity-linked annuity*.

**Equity-linked annuity**  Structured investment product that earns interest at rates that depend on the performance of a stock or a stock index.

**Equity-linked notes**  Bonds for which the final payout depends on the performance of an underlying equity or equity pool, which may be a stock, a stock portfolio, or a stock index.

**Ethical dilemmas**  Situations where values, interests, and/or rules potentially conflict.

**Ethical standards**  Principles that support and promote desired values or behaviours.

**Ethics**  A set of moral principles or the principles of conduct governing an individual or a group.

**Exchange rate**  The rate at which one currency can be exchanged for another.

**Exchange-traded funds**  Pooled investment vehicles that investors trade as common stocks on exchanges or through dealers.

**Exchange-traded notes**  Debt securities issued by investment banks that pay the value of an index, minus fees paid to the bank, when they mature.

**Exchanges**  Venues to which buyers and sellers submit orders for matching.

**Exercise price**  Specified in an options contract, the price to trade the underlying in the future.

**Expenses**  The cost of using up company resources (cash, inventories, equipment, etc.) to earn revenues.

**Exports**  Goods and services that are produced within a country's borders and then transported to another country.

**Fair value**  Value that reflects the amount for which an asset could be sold in an arm's length transaction between willing parties.

**Family office**  Private company that manages the financial affairs of one or more members of a family or of multiple families.

**Financial advisers**  Investment professionals who provide both financial planning and investment advisory services to their clients.

**Financial assets**  Claims on other assets and on future cash flows; for example, a share of common (ordinary) stock represents ownership in a company or a claim on the residual value of the company.

**Financial capital**  Funds provided to corporations and governments that allow them to purchase physical capital, to hire labor, and to acquire other inputs necessary to produce goods and services.

**Financial contagion**  A situation in which financial shocks spread from their place of origin to other locales; in essence, a faltering economy infects other healthier economies.

**Financial intermediaries** Financial institutions—such as banks, securitizers, and insurance companies—that channel funds from savers to spenders; they transform deposits made by savers into loans to borrowers.

**Financial intermediation** Process of collecting savings from lenders in one form, such as deposits, and transforming them into another form, such as loans, for borrowers.

**Financial markets** Places where buyers and sellers can trade securities; also called securities markets.

**Financial planners** Investment professionals who help their clients understand their future financial needs, and who create savings and payout plans appropriate to reach these needs.

**Fiscal policy** The use of taxes and government spending to affect the level of aggregate expenditures.

**Fixed costs** Costs that, in aggregate, remain at the same level regardless of a company's level of production and sales.

**Fixed exchange rate system** An exchange rate system in which the value of the currency is tied to the value of another currency or a commodity, such as gold.

**Fixed-income securities** Loans that lenders make to borrowers; also called debt securities and bonds.

**Fixed-rate bonds** A bond with a finite life that offers a coupon rate that does not change over the life of the bond. Also known as *straight bonds*.

**Floating exchange rate system** An exchange rate system in which the central bank does not intervene and lets the market determine the value of its currency.

**Floating-rate bonds** A bond with a finite life that offers a coupon rate that changes over time. Also known as *variable-rate bonds*.

**Foreign direct investments (FDIs)** Direct investments made by foreign investors and companies.

**Foreign exchange market** A decentralised network in which currencies are traded.

**Foreign exchange risk** See *currency risk*.

**Forward contract** An agreement between two parties in which one party agrees to buy from the seller an underlying at a later date for a price established at the start of the contract.

**Forward market** Foreign exchange market in which currencies are bought (sold) but delivered (received) at some future date.

**Forward rate** The exchange rate for forward market transactions.

**Foundations** Grant-making institutions funded by gifts and by the investment income that they produce.

**Fraud** Intentional deception intended to gain an advantage, such as deliberately causing or falsely reporting losses to collect insurance settlements.

**Front office** Client-facing activities that provide direct revenue generation, such as sales, marketing, and customer service activities.

**Front running** The act of placing an order ahead of a customer's order in order to take advantage of the price impact that the customer's order will have.

**Fund managers** Individuals or firms responsible for making and implementing investment decisions related to a portfolio of investments, such as a mutual fund or pension fund.

**Fundamental value** Present value of the cash flows a security is expected to generate in the future.

**Funded plans** Plans for which the sponsors make periodic contributions long before the benefits are paid.

**Funds of funds** Investment vehicles that invest in other funds.

**Future value** The amount to which a payment or series of payments will grow by a stated future date.

**Futures contract** An agreement that obligates the seller, at a specified future date, to deliver to the buyer a specified underlying in exchange for the specified futures price.

**General partner** Owner of a partnership who, unlike limited partners, is personally liable for all the debts of the partnership. In the context of private equity partnerships, general partners are the managers who make investment decisions.

**Geometric average** The average compounded return for each period; the average return for each period assuming that returns are compounding.

**Geometric mean** See *geometric average*.

**Global depository receipt** A security issued by a financial institution that represents an economic interest in a foreign company. The financial institution holds the foreign company's shares in custody and issues GDRs against the shares held. These GDRs trade like common stock on the local stock exchange.

**Goodwill** An intangible asset that arises when a company purchases another company and pays more than the fair value of the net assets (assets minus liabilities) of the purchased company.

**Gross domestic product** The total value of all final goods and services produced within an economy in a given period of time (output definition) or, equivalently, the aggregate income earned by all households, all companies, and the government within an economy in a given period of time (income definition). Nominal GDP uses current market values. Real GDP adjusts for changes in price levels.

**Gross profit** Sales minus the cost of sales.

**Growth equity** Private equity investments in existing companies that need additional capital to fund their expansion.

**Hedge** To reduce or eliminate risk by using derivatives.

**Hedge funds** Private investment pools that investment managers organize and manage. They are characterized by their availability to only a limited number of select investors, by agreements that lock up the investors' capital for fixed periods, and by their managers' performance-based compensation.

**Hedging** A risk management strategy used to limit the potential of loss caused by fluctuations in the prices of commodities, currencies, or securities.

**High-frequency traders** Market participants who trade very quickly using computer programs.

**High-net-worth investors** Individual investors who have investable assets over a certain amount (e.g., USD1 million or CNY10 million) and who are often, but not always, more sophisticated investors.

**High-water mark** Maximum level of a fund on which performance fees were paid in the past. The investment manager earns the performance fee only if the fund is above its current high-water mark.

**High-yield bonds** See *non-investment-grade bonds*.

**Histogram** A diagram with bars that are proportional to the frequency of occurrence in each group of observations.

**Historical cost** The actual cost of acquiring an asset.

**Holding-period return** The return generated for investors over a specific time frame, usually annually; a synonym for total return.

**Hyperinflation** Price increases so large and rapid that people find it difficult to purchase goods and services.

**Implicit GDP deflator** A gauge of prices and inflation that measures the aggregate changes in prices across the overall economy.

**Imports** Goods and services that are produced outside a country's borders and then brought into the country.

**Income effect** If the price of an item decreases, a consumer will have more purchasing power (i.e., their unchanged income can afford to buy more of the cheaper items), so the quantity they demand will increase.

**Income elasticity of demand** The proportional change in the quantity demanded divided by the corresponding proportional change in income.

**Income statement** A financial statement that identifies the profit (or loss) of a company over a given time period, normally one year.

**Index fund** A portfolio of securities structured to track the returns of a specific index.

**Index of leading economic indicators** A composite of economic variables used by analysts to predict future economic conditions.

**Index rebalancing** The process of adjusting the weights of the constituent securities in an index. That is, the weights given to securities whose prices have risen must be decreased and the weights given to securities whose prices have fallen must be increased.

**Index reconstitution** The process of adding or removing securities from an index list.

**Indirect investments** Purchase of securities of corporations, trusts, and partnerships that make direct investments.

**Industrial production** A measure of economic output by the following three segments of an economy: manufacturing, mining, and utilities.

**Inferior goods** A good whose consumption decreases as income increases.

**Inflation** The percentage increase in the general price level from one period to the next; a sustained rise in the overall level of prices for goods and services.

**Inflation risk** The risk associated with inflation.

**Inflation-linked bonds** Bonds containing a provision that adjusts the bond's par value for inflation and thus mitigates inflation risk.

**Information ratio** A reward-to-risk ratio defined as the portfolio's mean active return (the difference in average return between the portfolio and its benchmark) over its active risk (tracking error).

**Informationally efficient prices** Prices that reflect all available information about fundamental values.

**Initial margin** The amount that must be deposited on the day the transaction is opened.

**Initial margin requirement** Requirement set by the government, the exchange, or the exchange clearinghouse about the minimum fraction of the purchase price that must be deposited as the trader's equity.

**Initial public offering** The first issuance of common shares to the public by a formerly private corporation.

**Insider trading** Trading while in possession of material non-public information.

**Institutional investors** Companies, trusts, and governments that invest to advance their missions or to provide financial services to their clients.

**Insurance companies** Companies that sell insurance contracts (policies) that provide payments in the event that losses occur.

**Intangible assets** Assets lacking physical substance, such as patents and trademarks.

**Interest** Payment for the use of borrowed money.

**Interest rate risk** The risk associated with decreases in bond prices resulting from increases in interest rates.

**Interest rate swap** An agreement between two parties to exchange interest rate obligations for the benefit of both parties; usually exchanges a fixed-rate payment for a floating-rate payment.

**Internal audit** A function independent from other business functions that delves into the details of business process controls and ensures that IT and accounting systems accurately reflect physical transactions.

**Internal documents** Documents that are generally administrative and that direct an organisation's philosophy, approach, and activities.

**Internal risk limits** Limits that incorporate an organization's overall risk tolerance and risk management strategy—for example, the maximum amount of a risky security that can be held or the maximum aggregate exposure to one asset type or to one specific counterparty.

**Internalizing dealers** Broker/dealers who fill their clients' orders by trading directly with their clients rather than by arranging trades with others on behalf of their clients.

**International trade** The exchange of goods, services, and capital between countries.

**Intrinsic value** See *fundamental value*.

**Inventories** The unsold units of production on hand.

**Investment advisers** Investment professionals who provide investment advisory services to their clients, such as recommending investment strategies and suggesting trades.

**Investment banks** Financial intermediaries that typically provide capital raising and strategic advisory services, brokerage and dealing services, and research services to companies and governments.

**Investment companies** Companies that exist solely to hold investments on behalf of their shareholders, partners, or unit holders, including mutual funds, hedge funds, venture capital funds, and investment trusts.

**Investment industry** All the players that are instrumental in helping savers invest their money and lenders get the funds they require.

**Investment managers** Investment advisers who have authority to trade securities and assets on behalf of their clients.

**Investment policy statement (IPS)** A written planning document describing a client's investment objectives—return requirements and risk tolerance—over a relevant time horizon, along with constraints that apply to the client's portfolio. The investment policy statement serves as a guide to what is required and acceptable in the investment portfolio.

**Investment products** See *investment vehicles*.

**Investment risk** The risk of fluctuations in the value of investments.

**Investment structure** The structure of investment vehicles (i.e., how investors hold their investments and how those investments are managed).

**Investment vehicles** The assets, such as stocks and bonds, that investors use to move money from the present to the future.

**Investment-grade bonds** Bonds rated BBB– or higher by Standard & Poor's and Fitch or Baa3 or higher by Moody's.

**Issuers** Entities, typically corporations and governments, that sell securities, such as stocks and bonds, to raise money.

**J curve** The graphical representation of cumulative net cash flow (inflows minus outflows). It shows that for much of the early part of a private equity fund's life, there will be more cash calls from than cash distributions to limited partners.

**Junk bonds** See *non-investment-grade bonds*.

**Key risk measures** Measures that provide a warning when risk levels are rising; they require collecting and compiling data from various internal and external sources.

**Keynesians** Economists who believe that fiscal policy can have powerful effects on aggregate demand, output, and employment when there is substantial spare capacity in an economy.

**Lagging indicators** Turning points that signal a change in economic activity after output has already changed.

**Law of demand** The principle that as the price of a good increases, buyers will choose to buy less of it, and as its price decreases, they will buy more.

**Law of diminishing marginal utility** As a person increases consumption of a product (service)—keeping consumption of other products and services constant—there is a decline in the marginal utility that person derives from consuming each additional unit of that product (service).

**Law of diminishing returns** If the fixed inputs of production remain unchanged, the gain in output from adding variable inputs, such as labour, will increase at a decreasing rate.

**Law of supply** The principle that an increase in price usually results in an increase in the quantity supplied.

**Laws** Rules passed by a legislative body, such as Congress in the United States, Parliament in the United Kingdom, or the Diet in Japan.

**Leading indicators** Turning points that signal changes in the economy in the future, and thus are considered useful for economic prediction and policy formulation.

**Legal risk** The risk that an external party could sue for breach of contract or other violations.

**Leveraged buyouts** Buyouts that are financed with a high proportion of debt (or leverage).

**Liability** A monetary obligation of a company as a result of previous events.

**Limit order**  Instruction to a broker or exchange to obtain the best price immediately available when filling an order, but in no event accept more than the specified (limit) price when buying or less than the specified (limit) price when selling.

**Limited liability**  Liability that does not exceed an investor's initial contribution of capital. For example, shareholders are protected by limited liability, which means that higher claimants—particularly debt investors—cannot recover money from the personal assets of the shareholders if the company's assets are insufficient to fully cover their claims.

**Limited partners**  Owners of a partnership who, unlike general partners, have limited personal liability for the partnership's debts. In the context of private equity investments, limited partners provide capital, but they are not involved in the management of the underlying investments.

**Liquidity**  Measure of the ease of buying or selling an asset without affecting its price.

**Liquidity risk**  The risk that a financial instrument cannot be purchased or sold in a timely manner without a significant concession in price.

**London interbank offered rate**  The most widely used reference rate, defined as the average interest rate that banks charge each other in the London interbank market. *Also called Libor.*

**Long positions**  Positions in an asset or contract in which one owns the asset or has an exercisable right under the contract.

**Long-term debt**  Money borrowed from banks or other lenders that is to be repaid over periods of greater than one year.

**Loyalty**  An expectation that employees will place the employer's interests above their own and will not misappropriate a company's property.

**Macroeconomics**  The branch of economics that deals with aggregate economic quantities, such as national output and national income.

**Maintenance margin**  The amount that must be maintained in the margin account every day after the transaction is opened.

**Managed floating exchange rate system**  A floating exchange rate system in which the central bank intervenes to stabilise its currency, usually to maintain the exchange rate within a certain range.

**Management fees**  Fees that limited partners must pay general partners to compensate them for managing investments.

**Margin call**  Request for additional equity, such as to deposit additional cash or securities, to meet the maintenance margin requirement.

**Marginal cost**  The cost of consuming or producing an additional unit of a good or service.

**Marginal revenue**  The additional revenue from selling an additional unit of a product or service.

**Margins**  Cash or securities that are pledged as collateral.

**Market bid–ask spread**  Difference between the best bid price and the best offer price.

**Market equilibrium**  The condition in which the quantity willingly offered for sale by sellers at a given price is just equal to the quantity willingly demanded by buyers at that same price.

**Market makers**  Dealers who are willing to make a market (trade on demand) in specified securities at their bid and ask prices.

**Market manipulation**  Abusive trading practice that involves taking actions intended to move the price of a stock in order to make a short-term profit.

**Market order**  Instructions to a broker or exchange.

**Market risk**  The risk of changes in market conditions, which affect expected cash flows as well as supply and demand and, therefore, prices.

**Market-weighted**  See *capitalization-weighted indices.*

**Marking to market**  Settling of profits or losses based on current spot (market) prices.

**Maturity date**  Date when the borrower must repay the amount borrowed.

**Median**  The value of the middle term in a data set that has been sorted into ascending or descending order; the value for which as many outcomes are above it as there are below it.

**Merit-based**  Regulatory system in which regulators attempt to protect investors by limiting the products sold to investors.

**Microeconomics**  The branch of economics that deals with markets and decision making of individual economic units, including consumers and businesses.

**Middle office**  Core activities of a firm, such as risk management, information systems, proprietary trading, corporate finance, portfolio management, and research.

**Mode**  The most frequently occurring value in a data set.

**Model risk**  The risk arising from the use of models, including inappropriate underlying assumptions, unavailability and inaccuracy of historical data, data errors, and misapplication of models.

**Monetarists**  Economists who believe that the rate of growth of the money supply is the primary determinant of the rate of inflation.

**Monetary policy**  Actions taken by a nation's central bank to affect aggregate output and prices through changes in bank reserves, reserve requirements, or the target interest rate.

**Money laundering** A process in which criminals use financial services to transfer money from illegal operations to other legal activities; the money becomes "clean" in the process.

**Money market funds** Special class of open-end funds that for most purposes appear to investors as uninsured interest-paying bank accounts. Unlike other open-end funds, regulators permit money market funds to accept deposits and satisfy redemptions at a constant price per share if they meet certain conditions.

**Money markets** Financial markets for securities that have a maturity shorter than a year.

**Monopoly** A market in which there is no competition.

**Moral hazard** Tendency for people to be less careful about avoiding losses once they have purchased insurance, potentially leading to losses occurring more often when people are insured than when they are not.

**Mortgage-backed securities** A type of structured debt security created from a pool of underlying residential mortgage (home) loans.

**Multiplier effect** An initial increase (decrease) in spending produces an increase (decrease) in GDP and consumption greater than the initial change in spending.

**Mutual fund** Investment company that holds portfolios of investment securities and assets.

**Net asset value (NAV)** Total net value of a fund (the value of all assets minus the value of all liabilities) divided by the current total number of fund shares outstanding.

**Net book value** Calculated as the gross value of an asset minus accumulated depreciation, where accumulated depreciation is the sum of all reported depreciation expenses for the particular asset.

**Net exports** The difference between exports and imports of goods and services; also called balance of trade.

**Net income** The difference between revenue and expenses; income available to distribute to shareholders.

**Net present value** The present value of future cash flows less the cost of the investment, or the present value of cash inflows minus the present value of cash outflows.

**Net profit margin** An indicator of profitability; indicates how much (percentage) of each monetary unit of revenue is left after all costs and expenses are covered.

**Nominal GDP** A measure of GDP that uses the current market value of goods and services.

**Non-current assets** Assets used over a number of years to generate income for the company; examples include machinery, equipment, buildings, land, and intangible assets.

**Non-discretionary relationship** Relationship that permits the service provider to undertake only specific tasks that are authorised on a per task basis.

**Non-investment-grade bonds** Bonds rated BB+ or lower by Standard & Poor's and Fitch and Ba1 or lower by Moody's. Also called high-yield bonds or junk bonds.

**Non-tariff barriers** A range of measures, such as certification, licensing, sanctions, or embargoes, that make it more difficult and expensive for foreign producers to compete with domestic producers.

**Normal distribution** A symmetrical distribution in which the mean, median, and mode are the same value. The distribution is completely described by its mean and variance (or standard deviation).

**Normal goods** Goods that are consumed in greater quantities as income increases.

**Offer exchange rate** The exchange rate at which the bank or dealer will sell the foreign currency; also called the ask exchange rate.

**Offer prices** See *ask prices*.

**Oligopoly** A market dominated by a small number of large companies because the barriers to entry are high.

**Open market operations** Activities that involve the purchase and sale of government bonds from and to commercial banks and/or designated market makers.

**Open-end mutual funds** Investment companies that issue or redeem their shares when investors want to buy and sell shares.

**Operating income** Income generated by the company from its usual business activities before taking into account financing costs and taxes. It is often referred to as earnings before interest and taxes (EBIT).

**Operating leverage** The extent to which operating costs are fixed versus variable.

**Operating profit margin** A profitability ratio calculated as operating income divided by revenue.

**Operational risk** The risk of losses from human, systems, and processes failures and from events that are beyond the control of the organization but affect its operations.

**Operationally efficient markets** Markets in which trades are easy to arrange with low transaction costs. These markets have small bid–ask spreads, and they can absorb large orders without substantial impact on prices.

**Opportunity cost** The cost of any activity measured in terms of the value of the best alternative that is not chosen; the value that investors forgo by choosing a particular course of action. For example, the cost of not having cash to invest, spend, or hold; the cost of giving up opportunities to use cash.

**Option contract** An agreement in which the buyer of the option has the right, but not the obligation, to trade the underlying.

**Order-driven markets** Markets that use rules to arrange trades based on the orders that traders submit.

**Orders** Specifications of what instrument to trade, how much to trade, and whether to buy or sell.

**Outliers** Values that are unusual compared with the rest of the data set by being especially small or large in numerical value.

**Over-the-counter (OTC) markets** Another name for quote-driven markets dating from when securities were literally traded over a counter in the dealer's office.

**Own price elasticity of demand** The percentage change in quantity demanded as a result of the percentage price change of the same (own) product.

**Par value** The stated value or face value of a security; the amount the investor would be entitled to receive in a liquidation scenario, which also serves as the principal value on which coupon payments are calculated.

**Passive investment managers** Managers who follow a buy-and-hold approach and seek to match the return and risk of an appropriate benchmark.

**Pay-as-you-go plans** Pension plans in which the sponsors pay pension benefits out of current revenues.

**Payout policies** Guiding principles that specify how much money an institution, such as a foundation or an endowment fund, can take from long-term funds to use for current spending.

**Pension funds** Institutional investors who hold investment portfolios for the benefit of future and current retirees.

**Perfectly competitive** A market structure in which there is a high degree of competition.

**Performance bond** A guarantee, usually provided by a third party, such as an insurance company, to ensure payment in case a party fails to fulfill its contractual obligations.

**Performance measurement** The process of measuring the performance of investments, including the calculation of reward-to-risk ratios.

**Physical capital** The means of production; tangible goods such as equipment, tools, and buildings.

**Policies** Principles of action adopted by an organisation.

**Political risk** The risk of a change in the ruling political party of a country that leads to, for example, potential changes in policies that affect taxation, interest rates, investment incentives, public investments, and procurement.

**Pooled investment vehicles** Investment companies that pool funds from many investors for common management.

**Pooled investments** Indirect investment vehicles in which investors pool their money together to obtain the advantages of working together as part of a large group.

**Position** Quantity of an instrument that a person or institution owns or owes.

**Preferred stock** Also known as preference shares; a type of equity security that ranks between debt securities and common stock. It typically does not carry voting rights but has priority over common stock in the receipt of dividends.

**Present value** The present discounted value of future cash flows.

**Price index** An index that only measures changes in the prices of the constituent securities but ignores the income generated by the index's constituent securities.

**Price-to-book ratio** A valuation ratio calculated as market price per share divided by book value per share.

**Price-to-earnings ratio** The ratio of a company's stock price to its earnings per share.

**Price-weighted index** An index in which the weight assigned to each constituent security is determined by dividing its price by the sum of all the prices of the constituent securities.

**Primary dealers** Dealers with whom central banks trade when conducting monetary policy.

**Primary market** The market where new securities, IPOs, and subsequent offerings are issued and sold to investors.

**Prime brokers** Brokers who finance their clients' positions as well as clear and settle trades in addition to traditional brokerage services, such as arranging trades.

**Principles-based** Regulatory system in which regulators set up broad principles within which the industry is expected to operate.

**Private equity** Alternative investment class that specializes in the financing of private companies.

**Private placement** Offering type in which corporations sell securities directly to a small group of qualified investors, usually with the assistance of an investment bank.

**Procedures** What the organisation must do to achieve a desired outcome.

**Processes** Individual steps an organisation must take, from start to finish, to achieve a desired outcome.

**Producer price index** Reflects the price changes experienced by domestic producers in a country.

**Productivity gains** Increases in the ratio of gross domestic product (GDP) to units of labour expended to produce that GDP.

**Proprietary traders** Traders, such as dealers and arbitrageurs, who trade for the "house account" using their own account or their firm's account.

**Proprietary trading** When dealers trade using their own accounts and their own capital with buyers and sellers.

**Prospectus** Document offered by investment companies that discloses the investment policies, deposit and redemption procedures, fees and expenses, and past performance statistics.

**Purchasing power parity** Economic theory that a bundle of goods in two different countries should cost the same after taking into account the exchange rate between the two countries' currencies.

**Put option** The right (but not the obligation) to sell the underlying at the exercise price until expiration.

**Putable bond** A bond that provides bondholders with the right to sell (or put back) their bonds to the issuer prior to the maturity date at a pre-specified price.

**Quick ratio** A measure of liquidity that indicates a company's ability to satisfy current liabilities with its most liquid assets.

**Quotas** Limits on the quantity of goods that can be imported.

**Quote-driven markets** Markets in which dealers acting as principals facilitate trading and in which customers trade at the prices quoted by these dealers.

**Range** The difference between the highest and lowest values in a data set.

**Real GDP** The value of goods and services produced, measured at base-year prices; nominal GDP adjusted for changes in price levels.

**Real assets** Physical assets such as land, buildings, cattle, and gold.

**Real estate** Land or any buildings or structures on it.

**Real estate equity funds** Investment vehicles, very often open-ended funds, in which hundreds of commercial properties are held.

**Real estate investment trusts (REITs)** Public companies that mainly own, and in most cases, operate income-producing real estate.

**Real estate limited partnerships** Limited partnerships that specialize in real estate investments.

**Rebalancing** The process of adjusting the weights of the constituent securities in an index or the weights of assets in a portfolio.

**Recession** A period during which real GDP decreases (i.e., negative growth) for at least two successive quarters, or a period of significant decline in total output, income, employment, and sales usually lasting from six months to a year.

**Reference rate** An interest rate that serves as the benchmark to set the coupon rate of a floating-rate bond.

**Registers** Documents containing obligations, past actions, and future or outstanding requirements.

**Regulations** Rules that set standards for conduct and that carry the force of law.

**Reinvestment risk** Risk that in a period of falling interest rates, the periodic coupon payments received during the life of a bond and/or the principal payment received from a bond called early must be reinvested at a lower interest rate than the bond's original coupon rate.

**Relative returns** The difference between holding-period returns (absolute returns) and returns on a benchmark over the same holding period.

**Reserve currency** A currency held in significant quantities by many governments and institutions as part of their foreign exchange reserves.

**Reserve requirement** The requirement for banks to hold reserves in proportion to the size of deposits.

**Residual claimants** Investors whose claims rank last. Common shareholders are residual claimants. In the event of a company's liquidation, common shareholders share proportionately in the remaining company assets after all other claimants have been satisfied.

**Retail investors** Individual investors who have the least amount of investable assets and who are often, but not always, less sophisticated investors than institutional investors.

**Retained earnings** The accumulated net income that is retained by the corporation rather than distributed to its owners as dividends.

**Return on assets** A profitability ratio that indicates a company's net income generated per monetary unit invested in total assets.

**Return on equity** A profitability ratio calculated as net income divided by average shareholders' equity.

**Revenues** The amount charged (and expected to be received) for the delivery of goods or services in the ordinary activities of a business.

**Reward-to-risk ratio** Metric that divides a measure of portfolio holding-period return by a measure of portfolio risk. The higher the value of this metric, the more return an investment portfolio has generated per unit of risk.

**Risk** The effect of uncertain future events on an organization or on the outcomes the organization achieves.

**Risk appetite** Willingness to take risk.

**Risk budgeting** An approach to determining how much risk should be allocated among different business units, portfolios, or individuals.

**Risk matrix** A matrix that reflects the expected frequency of an event and the expected severity of its consequences and that can be used to prioritize risks and to select the appropriate risk response for each risk identified.

**Risk tolerance** The level of risk an organization is able and willing to take.

**Rogue trading** An example of operational risk that has a human component wherein traders bypass management controls and place unauthorized trades.

**Rules-based** Regulatory system in which explicit rules are provided that, in theory, offer clarity and legal certainty to industry participants.

**Sales loads** Fees paid to buy a fund.

**Seasoned equity offering** See *secondary equity offering*.

**Secondaries** Private equity segment that involves the pooling of investor assets to purchase already existing interests in private equity partnerships.

**Secondary equity offering** The issuance by a publicly traded company of additional common shares subsequent to the initial public offering.

**Secondary market** Market in which traders of a security trade with each other but not with the original security issuer; market in which investors buy and sell securities with each other.

**Securities** Financial assets that can be traded.

**Securitization** Creation of new financial products by buying and repackaging securities or other assets; the creation and issuance of new debt securities that are backed by a pool of other debt securities.

**Security lenders** Investors who have long positions and lend their securities to short sellers.

**Security market index** A portfolio of securities representing a given security market, market segment, or asset class.

**Sell-side firms** Firms, such as investment banks, brokers, and dealers, that provide transaction services and investment products.

**Seniority ranking** A priority of claims among a company's providers of capital, it affects the amounts investors will receive upon the company's liquidation and, in the case of equity capital, the order in which dividends are paid.

**Serial correlation** See *autocorrelation*.

**Settlement** Clearing activity consisting of the final exchange of cash for securities.

**Settlement risk** The risk that when settling a transaction, the counterparty does not complete its side of the deal as agreed, usually because of declaring bankruptcy.

**Share buyback** See *share repurchase*.

**Share repurchase** A transaction in which a company uses its cash to buy back its own shares from existing shareholders. This transaction reduces the number of shares outstanding.

**Shareholders** The owners of shares (stock) of a corporation.

**Sharpe ratio** A reward-to-risk ratio defined as the excess portfolio return (portfolio return minus risk-free return) over the standard deviation of portfolio returns.

**Shelf registration** Sale of new issues of seasoned securities directly to the public on a piecemeal basis, (i.e., over time when the issuer needs additional capital, rather than in a single transaction).

**Short positions** Positions in an asset or contract in which one has sold an asset one does not own or in which a right under a contract can be exercised against oneself.

**Shortages** When demand exceeds supply.

**Simple interest rate** The cost to the borrower or the rate of return to the lender, per period, on the original principal borrowed.

**Skewed** A distribution is skewed when the bulk (majority) of the values (possibly including the median) lie either to the right or to the left of the mean; the distribution is not symmetrical.

**Soft commissions** Use of commissions to buy services other than execution services, such as investment research used in the decision-making process.

**Sovereign risk** The risk that a foreign government will not repay its debt, because it does not have either the ability or the willingness to do so.

**Sovereign wealth funds** Funds created by governments to invest surpluses for the benefit of current and future generations of their citizens.

**Spinoff** A form of restructuring in which a company creates a new entity and distributes the shares of this new entity to existing shareholders in the form of a non-cash dividend. Shareholders end up owning stock in two different companies.

**Spot market** Foreign exchange market in which currencies are bought (sold) and received (delivered) immediately.

**Spot rate** The exchange rate for spot market transactions.

**Stagflation** When a high inflation rate is combined with a high level of unemployment and a slowdown of the economy.

**Standard deviation** A measure, in the same units as the original data, of the variability, volatility, or dispersion of a data set around the average value of that data set (i.e., the arithmetic mean). It is the positive square root of the variance.

**Standardised documents** Documents that are crafted for a specific purpose and consider various alternative uses. Some standard contracts are tailored by negotiation, but their form, content, and purpose have been pre-established.

**Statement of cash flows** A financial statement that identifies the sources and uses of cash over a time period and explains the change in the company's reported cash balance over the period.

**Stock dividend** A transaction in which a company distributes additional shares of its common stock to shareholders instead of cash. This transaction reduces the number of shares outstanding but does not affect the company's value because the stock price decreases accordingly.

**Stock exchanges** Organized and regulated financial markets that allow buyers and sellers to trade securities with each other.

**Stock split** A transaction in which a company increases the number of shares outstanding. For example, in a two-for-one stock split, the company doubles the number of shares outstanding and the stock price is halved, but the company's value is unaffected.

**Stocks** Ownership in a company; also called equity securities, shares of stock, or shares.

**Stop order** Order to which a trader has specified a stop condition. The stop order may not be filled until the stop condition has been satisfied.

**Straight bonds** See *fixed-rate bonds*.

**Straight-through processing (STP)** Processing with no need for manual intervention. Sometimes referred to as straight-through exception processing (STeP).

**Strategic asset allocation** The long-term mix of assets that is expected to achieve the client's long-term objectives, given the client's investment constraints.

**Strike price** See *exercise price*.

**Structured investment products** Securities that investment banks and insurance companies issue, whose returns replicate the returns of complex combinations of financial instruments that may include stocks, bonds, and derivative contracts.

**Substitute product** A product that could generally take the place of (substitute for) another product.

**Substitution effect** An effect caused by an increase in price of good X that induces a consumer (whose income has remained the same) to buy more of a relatively lower-priced good Y and less of a higher-priced good X. The consumer is substituting Y for X.

**Supply** The quantity of a good or service sellers are willing and able to sell at a given price.

**Swaps** Derivatives in which two parties swap cash flows or other financial instruments over multiple periods (months or years) for mutual benefit, usually to manage risk.

**Systematic risk** Also known as market risk, it is the risk created by general economic conditions that affect all risky investments. Systematic risk factors include changes in macroeconomic conditions, interest rate risk, and political risk, among others.

**Systemic failure** Failure of the financial system as a whole, including loss of access to credit and collapse of capital markets.

**Tactical asset allocation** The decision to deliberately deviate from the strategic asset allocation in an attempt to add value based on forecasts of the near-term relative performance of asset classes.

**Tariffs** Duties (taxes) levied on imported goods and services, which allow governments not only to establish trade barriers but also to raise revenue.

**Tax-advantaged accounts** Accounts that allow investors to avoid paying taxes on investment income and capital gains as they earn them. In exchange for these privileges, investors must accept stringent restrictions on when the money can be withdrawn and sometimes on how the money can be used.

**Term structure of interest rates** The relationship between the yields to maturity offered by government bonds and the maturities of these government bonds.

**Time-weighted rate of return** A measure of investment performance in which the overall measurement period is divided into sub-periods. The timing of each individual cash flow is identified and then defines the beginning of the sub-period in which it occurs.

**Total return indices** Indices that measure the total return investors would obtain if they bought and held the index securities. These indices include changes in price of the constituent securities plus any income received since inception.

**Tracking error** The standard deviation of the differences between the deviation over time of the returns on a portfolio and the returns on its benchmark; a synonym of active risk.

**Trade barriers** Restrictions on the free exchange of goods and services, often imposed by governments.

**Trade deficits** When the value of total imports exceeds the value of total exports.

**Trade surplus** When the value of total exports exceeds the value of total imports.

**Transaction costs** Costs that accrue from brokerage commissions, bid–ask spreads, and market impact; the costs associated with trading.

**Transfer agents** Entities, typically banks and trust companies, that maintain book-entry record of ownership of corporations' securities.

**Underlying** The asset, event, or outcome on which the value of a derivative is dependent.

**Underwritten offerings** Offering type in which the (lead) investment bank guarantees the sale of the issue at an offering price that it negotiates with the issuer.

**Uniform pricing rule** Pricing rule commonly used in call markets in which all trades execute at the same price. The market chooses the price that maximizes the total quantity traded.

**Unit elastic** An elasticity with a magnitude of 1. For example, when the price elasticity of demand is exactly −1, the percentage change in price is accompanied by a similar, but opposite, percentage change in the quantity demanded.

**Unit investment trusts**  Funds that are not actively managed. Instead, unit investment trusts hold a fixed portfolio of securities or assets until the trust expires.

**Unsystematic risk**  Also known as non-systematic risk, specified risk, or idiosyncratic risk, it is the company-specific risk associated with investing in a particular company or security.

**Value at risk**  An estimate of the minimum loss of value that can be expected for a given period within a given level of probability.

**Value-weighted**  See *capitalization-weighted indices*.

**Variable costs**  Costs that, in aggregate, fluctuate with the level of output of the firm.

**Variable-rate bonds**  See *floating-rate bonds*.

**Variance**  A measure of dispersion that is equal to the standard deviation squared (i.e., the standard deviation multiplied by itself).

**Venture capital**  Private equity investments in "start-up" companies that exist merely as an idea or business plan.

**Voting rights**  The rights of shareholders to vote—for example, to elect the members of the board of directors.

**Warrant**  An equity-like security that entitles the holder to buy a pre-specified amount of common stock of the issuing company at a pre-specified stock price prior to a pre-specified expiration date.

**Wrap account**  Accounts that give retail investors access to services of fee-based investment advisers.

**Yield curve**  Term structure of interest rates presented in graphical form.

**Yield to maturity**  The discount rate that equates the present value of a bond's promised cash flows to its market price.

**Zero-coupon bonds**  Bonds that do not offer periodic interest payments during the life of the bond. The only cash flow offered by a zero-coupon bond is a single payment equal to the bond's par value to be paid on the bond's maturity date.

Made in the USA
Charleston, SC
13 January 2014